# KISSES FROM A DISTANCE

# Kisses From A Distance
## AN IMMIGRANT FAMILY EXPERIENCE

**RAFF ELLIS**

Cune

*Kisses from A Distance:*
*An Immigrant Family Experience*
© 2007 Raff Ellis
Cune Press, Seattle
All Rights Reserved
(Hardcover $29.95: ISBN 978-1885942456)
(Softcover $17.95: ISBN 978-1885942463)

Library of Congress Cataloging-in-Publication Data
Ellis, Raff, 1931-
Kisses from a distance / by Raff Ellis.   p. cm.
ISBN-13: 978-1-885942-45-6 (hardcover : alk. paper)
ISBN-13: 978-1-885942-46-3 (pbk. : alk. paper)
1.  Ellis, Raff, 1931- 2.  Ellis, Raff, 1931---Family. 3.  Lebanese Americans--
Biography. 4.  Immigrants--United States--Biography. 5.  Christians--Lebanon--
Biography. 6.  Lebanon--Biography.
7.  Ellis, Raff, 1931---Travel--Lebanon. I. Title.
E184.L34E44 2007
305.892'75692073--dc22   [B]   2007014461

Cune Press
PO Box 31024
Seattle, WA 98103
www.cunepress.com

Other titles in the Bridge Between the Culture Series:

*The Road from Damascus: A Journey Through Syria* by Scott C. Davis

*Steel & Silk: Men and Women Who Shaped Syria 1900 - 2000* by Sami Moubayed

*A Pen of Damascus Steel: Political Cartoons of an Arab Master* by Ali Farzat

*Searching Jenin: Eyewitness Accounts of the Israeli Invasion 2002* by Ramzy Baroud

Thanks to the Salaam Cultural Museum for its support.

# Contents

Part III: The Hobeiche—Kmeid Union

Illustrations

*To those intrepid immigrants who braved the perilous journey to reach America's shores, while forsaking the familiar for the promise of the unknown, and whose contributions to the enrichment of the land they embraced has made this country what it is.*

# Foreword

*Remember from whence you came*
*lest you lose sight of where you are going.*

As often happens in people's lives, as it happened to me, members of succeeding generations of immigrant families suddenly find themselves pondering the question of who they are and how they got here. They begin to search for a co-identity, one that connects with their ancestral roots and uniquely cohabits with their American identity. My existential pangs were more strongly focused after my mother's death, when the multitude of saved correspondence from her family and friends was discovered among her personal effects. The 200 or so letters dated back to 1925. The sheer volume afforded us a glimpse into the thoughts and travails that my mother and her family and friends experienced over the years, insights that would not have been possible otherwise.

The discovery of the correspondence provided the spark that ignited my journey to discover the truth—truth about my heritage and the many stories I had heard. There were also numerous other questions that had lain submerged inside me for many years that needed to be answered, such as why my parents and the other Lebanese immigrants came to America, why they settled where they did, what the social and economic environment was like that received them, and what life was like for them and for those that remained behind in the "old country."

Thus, a voyage began that would take me to various libraries, both here and abroad, to archives both secular and religious, to an examination of census data and the Ellis Island ship manifests, to records housed at a foreign military installation, to hunt down and purchase old books from Internet sources such as eBay and Amazon, and to frequent obscure shops to obtain obscure histories written by obscure historians. Along with these accumulated written records, conversations with historians and recorded oral histories from village elders contributed mightily to this narrative.

The journey was at times frustrating, leading to many dead-ends and unanswered questions or conflicting stories that had to be checked, re-checked, and resolved. I often grew weary and many times abandoned the journey but after a short respite would take it up again, much like a Bedouin in search of new pasture for his flock just over the horizon. And the joy the nomad must have felt at his discovery had to be similar to what I felt when I unearthed fresh data for my story.

What intrigued me most on my quest for the truth about my Lebanese relatives and their fellow emigrants was their dogged desire for independence, a subject worthy of its own study. These are a people whose long history tells a story of continual cultural adaptation to foreign occupation, from the Hyskos in 1720 BC, followed by Egyptians, Assyrians, Persians, Greeks, Romans, Crusaders, Ottomans, and others too numerous to mention, all the way up to the French Mandate, which ended in 1943. We also get a glimpse into attitudes that were shaped from both sides of an archaic feudal system, from the sheikhs on one side to the lowly peasant farmers on the other.

The immigrant class of Lebanese in America was made up, for the most part, of rural people used to farming their own little carved-out-of-a-mountainside plot of land in a country where factory work was virtually non-existent and undesired. The freedom of running one's own business, even though the hours worked were often twice what would have been required in an American factory job, was much more preferable to the Lebanese immigrant. Thus it was that my father, after toiling for a short while in the paper mills of Northern New York at jobs he disliked intensely, sought the independent life of a peddler and shopkeeper.

I, like most children, was often told harmless fables—from Santa Claus to the Easter Bunny and the Tooth Fairy. When I finally found out that these myths were untrue, I was disappointed and became wary of "too-good-to-be-true" tales. In the fall of the year, when we seemed to have an abundance of fresh fruit, my parents would often remark that the apples grown in the mountains of their homeland were twice the size of those seen in the US. And, having been duped before by such "tall tales," including those from the old country, I would reply, "Yeah, sure they are." But I remember the first time I set eyes on those apples on my initial trip to my father's hometown in Lebanon, I blurted out, "Boy, the folks weren't kidding! These apples are huge!"

Thus, with a wary but hopeful eye, I set out to retrace the steps trod by my ancestors to see if what they told me was indeed true and to what extent those tales and their outlook on life were guided by a unique perspective embedded in their Lebanese ethos.

# Family Tree

## el Khazen  -  Hobeiche

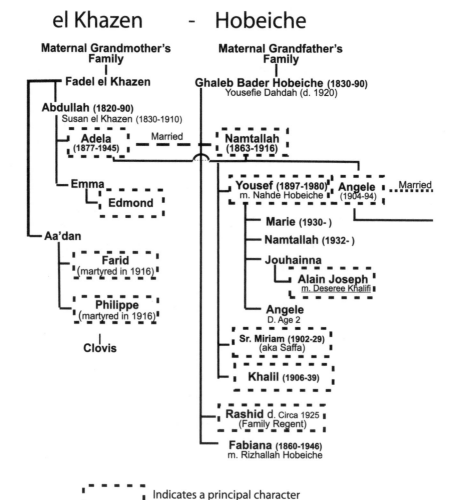

**Maternal Grandmother's Family**

**Maternal Grandfather's Family**

- **Fadel el Khazen**

**Ghaleb Bader Hobeiche (1830-90)**
Yousefie Dahdah (d. 1920)

**Abdullah (1820-90)**
Susan el Khazen (1830-1910)

**Adela (1877-1945)**  — Married — **Namtallah (1863-1916)**

**Emma**

**Edmond**

**Yousef (1897-1980)**
m. Nahde Hobeiche

**Angele (1904-94)** — Married

**Marie (1930- )**

**Namtallah (1932- )**

**Jouhainna**

**Alain Joseph**
m. Deseree Khalifi

**Angele**
D. Age 2

**Aa'dan**

**Farid**
(martyred in 1916)

**Philippe**
(martyred in 1916)

**Clovis**

**Sr. Miriam (1902-29)**
(aka Saffa)

**Khalil (1906-39)**

**Rashid** d. Circa 1925
(Family Regent)

**Fabiana (1860-1946)**
m. Rizhallah Hobeiche

- - - - - Indicates a principal character

# Family Tree

## Kmeid

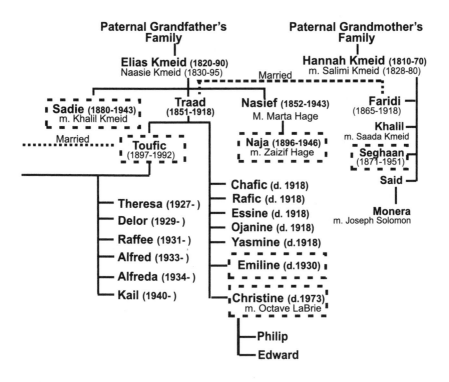

**Paternal Grandfather's Family**

**Paternal Grandmother's Family**

**Elias Kmeid** (1820-90)
Naasie Kmeid (1830-95)     Married

**Hannah Kmeid** (1810-70)
m. Salimi Kmeid (1828-80)

**Sadie** (1880-1943)
m. Khalil Kmeid

**Traad** (1851-1918)

**Nasief** (1852-1943)
M. Marta Hage

**Faridi** (1865-1918)

Married

**Toufic** (1897-1992)

**Naja** (1896-1946)
m. Zaizif Hage

**Khalil**
m. Saada Kmeid

**Seghaan** (1871-1951)

**Said**

**Theresa** (1927- )
**Delor** (1929- )
**Raffee** (1931- )
**Alfred** (1933- )
**Alfreda** (1934- )
**Kail** (1940- )

**Chafic** (d. 1918)
**Rafic** (d. 1918)
**Essine** (d. 1918)
**Ojanine** (d. 1918)
**Yasmine** (d.1918)

**Emiline** (d.1930)

**Christine** (d.1973)
m. Octave LaBrie

**Monera**
m. Joseph Solomon

**Philip**
**Edward**

- - - - Indicates a principal character

# PART I
## The Hobeiches

# 1

*A man is not a stranger because you do not know him.*

"KIDNAPPED!" she said.

"Kidnapped?" the wide-eyed boy replied.

She was my mother and I was the wide-eyed boy who filed the story away in the deep recesses of his developing memory, to be dredged up after her death many years later. The story was about her mother, a story that would be contemplated and retold many times as if the mere retelling could actually change what happened.

Back in 1895, my grandmother Adela el Khazen was a young girl who had offered herself up to serve God in a virginal life of chastity, contemplation, and prayer with the Sisters of St. Francis DeSales. She could neither have known nor realized that a chance meeting some two years before would be the force that would send her life careening in a wholly unanticipated direction.

The chapel bell at the stone-walled convent had softly tolled some ten minutes before but Adela didn't take notice. Why should she? This certainly would not concern her. The tall girl in her antiseptic white habit was busily dusting the marble statuary outside the chapel, thinking only about pending evening devotions. Her contemplation was soon interrupted by one of her sister religious aspirants who told her to go immediately to mother superior's office. The request was unusual, and Adela wondered what she could have done to warrant the summons as she scurried to Mother Anisa's workplace. At her knock, the reverend mother rose quickly and led the puzzled postulant* to the visitor's room.

There, Adela was shocked to see her cousin Farid el Khazen and Fr Boulous, her parish priest, seated on the other side of the cloistered divide. Someone in the family must have died was her first reaction, for surely it was the wrong

---

*A candidate for admission into a religious order.

time of the year to be getting visitors, relatives or not.

Cousin Farid, the neatly coifed, handlebar mustachioed young man who had been busy making a name for himself as a journalist in Jounieh, rose to greet Adela as she rushed up and stuck her fingers through the carved wooden lattice. She clutched the barrier tightly as if to strangle her mounting fear. In a voice trembling with apprehension she asked, "What has happened?" Farid quickly assured her it was not bad news that had brought them. "Why is the priest here," she then asked. The rather rotund cleric, who remained comfortably seated, had never visited her before, so this was another cause for concern. Fr Boulos, in his turn, also assured the young girl that there was nothing to worry about as they had come on a joyous mission.

Despite being puzzled by the unexpected visitation, the anticipation of dire news, and now the announcement of a joyous mission, Adela forced herself to appear calm. She warily asked the priest, whom she had never completely trusted despite his clerical collar, what he meant. Fr Boulos astonishingly replied, while mindlessly stroking his bushy beard, "We have brought you a suitor!"

Of course this shocked the girl who, like anyone properly motivated to a religious vocation, would certainly not be contemplating matrimony or any of its consequences. Her first reaction was to scream a refusal of this suggestion, but her tongue grew thick and refused to cooperate. Mother Anisa guided her to one of the rude, stiff-backed chairs and bade her sit down. Once seated, Adela looked imploringly at mother superior but did not receive the expected reassurance or support. The nun was being obsequiously deferential to the visiting priest, and avoided looking directly at her charge who was now busy praying that this was but a nightmare that would soon pass.

After what seemed an eternity, Adela composed herself enough to speak and sharply told the priest, "This is impossible!" She took pains to explain that she was to be professed* in two months, God willing, and that she had never considered the married state. Her voice trailed off as she turned to the uncharacteristically stone-faced reverend mother, a woman whom she trusted would certainly save her.

Mother Anisa, however, told Adela that she didn't think it would do any harm to listen to what *aboona* (Father) had to say. After all, he had come a long distance and they would not want to be so rude as to dismiss his words without consideration. The nun then rose, taking Adela by the elbow to lead

*Having taken the vows of, or been received into, a religious order.

20

her to a side door that exited from the cloistered area of the convent—an area that Adela had not breached since entering the nunnery. Farid and the priest soon joined her there and guided the trembling Adela down the path to the iron-barred portal that guarded the convent. She was unable to concentrate on the priest's droning dialectic about the holy sacrament of matrimony or the suitor he had brought. Sheikh Namatallah Hobeiche, he said, came from a good family, one that was *as white as the inside of a turnip*. He also pointed out that they had met some time before at her parents' home in the Mazraat, and she had served him a meal. The sheikh was sure she would remember.

Adela tried with great resolve to dam that particular memory stream, but the long-ago encounter would not be held back and burst forth in a flood of shame, reddening her cheeks along the way. Men were not to be thought of in any context, much less romantic ones by girls in her situation. She demurred by saying she was not sure she recalled any such encounter.

But, in truth, she did remember that day two years prior when she first encountered Sheikh Namatallah Hobeiche. Encountered, not met, best describes this meeting, for Adela, like any well-brought up young sheikha, knew better than to make eye contact with a strange man, no matter how inviting. And, engaging him in conversation was totally out of the question. The encounter would never have occurred had not one of the peasant servers taken ill and Adela been pressed into service in her place.

Adela's parents ran a hostel* at their home in the little town of Mazraat Kfar Debiane up in the mountains of Lebanon. Why the Hobeiche sheikh showed up that day is a mystery. The notable clans of el Khazen and Hobeiche certainly were not strangers, and Nami, as Sheikh Namatallah was called, could easily be at home with them.

The tall, certainly by the standards of the day, imperious, strutting sheikh marched in, inhaling deeply of the aromas that promised to quiet the rumblings of his substantial appetite. The Hobeiche sheiks were large men with large appetites, and not only for food. Just past thirty years of age, he was dressed in the gentleman's costume of the period, a white collarless shirt, baggy pantaloons, and boots, his riding crop dangling loosely from his left hand. He immediately crossed the small room to introduce himself to Adela's father, seated on a stool opposite the front entrance.

Of course the few guests noticed and quickly turned to observe the new

---

*My mother called it a hostel even though it was their principal residence, as they provided a meal or a bed for traveling notables.

arrival as Adela's father, Sheikh Abdullah el Khazen, exchanged a greeting with his latest visitor. The other guests began vying to exchange salaams with the sheikh. Hardly anyone in Lebanon did not know of the Hobeiche family's preeminent past, for they were not bashful in boasting about their exploits. They bragged, for instance, about having acted as guides for the Crusaders when they appeared in the Middle East at the end of the eleventh century.

While serving lunch to the confident stranger, Adela suddenly became aware of an odd attraction to him. Although she betrayed not the slightest emotion, she noted the way he parted his close-cropped wavy hair near the center of his scalp, just like the European priests she had seen when at school. Although she could feel this stranger's deep brown eyes upon her as he wolfed down his meal, she kept her head slightly bowed and tended her chores as if without notice. Neither she nor the sheikh uttered a word to each other, but this did not stop him from staring at the sixteen-year-old girl with long, and not so furtive, glances.

Only after Sheikh Nami had finished his lunch and downed his Turkish coffee, paid his final respects to his host, retreated through the door to mount his steed and ride off on his mysterious journey, did Adela hurry outside to catch a glimpse of the departing stranger. She could see only his long erect back disappearing into a shroud of dust kicked up by his galloping steed. A dashing figure, she thought to herself innocently enough, and soon put the encounter out of mind.

It was now two years later, and Adela was a hopeful candidate at a convent where many members of her clan had also chosen similar vocations. There were many el Khazens who had become priests, monks, and nuns, forsaking the life of the privileged class, as diminished as it had become.

But Adela was not one who dwelled on history and had given little thought to that chance encounter with Sheikh Namatallah Hobeiche. Fr Boulos, who had assumed the role of director in this unfolding drama, dismissed Adela's reservations, saying it wasn't so important that she remembered the man, and that the gentleman in question was waiting by the hitching rail to get reacquainted. He also mentioned that they had come directly from her father's house and that he had given his blessing to proceed with the courtship, feeling that this union would be good for both families. The presumptuous priest thought it would be a shame for Adela to waste away in the convent because there was no shortage of religious candidates in those difficult times, and the girl had to consider her family first.

Adela weakly protested that she had to get ready for vespers and fleetingly wondered why this "suitor" had remained outside. She asked the priest to tell

22

Sheikh Hobeiche that she was sorry for his trouble and turned to return to the convent. But the priest barred her escape and her protracted protestations made him so angry that his mottled brown eyes turned black and his voice took on a menacing tone.

With words muscling their way across his hair-framed lips, the priest admonished Adela not to dismiss them so lightly, reminding her that they had come a long way and had followed all the steps of propriety. Fr Boulos added that she would not be permitted to insult them and turned so violently to grab Adela's arm that his flat-topped priestly cap nearly fell off. Farid was sympathetic to his cousin but now seemed to have accepted a supporting role in the priest's production. Her urgently whispered pleas to him for help, although visibly unrequited, genuinely disturbed him as he trailed the pair down the path into the courtyard.

When the trio passed through the wrought iron gate, Adela could see Sheikh Nami standing with his elbow draped over the saddle of the same speckled white horse he was riding on that day in the Mazraat two years before. She remembered him now. So nonchalant, so sure of himself, she thought, and quickly studied his face anew, noting his symmetrical features, firm jaw, modest nose and close-cropped, dark, wavy hair. She conceded that he indeed was a handsome man, even if she didn't particularly care for his brushy moustache.

She also saw two other animals, her cousin's horse and the priest's donkey, tied to the hitching rail. Regaining his composure, the priest sought to make the proper introductions in his usual sycophantic manner. Nodding to Sheikh Nami, he presented the girl as Sheikha Adela el Khazen, the young woman who had attracted his eye in a previous encounter.

Sheikh Nami, in his unaccented French, described what a pleasure it was to meet her again. His voice was firm and melodious as he reached out and grasped Adela's right hand, rosary and all, brought it up to his lips, and kissed it, emulating the manner of his Continental tutors. Adela trembled as Nami's lips and moustache touched her hand, and she reminded the sheikh that she didn't speak French. Adela didn't have the presence to add that she did, however, have some facility in Italian, taught in her school by nuns from Rome. Quickly and effortlessly reverting to his native tongue, Nami reminded Adela that they had met two years before at her parents' home when she was busy serving in the dining room. He claimed to have never forgotten that meeting and asked if she remembered.

Adela appeared puzzled, so puzzled in fact that her face wrinkled up, tightly forming a countenance that could have passed for a road map, one that blocked all paths leading to this repressed memory. "It is hard to remember, especially from that long ago," she said and urgently added that she had to go in for evening prayers. With that pronouncement she turned again to reenter the convent and bumped into the bulbous Fr Boulous who had stationed himself between her and the gate.

Nami quickly admonished her not to be in such a hurry as he again reached for her hand, but Adela was ready for him and deftly avoided his grasp. Nami began to talk of his family's history and how, for many generations his ancestors and Adela's had fought side by side in the name of their Maronite* religion and for the independence of Lebanon. Every so often, the priest would nod his head and make an exclamation in praise of God. And each time he invoked God's name, Adela would make the sign of the cross and kiss the crucifix attached to her rosary.

As the light in the sky cooled from orange to gray, Adela began to fidget and again looked imploringly at her cousin Farid, but his face betrayed that he had partnered with the priest and the sheikh. As insincere as it sounded, he told Adela, "Listen carefully, because this is very important to you and to the family." Adela responded by bowing her head and staring at the ground with a look of despair.

The beleaguered girl now felt smothered by the shroud of words that the sheikh and the priest had so adroitly knit about her. And, no matter how much she flailed and fidgeted, she became immersed deeper and deeper in its folds. When dusk suddenly took hold of the heavens, one of the nuns quietly, and unnoticed by everyone but the priest, slipped out of the convent and slammed the iron gate shut with a resounding clang!

Simultaneously the chapel bell began to peal, startling both Adela and the priest's donkey, and the girl quickly wheeled to reenter the convent. The priest had now stepped aside, but the gate was locked. With the braying of the donkey as accompaniment, Adela cried out to the sister, "I can't get in!" But, without so much as a backward glance, the nun disappeared inside the convent, banging the heavy oak door shut behind her.

The harsh metallic sound of the gate's closing was still reverberating in Adela's ears as she continued pleading for the nun to open the gate. With tears in her eyes, she began to beat on the gate with her fists. A burr on one of the bars opened an oozing cut on the heel of her right hand, which left short

---

*One of many Eastern Rites of the Roman Catholic Church that are in union with the Pope of Rome.

bloody smears on the iron gate.

The priest reminded Adela of the rules that her convent had enacted to insure a postulant's chastity, namely that once outside the gate after sundown, communal rights were forfeited. This was, after all, a cloistered convent, designed as a place for seclusion and purity, and Adela now had no option but to return home.

The very idea that the sisters would no longer take her back stabbed at Adela, and she clutched her breast as she banged her head repeatedly against the gate. The distraught girl was now sobbing uncontrollably as the priest, who with sudden and uncharacteristic tenderness, led her from the gate to her cousin's horse. He tried to reassure her that all would be well and there would be rejoicing in the Mazraat when they returned.

Now astride Farid's horse, Adela suddenly composed herself and fell deathly silent. But her face could not have revealed her inner feelings, the feelings of one betrayed not only by her family and her priest, but also by her aunt Mother Superior and the beloved Sisters of St. Francis De Sales. Farid gazed sadly at Adela, and while bandaging her hand with his kerchief, whispered reassuring words to her. He then gently caressed the swelling welt on her forehead, an ugly bruise that was quickly metamorphosing from red to purple. But Adela said nothing.

The jubilant Nami mounted his horse while triumphantly grinning from ear to ear. He had, after all, made a bridal conquest in the finest romantic tradition of his country, and he did not let Adela's depression diminish his joy. In the Lebanese culture, kidnapping brides was not an uncommon occurrence, and many stories of such escapades are told in what are considered romantic folktales. It remained to be seen if, in the years to come, Nami would continue to savor this conquest with the same grinning gusto.

So, with the clanging closing of the cast-iron gate, absent which I would not be here to tell this tale, a new chapter in the history of my family had begun.

# 2

*I am in the west, but they call to me from the east.*

"WHAT? YOU'RE GOING TO LEBANON! ARE YOU CRAZY? What are you going to do, ride a camel?"

That was one of their first responses when friends heard of my latest impending trip to the homeland of my ancestors. Unfortunately, all that most Americans know about that troubled country is what they see on TV or read in the newspapers. And that coverage tends toward the sensational: terrorism, bombings, and kidnappings. Indeed, these were a part of Lebanon's past, and periodically reappear in its present. It is an enduring image. The State Department didn't think Americans should travel to Lebanon, and had only recently lifted the passport ban that had been in effect since 1985. I didn't care; I was going anyway. It is what I had to do if I was going to pursue the truth.

Descending into Beirut by air, our glide path takes us perilously close to the rooftops of the apartment buildings below. Out the window I see a city in transition, struggling to balance the forces of modernity and antiquity. Construction cranes dot the skyline like a flock of giant birds. It is hard to believe that so many projects could be going on simultaneously. The skeletons of buildings, casualties of the long civil war, incongruously exist alongside emerging high-rises.

Lebanon not only has a long and interesting history but a unique topology as well. The country measures 125 miles from top to bottom and from east to west averages only forty miles in width. That space includes two mountain ranges, a coastal strip, an inland plain, and many rivers and lakes.

My cousin Alain Joseph and his wife Désireé meet me at the airport, and after the usual Lebanese greetings with triple kisses, I am whisked off to their chalet on the Mediterranean seashore north of Beirut. The ride is exciting with Mercedes-Benzes and BMWs racing over roads under construction to achieve a single car-length advantage. The game of "chicken" is alive and well in Lebanon, and those who drive must be prepared to play. The one or two traffic signals I saw are totally ignored. Highways have no route designations that I could discern. Signposts are scant to non-existent. Cars on three-lane roads squeeze together to forge a four-lane highway. The drivers seem not to understand the purpose of the painted white lines as they straddle them for long distances, abandoning the practice only to pass other cars, on the right or left. If Lebanon has police cars, they are invisible, and the few patrolmen by the roadside seem oblivious to the traffic whizzing by.

Désireé asks me what I hope to accomplish on this trip. After I tell her of my plan to follow the ancestry trail, she nonchalantly says, "No problem." She thinks nothing of adding my itinerary to her already busy schedule, which includes balancing her time between two jobs and homemaking chores for three children and a husband. She will prove to be positively indefatigable, and I will get tired just following her around. "We go tomorrow," she says, "and we will find Adela's house."

We start our trek up into the mountains the next morning—and I do mean up—abandoning the hectic coastal road for a different kind of adventure. The road rises steeply, and in less than fifteen minutes we ascend from sea level to an altitude of 2,900 feet. I keep expecting oxygen masks to drop down from above as we climb, but that proves unnecessary. The narrow, twisting roads reveal a majestic view, both of the sprawling valleys below and the sparkling blue Mediterranean, now in our rear view. Désireé's little Peugeot dashes up and down the ancient, paved-over donkey trails, lurching in and out of the characteristically small settlements that dot the hillsides of mountainous Lebanon.

I call Désireé my cousin, even though the relationship is through marriage, because she seems more interested in helping me trace the family history than do my blood relatives, something I find rather curious. Although her English is a bit accented (Désireé's three sisters and brother make fun of her lack of fluency), it is more than passable, and whatever she lacks in command of American idioms is more than made up for by her unabashed enthusiasm for the chase.

Thirty minutes into our journey the road veers sharply to the right, just past the town of Faitroun, the site of a limestone quarry, probably the one where my father worked as a young man. The road has slimmed considerably and the curves become more pronounced. Désireé is undeterred, however, honking the horn as she negotiates each blind curve, warning everyone of our coming. "Mazzrat Kfar Debiane," Désireé says, and a quick glance at my watch shows we have been on the road for three quarters of an hour. As we rolled into Adela's undistinguished hometown, I couldn't help but wonder if it had changed much in the last 100 years, and if the old el Khazen hostel still stands.

The Lebanese custom, as I often observed is when in doubt, inquire. We stop and ask if there are any el Khazens about, and after finding a few distant cousins, we are pointed to a house that sits below the main highway and is accessible only by descending a long flight of stone steps. This is strange, I think, for how could the story about my Grandfather Sheikh Namatallah Hobeiche riding his horse to the door of the el Khazen's hostel be true? He certainly wouldn't have traversed this steep hill on horseback, nor would my great-grandfather have put his house in such an inaccessible location.

"Is this Sheikh Abdullah el Khazen's house?" we ask. Yes, the lady of the house answers and assures us this is indeed the home where my Grandmother Adela lived over a hundred years ago. "Where did the old road go?" I ask. Of course, I'm told, it ran right along next to the house through what is now an orchard of plum and pear trees. It seems there was a boundary dispute twenty years prior, a common occurrence in Lebanon, and the old road became a casualty of the legal settlement.

The house, although large for Lebanon of the nineteenth century, is not opulent unless matched against those of the sharecropping peasants of the time. To this day the structure has a commanding view across a steep chasm to the neighboring town of Bqaatouta, a town we'll hear more about later on.

The dwelling has changed from when Grandmother Adela was living there. A gabled roof was added sometime after the First World War. Most of the flat, earthen roofs of that period have been replaced with relatively care-free pitched metal ones. Even a hundred years ago, charming architectural antiquity was giving way to labor-saving modernity. The benefits of not having to place stone jars under a leaking flat roof, or to periodically roll that roof with a heavy *mahdalla* (stone cylinder) to clog up the leaks, were compelling. To me this is a cultural loss, but I wasn't the one who had to push the granite roller around the rooftop. Most Lebanese seem willing to sacrifice quaint construction aesthetics for modern practicality.

There also appears to have been a substantial addition made to the original house, creating a new front entrance and relegating the earlier dining room to storage room status. Looking up, once inside the old entrance, I can see the antique structural beams made from tree saplings still remain, including the soot-blackened timbers above what was the kitchen. The area seemed small and wouldn't have accommodated more than a dozen guests. It is no longer connected to what has become the main house as the quite discernable arched former passageway has been sealed off. The storage area is now chock full of relics of the past—straw baskets, old tools, and a balance scale complete with a set of weight stones.

At this moment the vision of Sheikh Namatallah Hobeiche riding up to the house becomes quite clear. This was the very room that he was in when he first met Adela el Khazen back in 1893. But the relatives living here now have never heard the story, and quite frankly, it generates only polite interest, the kind that Lebanese hospitality demands, and no more.

After more courteous conversation with our hostess and an adequate sampling of the ubiquitously offered fruit, Désireé and I wrap up our visit to the old el Khazen homestead and start down the mountain trail to Zouq Mikhail where the next chapter in Grandmother Adela's saga would take place.

My amiable chauffeur wriggles our little car down the zigzag twists and turns with reckless ease. It seems as if the Peugeot can navigate its way without prompting because Désireé keeps turning to speak to me as the car careens around the curves on the narrow road. It sets me thinking that a deliberate, braying donkey, albeit a lot slower, would be the safer, and my increasingly preferred, way to reach our destination.

Désireé brakes the car suddenly, a practice that any traveler in Lebanon will come to know well, to seek directions from people along the roadside who look just as lost as we. A surprising characteristic of the Lebanese, from my perspective at least, is their innate suspicion of most things, including maps. Perhaps this peculiarity has been genetically imprinted through their long and tortured history, but it is nettlesome nonetheless. I don't know if they can't read maps or just don't trust them—probably a bit of both. The conversations when asking directions are always polite and animated with a lot of finger pointing, hand waving, and well wishing. Having received the latest set of directions, our Peugeot slithers up a serpentine road into the heart of the little town of Zouq Mikhail where my family tree branched more than a hundred years ago.

We pull up in front of the convent of Sayadet el Becharra, with its iron gate yawning lazily in the afternoon light, and on the hinges of which my family's history pivoted those many years ago.

Strolling through the courtyard we encounter a nun by the name of Sr Margarite Marie Issa Juan. She is one of two nuns at the convent permitted to mingle with the outside world. They are in charge of acquiring provisions and seeing that the grounds are kept up. Sr Juan gives us a tour of the premises, sans the cloistered area of course. We end up in the visitors' room with its floor-to-ceiling grate separating us from two nuns seated on the other side. There is a cute little turntable built into the wall at the far end of the room that is used to pass refreshments to the guests without violating the cloister. And soon the device swivels to present us with hot tea.

An elderly nun enters and takes a chair across from us. Sr Takla has been at the convent since 1925 and remembers meeting my grandmother Adela when she was visiting her four nieces who were nuns there during the 1930s. "She was always dressed in black," Sr Takla remarks. "Do you know why?"

I ask Désireé to tell the nun that she was probably still mourning the death of her husband Nami. Emotions begin to build as the deaths and mourning of relatives are recalled, and Désireé begins to silently weep. I can only put my hand on her shoulder to comfort her, trying not to let her see the tears forming in the corners of my eyes. She tells me later that she is embarrassed because it's not like her or members of her family to show their sentimentality in such situations. This I find hard to believe because, from my vantage point, the country of Lebanon is a bundle of emotions. A walk down any street showcases the incessant hand gestures, shoulder shrugs, and exaggerated facial expressions, along with a profusion of shouts and rejoinders.

Our conversation with the elderly nun makes it easy for me to go back in time and conjure up images of the people in my grandparents' day. I see them walking or riding their mules along those same roads we traversed to get to the convent. I see them working the land, putting their hands into the obstinate earth, and wrenching from it the bare essentials of life.

And there is Adela, poking her fingers through the grate, alarmed at what her visitors have just told her. The movie has started playing in my mind, a movie that will take me across the divide of time into the lives of my ancestors.

# 3

*If you marry well, you should be able to treat her well.*

TRAVELING THOSE MOUNTAIN ROADS AFTER DARK was impossible, so the priest insinuated his party into the residence of the pastor of the local church. When the cock crowed, the party quickly arose to continue their journey. At an average speed of five kilometers per hour, the trip would have taken six hours. Thus, Nami's caravan would arrive at the el Khazen destination in the Mazraat an hour or so past lunchtime.

The el Khazens, having anticipated the results of the goings on at the Zouq convent, were ready for the entourage. Adela's mother consoled her daughter, while wringing or wiping her hands on her ubiquitous apron. She was quite concerned about the sight that greeted her—Adela's bloodshot eyes, a purple bruise on her forehead, the makeshift bandage on her hand, and dried bloodstains on her white religious habit. She had to wonder just what went on down at Zouq. Farid, of course, reassured his aunt that there was nothing to be concerned about. Adela reportedly remained silent.

Only two weeks went by before the nuptials for Nami and Adela were held with the usual fanfare in the Patriarchal Chapel in Bekerke, the little town that to this day houses the command center for the Maronite patriarchy. It was de rigueur for notable families to be matrimonially joined in the impressive, stone-vaulted Maronite church where both the el Khazen and Hobeiche patriarchs would have prayed. Yes, a Hobeiche had immediately preceded an el Khazen patriarch, and he was also named Yousef, the same as Nami and Adela's first-born would be christened.

Fr Boulous was allowed to concelebrate* with the bishop of the church, and all during the ceremony Adela averted her eyes, even when she was asked to

---

*A mass is said to be celebrated and when there are two or more celebrants, it is referred to as a concelebration.

33

repeat the marriage vows. As was the custom for a Maronite Rite high mass,* there was a great deal of echoic chanting and pendulation of the smoldering incense censer throughout the ceremony. The ritual was accentuated by the thurible's aromatic odors, which readily combined with the scent of scores of flowers arrayed about the church. The resulting aroma that permeated the atmosphere surely added to the solemnity and importance of the occasion.

A large contingent of Hobeiches, el Khazens, and Dahdahs, the three major historic families of sheikhs in The Mountain (a synonym for Lebanon), made the trek from Ghazir, Jounieh, Byblos, Ajaltoun, and surrounding areas to attend the wedding. All were anxious to partake of the obligatory celebrations that followed the nuptial rites. This would include dancing, drinking, and discharging firearms, a necessary accoutrement to the festivities, that would go on well into the night and for three days thereafter. The celebration was carried on with a gusto that increased in direct proportion to the amount of *arak* consumed (that anise-flavored, heady brew that Lebanese love). All, save Adela that is, reportedly had a good time.

No mention was made whether Adela's mother-in-law retrieved the sheet from the wedding bed to hang out for all to see. That bloody ritual, proving the virginity of the bride, was omitted from the folk tale handed down to us.

So, Désireé and I turned tail from the convent at Zouq Mikhail and headed up the mountain to the former country home of the Hobeiches of Kattine. What lay in store for Adela I could only imagine, for the union had gotten off to a rocky start, what with a reluctant bride and a groom that she knew very little about.

The trip up to Kattine is graced with spectacular scenery. Across the valleys I see honeycombed gardens terraced into the hillsides with meticulously assembled stones, the very structure of which seems to defy gravity. Those traveling these roads to the wedding celebration were certainly used to these sights and probably gave them no thought at all. I can't help but think that the yanking of a single stone could send the entire assemblage tumbling into the valley below.

Wild flowers in red, purple, and golden profusion populate the road's

*A high mass is celebrated according to the complete rite, in which the liturgy is sung by the celebrant.

narrow shoulders and even peek out from the microscopic cracks in the sheer cliffs. Thistles, vetch, lavender, pimpernel, and heather in various colors, watched over by the long-necked Spanish Broom, poke their noses up at us as if to wonder why we are in such a hurry. "Stop," they seem to say, "and take in the beauty!" But Désiree hurries on regardless, having seen it so often that she has become invulnerable to this simple but majestic display of nature's bounty.

I suddenly remembered asking my Uncle Yousef many years before if there were a lot of accidents on these roads. "No, no," he laughed, "more accidents on good roads!" Soon I spy the Hobeiche villa off in the distance, peering out of the mountainside. I thought it was fairly remote when I first saw it twenty-five years earlier and could only imagine what it must have been like when horses and mules were the only means of travel and the house was a one-room dirt floor affair with curtains strung up as room dividers. Like many of the houses of that period, it has undergone substantial expansion and modernization but still retains the flat roof, although the earthen construction has given way to a more weather resistant bituminous material.

The married couple, once the celebrations were over, would settle into the routine of daily living at the small country house. Nami, upon his father's death five years before, had been given one of the four houses in the family compound, the one that was tucked into the side of a large rock outcropping. Along with the rude country house and a few tenant dwellings, there were orchards and gardens and a spring for irrigation. With the increment of Adela's small dowry, the couple began life as the most prominent, if not wealthiest, family of the small village of Kattine.

In those times, the bitter chalice of unhappiness was being freely passed around Lebanon's countryside, and it didn't take Adela long to take a sip. Expectations that this man whose honor was *whiter than the inside of a turnip*, but whose wallet was as threadbare as a pauper's coat, would make her better off than her past circumstances were soon to be dashed. This in turn caused Adela to imbibe more deeply from the distasteful cup. Her feelings, usually never more distant than the next bead on her rosary, had been repressed in the hope that this escapade might turn out well. The house was smaller and quite different from the one she had left in the Mazraat, and it was enough to make her mutter a common Lebanese curse that damned the responsible priest and the man who sired him.

Those who came to know the couple soon recognized a disparity of strength and purpose between them. Nami the insistent suitor became the easygoing

35

gentleman farmer. He had the usual contingent of sharecroppers working his gardens and orchards, and he treated them in a jovial manner that belied the discrepancy in their social status. As was the norm in that day, they were paid with a portion of the produce. Adela, despite her religious zeal and attendant charity, was unused to this familiarity with the help. The el Khazens she was bred amongst had well-deserved reputations as stern taskmasters who brooked no such easiness with the help.

Adela was a hard worker, and along with the favors shown to the sheikh and his wife by the neighbors, was able to assist in the cultivation of a modest standard of living. People were paying their regular and obligatory visits, bringing foodstuffs and even, on occasion, entertaining the couple in their own modest homes. These were the accepted perks of belonging to a noble family, perks that obtained no matter what their material circumstances were.

In some ways, it reminded me of my youth when the ladies of the Lebanese community would visit my mother, bearing food and whispering among themselves about the "sheikha." I always knew that something un-egalitarian was going on but accepted it as a cultural custom, one that I didn't need to fully understand. These traditions meant little to me, and in fact, I thought they stood in the way of my becoming a fully assimilated American. Therefore, these customs were something to be tolerated, not adopted for the long haul.

Adela, who would teach those traditions to my mother, not only understood but also expected this kind of treatment. It was an interesting turn of events for someone who had just left the humble cloistered convent life of worldly denial.

As time passed, the children came. The first born, a boy, Yousef, arrived just short of the couple's second wedding anniversary in 1897. And what Maronite boy wouldn't be proud to bear Patriarch Yousef Hobeiche's given name? Pointing out a former patriarch on your family tree was like saying you were related to the pope.

Times were tough but living beyond a person's means was not foreign to Nami, or indeed to many of the other sheikhs in Lebanon, a habit that I observed still prevails to the modern day. He took a mortgage on the homestead with the Hobeiche church, Mar Elias. He also bartered resources such as lumber and did whatever he could to obtain the wherewithal to showcase the style he knew was expected of him. Reportedly this resulted in constant haggling with Adela and incessant struggling to make ends meet. A girl, Safa, was born, followed by another, my mother Angèle, three years later. And when, just twelve months later, another boy, Khalil, was produced, Nami's thoughts began to probe ways to make do. Such thoughts soon drifted to the streets of gold that were buzzed about, in "*Amreeka*."* He would have to find additional sources of income, as times were getting tougher in Lebanon.

The population had long since exceeded the land's ability to sustain it, and soon the few pebbles that tumbled down the mountain and rolled on to ships heading west became an avalanche of humanity seeking passage to the land of opportunity. Two of Nami's cousins had gone to *Amreeka*, wherever that was, and the stories of which they and other émigrés wrote in their letters kept the population buzzing about the riches to be had in the New World. Those left behind took note of the remittances being sent back and saw what it meant to their families, so they also began to dream. Steamship companies sent agents to comb the hills of countries such as Lebanon for those seeking the "good life," candidates to fill their passenger rolls. Silly rumors about gold growing on trees just waiting to be plucked were rife, and willing harvesters crowded the wharves anxious for a chance at the plucking.

From a reading of the history of this period, it is obvious the Ottoman Empire was undergoing critical change. In the previous thirty-five years of relative calm, the population of Lebanon had mushroomed and many of the residents had no option but to seek work elsewhere to help support their families. The Ottomans, for their part, felt it didn't look good for the Empire to have their subjects leave in noticeable numbers so, for a period of time, they banned emigration altogether. Heaven forbid that it should look to the outside world that there was misery in a land that encompassed the original Garden of Eden.

The emigration phenomenon, to me, was hard to fathom. Why my ancestors, in search of their fortunes, were impelled to travel 6,000 miles to a country whose language they knew not, with but a pittance in their pockets and no knowledge of when or if they could return, amazes me to this day. It took an enormous amount of courage or desperation to embark upon such a journey. And millions from around the world did just that.

There was, of course, an ancient version of Catch 22 at work in chasing this dream and that catch was the price of passage. Those who needed money the most ended up needing more money just to get the needed money—a

---

*Pronounced Am·reé·ka by Arabic speakers.

vicious circle indeed. One couldn't just jump aboard a steamer to escape poverty, although stowing away was not unknown. The usual method was coming up with the required payment of ten gold Turkish liras (at the time $44). It was no small sum to people struggling to feed their families where the average peasant's income was the equivalent of 10¢ a day.

Many whose families owned land and could use their property as collateral for a loan did so. Families pooled resources to send their able-bodied members abroad who, in turn, would send money to pay off their debts and confer passage on others to join them. It was a pyramid scheme of sorts, and the bagmen for the steamship companies were but stepping-stones on the climb to its apex. The needy would have to scale those heights to get to the "Promised Land," and for them the climb was much steeper than for the relatively affluent few who had little reason to emigrate.

Nami depended on his brother Rashid to help better manage his affairs, and even with his help, was barely able to keep the snarling jackals of hunger and deprivation from his door. And this was a time when fulminating packs were freely roaming the countryside in search of prey. So, he had to be as vigilant as a shepherd tending his flock in the mountains, who had to keep watch not only for jackals, but wolves, hyenas, lions, and bears that were waiting to pounce on weak or unprotected lambs. It was a wearying task for the gentle Sheikh Nami.

Adela, not unlike the majority of highborn women, could not read or write her native Arabic. She was therefore always curious about the contents of letters that arrived sporadically, bearing foreign stamps and a different script. It was in the summer of 1909 that one such letter arrived.

# 4

*One's feet carry him only to places he wants to be.*

THE FACT THAT THE WRITTEN AND SPOKEN ARABIC are in essence two different languages always puzzled me. It's a foreign concept to someone educated in the English language. From time to time, there have been struggles in the Arab world over this dichotomy, with various factions promoting the idea that the written language should be more colloquial. But the guardians of the language of the Quran have always squelched such ideas. This linguistic dichotomy, of course, is not unique to Arabic, as many countries of the world have had higher and lower versions of the same language.

I saw the Lebanese immigrants of my time struggle with their adopted English, and it was because of this that many of them came to prize the ideal of education. Something that was not emphasized in the old country became a necessary lynchpin for success in the new one. I would often hear my father say that so and so was "edikated." He also would often remark that he had no "edikation," equating that notion not only with the facility of literacy but also with the ability to accrue a fortune in *Amreeka*. He believed this even though many uneducated immigrants, including Lebanese, amassed large fortunes in their new country without the benefit of formal "edikation."

In Lebanon in the time of my grandparents, many were not "edikated" to the point of literacy in their native language, and Grandmother Adela was but one of them. Thus, the mysterious letter that was awaiting Nami's return from another of his mysterious trips piqued Adela's curiosity. Her husband had not heretofore confided to her the contents of correspondence that messengers had brought him from time to time from his cousins in the New World. The one in Mexico City was doing well in the export/import business, and the other, a Maronite priest in Cincinnati, Ohio, was ministering to the growing Lebanese immigrant community there.

The perception that Sheikh Nami was troubled about his economic situation was not evident to the casual onlooker. The way he indulged his son Yousef belied his unease, for the boy could do no wrong in his father's eyes. Adela openly fretted that he was being spoiled. Nami said she should mind the girls, and he would take care of the boys.

Yousef, the Arabic name for Joseph, was a large boy who seemed to grow like the weeds that infested the Hobeiche gardens. Even in his pre-pubescent days, he relished riding his father's horse recklessly, even over the neighbor's grounds, unconcerned with the consequences. Sent off to school in Aintoura to study at St. Joseph's, he took his pampered demeanor with him and quickly let his classmates know just who he was. Not studious by nature, but doing well thanks to a prodigious memory; brooking no slight; temper flaring; bloodying noses; cracking jaws; receiving a wide berth from the other boys; a wicked right hand earning its own reputation; showing surprising leadership qualities; and earning many a disciplinary action. His reputation was building at an early age, and as our story will reveal, would continue until the day he died.

Yousef was twelve when the curious letter arrived and his father took him aside and explained that since the Young Turks revolted, the Ottoman Empire had begun to change. He was, of course, referring to the turmoil in Constantinople (named by the Emperor Constantine after himself in the fourth century AD and officially changed to Istanbul in 1930) caused when a group of dissident army officers dropped a rock in the Ottoman sea that caused ripples throughout the Empire, especially in Lebanon. Heretofore, the separately governed Lebanon had enjoyed special privileges that were granted in the Réglement* of 1861-63, and those were now endangered. Nami added, with some resignation, that times were getting harder in the mountains and that he might have to seek opportunities elsewhere to provide for the family.

As they sat out on the veranda, Nami inhaled deeply from the *nargelie*** that ubiquitous brass and glass water pipe that was always nearby and usually stoked up after the evening meal. The ensuing conversation seemed to be embraced by the smoke and the gurgling bubbles produced by the smoldering device. Although only twelve, smoking was not unknown to Yousef (a habit that would cause persistent hacking throughout his later years). He was a boy eager to taste life, and he watched expectantly as his father nursed the pipe

*Among the privileges was freedom from military conscription, lower taxes, and a Christian Ottoman subject as their governor.
**Also called a *hookah* or hubbly-bubbly.

stem, hoping to get a drag or two for himself.

Nami began with a family story that explained to Yousef that he was descended from a long line of sheikhs who helped create the history of the country. His family, (and he repeated what we already know), had some 800 years before helped guide the Crusaders over the mountains when they came to recapture the Holy Land.

Yousef had also heard these stories in history classes at school. But his father, seemingly entranced by the deepening shadows cast by the setting sun, almost hypnotically began to repeat the tales that were told him by his father from his father before him. It was time to make sure that his eldest son and heir knew their cherished history, just as every child of the notables would be made to know.

It was easy for me to visualize this scene because my mother spent many evenings on our front porch, sans *nargelie* of course, spinning the same tales to her brood. History in the form of storytelling was an integral part of Lebanese culture in those days.

Nami was reputedly a good storyteller, and when he began his tale, he had the knack of transporting his listeners to the time and place of which he spoke. He recounted that the Hobeiches came from North Lebanon, having been invited to Ghazir by Emir Mansour Assaf in the early 1500s from the valley of *Nahr Ibrahim* (Abraham's River). Then, twenty years later, as a reward for doing the business of the emir, they came to Kattine. The stark and sometimes lurid facts of "doing the business" were not something they were ashamed of, not in the least. Rapidly exhaling the *nargelie's* gloomy smoke, Nami was unmindful that it was enveloping both him and his son in a cloud that seemed to transport them to another time, while also providing cover against the marauding mosquitoes that came out in droves after dark.

The story was that the emir, whose castle was in Ghazir, had a traitor in his ministry who was conspiring against him. Two Hobeiches, Sheikhs Yousef and Soleiman, were asked by the emir to "take care of the problem."

My imagination took flight when I first heard the story from my mother, and I pictured an advertisement in a newspaper under Personals or tacked up in the public square. "Got a personnel problem? Call the Hobeiches." So, they were the emir's hired guns!

Much to Adela's chagrin, Nami showed no hesitancy in telling the story to the young Yousef. He proceeded to regale him with the tale of a certain minister who was planning the overthrow of the emir and how the two Hobeiche boys attacked the minister's residence one night, broke down the door in that part of the citadel, grabbed the perpetrator by the neck, took him to the edge of the castle's cliff, and along with eleven other members of his family, slit their throats and threw them into the valley below.

On one of my trips to Lebanon I visited the place where the Tower stood, and it is now the site of a church, "Our Lady of the Tower." I had a hard time picturing what the castle looked like in the 1500s when this event transpired but the idea of a church overlooking the place where a dozen murders took place seemed a bit incongruous.

Adela knew the history well, having heard it even before she married into the Hobeiche clan. She thought it was a gruesome story and didn't like it being told to her children, and said so to her husband.

Gentle Nami could be patronizing and condescending when provoked and insisted that the stories be told as they were told to him. He turned his attention back to his raptly attentive son and let out yet another long stream of grayish-white smoke. Yousef, for his part, was not shocked, just inquisitive. Even discounting what I knew to be the accepted practice of exaggeration in Lebanese storytelling, this gruesome recounting seemed a tad strong, but Yousef would not think so.

Nami chalked up the consequences as the price of treachery where, in a traitor's family, everybody paid. And part of the reward was the very land they now inhabited. I guess you could call it a blood payment, but to Nami the lands came down through the bravery of his ancestors, men of honor, a people to be reckoned with.

Seeing his father in a storytelling mood, Yousef asked if the tale about Sheikh Torbey was also true. His father smiled widely, his moustache curling around the perimeter of his mouth, and wondered where the lad had heard this legend.

The event had been recorded in a book authored by Fr Henri Jalabert, a Jesuit historian and faculty member at St. Joseph's. Yousef gave a sketchy account of what he had heard about Sheikh Torbey shooting a muezzin (the caller of Muslims to prayer) from his minaret in Ghazir. Incidentally, Torbey was Nami's great-great-great-grandfather.

Nami was prompted to embark on an animated story about the need to fight for every inch of privilege in order to practice their religion and keep whatever semblance of independence they had. He said that one Sunday morning the sacristan of their church was banging the *naqous* (a metal bar vertically suspended from supports, like an overgrown wind chime), to call the people to mass. At the same time the muezzin, from his nearby minaret, was singing a call to prayer. Reportedly the muezzin became angry at the racket the *naqous* was making, so he began to sing louder and louder. In typical sectarian escalation, the sacristan began to beat the iron bar harder and harder. This angered the muezzin, who descended the circular staircase of his minaret and promptly toppled the offending instrument.

Because of all the shouting, a crowd gathered and was on the verge of riot. In the meantime, someone ran off to tell Sheikh Torbey, who promptly came to the scene armed with his rifle. He spied the muezzin, who had returned to his minaret to resume his loud singing, drew a bead, and shot him dead on the spot.

Adela, rolling her eyes to the darkened sky and then back to her husband along with a reproving glance, turned to go back into the house to ensure the younger children said their prayers and were tucked into bed. Nami reciprocated her glance and wearily responded that she should come back when finished because he had something important to tell her.

I would have rolled my eyes as well, for I didn't quite see the valor in shooting the unarmed muezzin for tipping over the *naqous*. This incident, the recording and exaltation of it, exemplified the depth of religious strife between Maronites and Muslims of that time. One would also have to wonder how the glorification of these divisions would affect an impressionable youngster like Yousef later in life.

The storyteller and his son followed Adela into the house where Nami lit a fire in the crude fireplace. The mountain air had invaded the house and brought on a chill, as it often did on those summer evenings.

When Adela had finished her chores, she returned, muttering something about "all this throat cutting and shooting" while taking her place by the fire. She picked up her needlework, a popular cross-stitching of the Cedar of Lebanon for a pillowcase, and looked up at her husband, who had pulled his chair closer to the fire. Yousef sat on a floor cushion, drawing his knees to his chin, not wanting to miss any new announcement. Sensing something momentous, Adela apprehensively asked her husband what it was he wished to tell her.

The room grew quiet save the crackling fire that seemed to keep time with the pulsating tension, a tension that emerged as soon as Nami had forebodingly told Adela of their need to talk. After a few more long puffs on the water pipe, which Yousef had dutifully towed in from the veranda, the mysterious letter was withdrawn from Nami's tunic, and he began to read. It was from his Mexico City cousin, and along with the offer of shelter in the New World, a bank draft for sixty pounds was included to defray the cost of passage.

How the cousin got to Mexico was an interesting story in itself. With no visa available to him because the Ottoman government was severely curtailing emigration at the time, he turned to the black market. The paranoiac Ottomans, as mentioned before, felt that a mass exodus of people from Lebanon reflected badly on the Empire, so they discouraged it at every turn. If, however, one had the money, there were entrepreneurs, such as Hassan Khrairo (a local Mafioso capo, or so it seems), who could get you on a boat, for a price. As the legend goes, Khrairo met his end the same way many a gangster did in America; lured to a dinner meeting and given a bullet for his bother.

With money changing hands at every point along the way, the cousin, under cover of darkness, sat in a short-sailed dinghy in the bay of Jounieh for several hours, waiting for a certain vessel on its way out of the Port of Beirut. Upon spying the ship, the boatmen sailed and rowed as hard as they could to get to the ship before it was completely out of the harbor. An arrangement had been made with the captain, and the passenger was hustled aboard. When he asked where they were going, he was told, "*Amreeka.*"

The ship, after several intermediate stops, docked two weeks later at the port of Vera Cruz in Mexico. The Mexicans weren't as fussy as the Americans on matters of immigration, and a man, even one with dubious papers, would be hustled through the scant procedures to seize any opportunity that awaited. Thus, Nami's cousin had arrived in Mexico four years before and was apparently doing quite well.

Adela moaned as she dropped her sewing and began to beat her breast while pointing out that he was nearly fifty years old and untrained in any trade. She derisively asked if he was going to be a peddler like the rest of those Lebanese peasants.

Nami tried to calm his wife, fearing that she would alarm the children. He coolly pointed out that things were hard in Lebanon, and they weren't getting better. He added that the French who had been protecting them might not be able to continue to do so.

Adela, maintaining her faith in her perceived patrons, replied confidently that the French would take care of the Turks as they had in the past. It was largely through France's intervention that the Capitulations* were enforced with the Ottomans.

Nami said it would be foolish to think the French were invincible just because they helped them get and keep concessions from the Turks in the

*Contracts forced on the Ottomans conferring rights to European (and American) subjects residing or trading in their dominion.

past. He said France would think of herself first and that Turkey would have powerful allies. Nami took pains to emphasize their obligations to educate the children, realize income from the property, and keep the estate in good running order. More money would make it easier all the way around. He also noted how well the families of the expatriates were doing, which was a large incentive for him to make the move. She could continue sharecropping the land as in the past, and they would have more food with his absence. His brother Rashid would look after the family while he was away.

Adela told her husband that since his mind was made up there was nothing more to say except, "God be with you."

# 5

*Things to come are nearer than things that are gone.*

A N EXAMINATION OF THE ELLIS ISLAND RECORDS attests that people of all ages were immigrating to the US during the period 1880-1914. The most common recorded occupations for men from Lebanon and Syria were laborer and farmer, with an occasional shoemaker or merchant. In those days being a member of the merchant ranks wasn't exactly considered high class. Families including babies and grandparents also emigrated, but the notion of a notable of Nami's age choosing to leave was puzzling. What would he list as his occupation? Hmm... Sheikh? Could the situation have incubated such hopelessness that it would give birth to desperation? "I don't know why," my mother said years later. "We don't know why," my cousins echoed. It is a family mystery that went to the grave with the enigmatic Sheikh Nami.

What we do know for sure is that the economic hardship endured by most of the aristocrats in Lebanon was a legacy of the Peasant's Revolt. That inheritance was due to a number of factors, not the least of which was the Lebanese class structure itself. In pre-revolt days, the sheikhs could extract labor, "gifts," and taxes from the subservient peasants virtually at will. There were also many artificial strictures that defined the disparity between the two classes. The peasants couldn't, for example, even dress to the same standards as the notables because they would be seen as encroaching on their turf, or in American parlance, "being uppity." There were even legal penalties for such transgressions.

The sheikhs, for their part, wouldn't be seen engaging in traditional peasant activities that required working with their hands. Thus, when the economic balance was upset, the inclination for continued adherence to these ancient class constraints served to impoverish those of the notable class. Nami was but one among them that fell in to this category, and a dejected Adela knew the story all too well.

I could appreciate the depths of despair this setting induced by seeing it through the eyes of my mother as she recalled her family's plight. Even though a half-century had elapsed, time did not dim the experience for her.

Anyone who knew Angèle certainly would know that in times of stress she turned her prayers to the Virgin. She wore her typically Lebanese devotion to the mother of Jesus proudly, a devotion that was eminently observable throughout her life. There would be statues, pictures, and iconographs of the Blessed Mother placed about our home, and even a small shrine with a votive candle. She spent many an hour making miniature clothes for the statue, clothes that were made of the finest silk. "*Ya Adra,*" Oh Virgin, was an intonation that was never far from her lips.

So too on this occasion Angèle turned to the Virgin, imploring intercession on her father's behalf. She was too young to understand that her father felt he would never achieve the promise of his station in his home country and was driven, in fact compelled, to find success elsewhere. Compounding the problem was the wearying effect of his relationship with the strong-willed Adela. The older Nami got, the less he seemed able to put up with her overbearing ways.

As soon as she was up, Angèle confronted her Baba. Nami sat the little girl on his lap and tried to soothe his daughter's fears by caressing her long hair, telling her not to worry, and that he would return soon.

The little girl was not easily mollified and wondered aloud what she would do after her protective Baba was gone. Her mother had become totally obsessed with making sure that her children would be in position to overcome the vicissitudes of economic misfortune that had plagued the family from the beginning of her marriage. This resulted in the use of a stern hand, one that would discipline while pointing the way ahead. Angèle chafed at this treatment and suddenly confessed out loud that she hated her mother, which took her father aback. Nami knew better than to buttress his daughter's animosity toward her mother. He mildly admonished her not to say such things, reminding her that her mother meant well and was just making sure that she grew up educated so she could reach her potential.

These words may as well have been spoken to the female goat, which was tethered just off the veranda, for they made as much sense to Angèle as they would have to the nanny. Her feelings toward her mother were especially strong at the moment, and she continually marveled at her father's forbearance. She also impishly reminded him of a proverb that she oft heard him repeat, "*That which is in the heart is on the tip of one's tongue.*"

Her father smiled but added that Angèle must help her mother all she could and take care of her little brother after he was gone. She had to remember that she was a sheikha and had a duty to her family and her heritage. Angèle retreated to the room where her mattress had already been rolled up and piled into a corner, and stared into the small mirror that hung on the wall. She basked in the notion of being a sheikha, liking the sound of the word so much that she repeated it over and over.

# 6

*She finds fault in a bird even when it's flying.*

BASED ON EVERYTHING I COULD READ AND OBSERVE, being a sheikh or a sheikha continued to lose its cachet as the country became further and further removed from the feudal system. And, like the exiled royalty of Russia, the trappings of class for the Lebanese notables were difficult to relinquish. In Angèle's case, her parents did not make the transition any easier. Neither did the outwardly obsequious peasants who had long been taught to defer to these people whom they considered their betters, not only by birth or perceived wealth but also by the benefit of education.

But reality was the order of the day for the Hobeiche household. Adela, trying to be faithful to the instructions her husband had left, sent the children off to school. It is rumored that the el Khazens of that period didn't place the same premium on education as did the Hobeiches.

Angèle continually asked her mother why she had to go away to school while her little brother Khalil stayed at home. Why should she, still short of her fifth birthday, have to leave home? Her crying and whimpering were to no avail, and she was trundled off to Ajaltoun with her sister Safa. Normally the nuns wouldn't accept a youngster that age, but the el Khazen family had also endowed St Vincent's school. Adela's lineage still held a modicum of sway with them, influence that she was willing to use.

The fall air was crisp and the long ride on the mule was an adventure for the girls. Birds were on their migratory swing, making alternately large and small specks in the sky as they zoomed in and soared out. The plodding mule paid no attention, keeping his head steadfastedly down, hewing to the steady climb. Hours later, when they arrived at the convent school, Angèle's tears began to flow anew.

Imagining my mother in these circumstances reminded me of my first experience with school at the Augustinian Academy in Carthage,

New York. My brother was a year-and-a-half older than I, and because of my attachment to him, I would follow him to school every chance I got. In those days my stay-at-home mom was so busy with two kids under the age of two that it was easy for me to slip unnoticed out the door and up the block to the school. Unlike my mother, I was eager to escape the home environment and find refuge in the blackboard jungle. The nun finally tired of sending me home so she sat me down in the back of the room as an observer. I remember on moving-up day crying my eyes out when I learned, at age four, I would have to repeat the first grade.

Wherever I went in Lebanon, I noticed that virtually all adults, old and young, relatives and strangers, have an indulgent fascination with children. They break out in broad smiles and call to them with words of encouragement, hugs, candy, and even loose change. "*Ta, ta, ta,*" they call, much like a shepherd calling his sheep. It seems so different from the wariness in America where children are admonished not to talk to strangers, or at the other extreme, considered annoyances who should be seen but not heard. In Lebanon it appears to be a long-standing cultural tradition to dote on children, a tradition my parents didn't carry with them to the New World.

It is easy, therefore, to imagine the crying and pouting Angèle being courted by the gaggle of workers who were always busying themselves outside the convent school. Everyone sympathized with the sad little girl, and when the children walked between buildings, coming from or going to class, the laborers would call out "*ta, ta, ta,*" bidding her to come and join them and telling her not to cry. She was cute and attracted lots of attention but continued to cry nonetheless.

In school, a stern nun sat Angèle on a small stool off to the side, out of her way and that of the other students. She didn't expect much from the little girl who continually rubbed her runny nose on the sleeve of her dress. Despite the low expectations, Angèle had a percolating brain that would learn in spite of her misery. The instruction was in French, and Safa, in the off hours in the dormitory, would practice her vocabulary on Angèle. So, it wasn't long before the little girl began to sound out the words and one day, a few months later, Angèle astonished the nun by blurting out the answer to one of her French vocabulary questions before anyone else could raise their hand. Her teacher was so impressed that during recess periods she began taking the little girl around to other classes to show her off. It was a tribute to the proud nun's teaching skills, or so she presumed, even though she had made no conscious attempt to teach the little girl anything.

Despite the increased attention, Angèle never forgot the unhappiness of that experience (even making a point of telling the story to her grandchildren many years later). One evening she exclaimed to Safa that mama didn't love her, to which her sister replied that she was being foolish. Angèle often wondered aloud why she was there and her brother Khalil was at home and had concluded that mama loved Khalil more.

Her sister threw up her hands. The three-year difference between them was magnified at that age and the taller Safa, following her mother's cue, took on the role of both counselor and disciplinarian. She warned her sister not to speak of those things. But the homesick Angèle chafed under her sister's admonitions, although not quite as much as she did at home with her mother.

The school year dragged on and the little girl grew, both physically and intellectually. By the end of the year she had mastered the alphabet and numerals in both French and Arabic, and was pronouncing the mandatory French responses quite well. When it came time for the duo to make the trek back to Kattine for the summer, the *mukre* (muleteer) was waiting with his animal, lunches were packed, goodbyes were said, and the girls started the journey back to Kattine.

It was the first of June, and the pleasant weather allowed the mules to make six kilometers per hour down the dusty, stone-strewn trails. When they stopped to eat and rest the beast, the girls played tag and picked wild flowers by the roadside. They were both happy to go home even though Angèle continued nursing the perceived slight from her mother. This was easy to believe because I can personally attest that she had a lifelong propensity for remembering slights that were best forgotten. After having read her brother's thoughts in his letters to Angèle, I have come to conclude that this is a genetic peculiarity that saturates the roots of the Hobeiche family tree.

*Better to attend a funeral than a marriage.*

The Arabic language is rich in proverbs and seldom does a situation arise that a time-tested adage is not available to hammer home a point. Such was the case when Adela found herself bitterly lamenting her "arranged marriage." She would often say, *It is easier for a sieve to hold water than for a woman to trust a man.* And once the dark mood took hold of her, it would not easily let go. Bad enough the marriage had not been materially prosperous, but the presaged riches available for the plucking in *Amreeka* had failed to appear as well, certainly not in sufficient quantity to keep worry from Adela's visage. Nami had been gone two years, and his letters and remittances were intermittent at best.

Angèle said she was always surprised when such candid outbursts erupted and would ask her mother if it was really true that she didn't want to get married. She thought her mother was just exaggerating out of frustration.

Adela's voice would falter as she recounted the tortured tale of her "abduction" from Saydet el Becharra and the Sisters of St. Francis De Sales. And, as always with this recitation, she ritualistically blessed herself, tracing the sign of the cross with all five fingers of her right hand, ending with them pressed to her lips while looking to the heavens. She claimed that she was very happy at the convent, but the family had insisted that Sheikh Namatallah Hobeiche would be a good match, even though she came from a family that, it turned out, was far better off. In response Angèle would often say that being forced into marriage would never happen to her. In fact, she might never marry at all.

Adela dredged up this memory whenever her unhappiness bottomed out, instances that increased in concert with the march of time. Of the miscreant, but now passed-on priest, Fr Boulous, she never failed to remark through clenched teeth that if she knew where he was buried she'd make a pilgrimage just to piss on his grave (I assumed this was the ultimate insult). At the end of the day, she placed blame on him for her having to leave the convent and the troubles she inherited as a result.

The image of Grandma Adela relieving herself over the priest's grave is not a pretty one. It also never ceased to shock me how, for all her Christian devotion, my mother would relish repeating such a story. Often times these tales would be intermixed with religious ejaculations, the irony of which went unnoticed. The contradictory juxtaposition of the sacred and profane reminded me of General George S. Patton who, when asked by a chaplain if he read the Bible, reportedly replied, "Every goddamn day."

Many years ago when I regularly frequented a Middle Eastern restaurant in Pittsburgh, I would often practice my meager language skills with the two proprietors, Ivan and Nadim, both of whom were college students from Syria. Occasionally I would let out a stream of expletives in their native tongue that would fairly singe their eyebrows. "Where did you learn this?" Nadim asked me one day. "From your father?" "No, from my mother!" I replied with a grin. Where else but from Grandmother Adela could Angèle have learned such conversational niceties?

The young Angèle's thoughts often turned to her father, and she never tired of asking her mother when he was coming home even though she knew the answer—"only God knows."

One of Angèle's most important tasks when at home was the care and feeding of the silkworms. Sericulture, even with its periodic economic oscillations, had become a primary source of income for the Lebanese, and nearly every household in the mountains participated—even those of the notables. The expansion of this cash crop, after the fall of the nobility in 1863, allowed the peasantry to achieve a moderately higher income and actually set the stage for further social upheaval in the country.

Traditionally, the Lebanese conducted daily life under a patriarchal imperative where all decisions of any import were made by the male head of the family or the village sheikh. These decisions included arranging marriages for all the children, both male and female, and the remittance of any wages to the head of the family. But once the economic balance between the *m'sheikh* (nobility) and the *fellahin* (peasants) was sundered and female members began working in the burgeoning silk manufactory, many of the girls began rebelling against this system. But Angèle, at her tender age, was unaware of the social implications the little silkworm had wrought on her country and how her own rebellious nature would comfortably weave into this web.

Angèle liked her sericultural duties. The hatchery had become a comfortable refuge for her, one where she could escape Mama for a while. She would bring book and candle with her, and after meticulously cutting up the mulberry leaves to feed the freshly hatched worms, she would stay and serenade them with words pronounced from her French primer as the candle's flickering glow bounced off the droplets of water that inched down the dank cellar walls. Although she had to strain to see in the dim light, she was out of Mama's sight, and more importantly her reach, a reach that Angèle had learned to avoid as much as possible.

In a few weeks the worms would be able to feed on whole leaves, and this would save Angèle even more time away from the never-ending hustle and bustle of the household. She also had to hang boughs around the room for the worms to crawl upon to spin their cocoons, a part of the never-ending silk production cycle. Most of the little white fur balls produced would be sold to silk-reelers who would boil the cocoons and wind the released thread onto spools for export. All the activity had to be timed to take place before the caterpillars metamorphosed into butterflies. Some cocoons would be kept, as a sort of seed crop, and then the emerging butterflies would lay eggs to start the process anew.

As she grew older, the precocious Angèle proved to be quite good in school, actually better than her older sister Safa. She exemplified her father's traits of intelligence and wit, along with a facility for languages.

Angèle came to prefer speaking French over her native Arabic—a trait that would be emulated years later by her brother's children—even though her mother did not speak it at all. This attitude strengthened over time, and she took to muttering French responses when she didn't want her mother to understand her retorts.

A preference for the French language among certain of the Lebanese was just another way of distancing themselves from what had become the pejorative Arab classification. This affectation was also popular in European countries at that time, especially amongst the aristocrats of Czarist Russia who felt by speaking French they were kept well above the peasant throngs.

I recall on my first visit to Lebanon being invited to dinner with a large group of my cousin Jouhaina's friends. Her English wasn't very accomplished so she resorted to speaking to me in Arabic, most of which I could surprisingly understand because of her Kesrouani dialect. One of her contemporaries became annoyed at this and asked my cousin what was wrong with her— "Have you forgotten your French?" I wondered why the Arabic tongue was so repugnant to this woman. Also, even neglecting that she knew I didn't speak French, I thought it was rude and betrayed some deep-seated identity problems.

The ever-vigilant Adela would seldom relax her disciplinary ways and took every opportunity to lecture Angèle, pointing out there was always something else to do. The girl would sigh and wonder if there was no escape from all the drudgery and think of places where she could hide from her mama's reach.

Far up the hill in back of the house was a cool, sweet mountain spring, called the *jazzat*, that her father had dammed up to create a mini-reservoir. The workmanship was not a craftsman's dream, for it didn't hold much water and leaked incessantly. However, the steep ascent deterred her mother from looking for her there so it became an enticing hideaway for Angèle. But the unique terrain also allowed her mother to easily communicate with her by calling to her up the mountain. The sound carried so well that Adela knew Angèle would hear her even though she might pretend she did not. The girl enjoyed her respites at the *jazzat* even more than her duties with the silkworms.

Work in the kitchen when home from school was not one of Angèle's duties because the household was small and the amount of food preparation was minimal. Her older sister Safa managed the kitchen so well that Angèle spent her time learning the finer points of crochet, embroidery, cross-stitching, and of course, sericulture. In one of her rare contributions to food gathering, the little girl would go out to pick escargot on dewy, late summer mornings.

Although Adela struggled to keep worry from fouling her features, the family finances and amassing the means to keep the children in school was never far from her mind. She told no one that she had decided to sell the property she inherited in Mazraat to help keep up that effort. Her brother-in-law Rashid, the lawyer turned family regent from Ghazir, especially didn't have to know.

*Put your foot on the path of the fortunate*
*and you too will be fortunate.*

The peripatetic Nami had now been gone nearly three years when Adela got fresh news from Rashid that Nami had left Mexico for a place called Cincinnati in the US. It didn't really surprise her because she knew that Nami's relationship with his cousin in Mexico was a tenuous one. Rashid reported that Nami had crossed the border to join his cousin Fr Toubiya Dahdah in the United States. As was often the case with Nami, no one knew or recorded what transpired to cause this latest rift between him and his cousin. Nami pulled up stakes, bussed his way up to Texas, then traveled by train to Ohio to be with the Maronite priest. Fr Dahdah was a first cousin on his mother's side who was ministering to Lebanese émigrés in the Cincinnati area. As they had been doing since the time of Columbus, clergymen lost no time in following their migrating flocks to America to attend to their spiritual needs.

It really meant little to Adela whether her husband was in Mexico or the United States. What she looked forward to were the infrequent remittances that would help her family survive. I realized at an early age how important remittances were for the Lebanese, a practice that continues to be a large part of their economy to the present day. I can recall the many letters that I addressed in a deliberate hand for my mother, all of which contained some small amount of money for her relatives back home, money that she could hardly spare but knew would alleviate a bit of misery in the "old country." It didn't occur to me until I was much older that Angèle was taking up, however meagerly, where her father left off. It was a practice that she would continue until late in life, when there were no longer any needy beneficiaries left.

# 7

*A noble person is noble though privation touches him.*

THERE WAS A CERTAIN WISTFULNESS IN HER VOICE whenever my mother recalled her family's travails during the Great War. "It was hard, very hard," was her most common expression. Letters from her brother Khalil twenty years later, sent during the midst of the Great Depression, still mentioned those difficult days.

> Khalil to Angèle, 6 September 1933 – No matter how bad the situation, it couldn't be worse than the days we had to go through when we were children. We should not worry now.

The situation took a turn for the worse in the fall of 1914 when Turkey finally declared war on Great Britain and France, allying itself with the Central Powers of Austria-Hungary, Germany, and Bulgaria. This momentous event presaged great changes for Lebanon. The French institutions were the first to feel the effects of an increasingly hostile Turkish regime. All of the French schools were closed and their citizens, including nuns, priests, and administrators were deported.

Soon afterward, brother-in-law Rashid announced to Adela that hard times were upon them, and they had to change to accommodate them. He had leased the stand of hardwood across from the Hobeiche homestead to a man who would use the timber to make charcoal. The moneys he received, he said, would allow him to store enough wheat to see the family through the perilous times ahead. He further told Adela that he would ration out the wheat on a weekly basis, and they would have to augment these rations with whatever crops they could raise.

Adela had no head for business, but she was wise enough to defer to her brother-in-law in this instance. If he thought this was the sensible thing to do, then that's what they would do.

Adela's oldest son Yousef, who had been sent home from school, was perplexed by these developments. Turkish soldiers had arrived at St. Joseph's two months into the fall term and summarily shuttered the school. Since he was the man of the house now, his uncle Rashid reminded him that he had to take care of the gardens and help make sure that the family had enough to eat. Rashid, mindful of Yousef's imprudence, reportedly lacked confidence in Yousef's ability to handle such responsibility.

### *Am I riding a camel and no one sees me?*

In April of 1915, nine months after the war began, hordes of marauding insects descended on Lebanon in what became the great locust invasion. In a futile attempt to save her garden, Adela had spread blankets over the crops. The next morning, not only were her vegetables gone but in the feeding frenzy the blankets were consumed as well.

A month later Adela walked down to Ghazir to see her brother-in-law Rashid. As she surveyed the landscape, she saw that the locusts had devastated the crops at all elevations. Some people were still beating laggards with switches, burning them and futilely stomping them with their feet.

The purpose of Adela's visit was to ask Rashid where their allotment of wheat was that he said he would send each week. Her brother-in-law reminded her that he would ration it as needed and cautioned her not to speak too loudly because there were thieves and desperate people all around. With those words he turned back to the papers on his desk, leaving Adela to understand that the audience was over. The woman left with the same heavy heart she had when she arrived and began her return journey home.

The utter despair Adela must have felt was in my mother's voice when she told of the hardships she and her family endured during the war. But unbeknownst to Adela and others in her situation, a little help was on its way, and the conduit for this beneficence would be the Protestant missionaries, the selfsame people that their priests railed against, accusing them of trying to proselytize their flock.

The Presbyterian American Missionary Press in Beirut, known simply as the American Press, had observed the developing misery and began planning to circumvent the Ottoman policy of embargoing mail and all other help from the West. American Press personnel, whose main mission was to translate English language religious books and tracts into Arabic, decided to become the conduit for remittances to Lebanon and Syria. An ad was placed in several newspapers in the US alerting Lebanese and Syrian émigrés of this service. "*The treasurer of the Presbyterian Board of Foreign Missions will accept for transmission any sums of money that Syrians [including Lebanese] resident in America wish to send to their relatives. Moneys may be sent to the Board's office in New York City.*"

The advertisement also gave the New York City address for the Board of Missions where remittances would be accepted. The Presbyterians would collect and forward monies to Beirut where members of the Press would convert and distribute the funds to the designated donees. This was no simple task as it involved collecting the money in various forms (checks, bank drafts, even wads of cash), providing receipts, identifying the recipients and their whereabouts, negotiating the most favorable exchange rates, routing the money to the proper mission station, and assigning an individual to trudge through hostile terrain in all kinds of weather to deliver the payment.

The American Press staff played a heroic role, at no small cost to themselves, in relieving the suffering of many of the destitute residents across Lebanon and Syria. They traveled to remote villages in winter and summer to see that the aid got through. They risked their personal safety and suffered harassment and arrest because the Ottomans looked with extreme disfavor on their activities. And they did it without regard to religious denomination or affiliation. They also took great pains to ascertain that the recipients who got the aid were who they said they were, for when it got round that a particular individual was being sought, imposters would appear posing as the rightful claimants.

Adela had traveled less than a mile toward home when a one-horse shay with an elderly gentleman holding the reins pulled up alongside and asked, "Would you like a ride?" Adela sensed the stranger was a gentleman of breeding because of his impeccable dress and the way he spoke the language. The man's gray hair and mustache were neatly trimmed, and he was dressed in western garb with a dark gray suit coat, striped tie, and red fez atop his head.

Adela was tired and would dearly like a ride but was unaccustomed to accepting lifts from strangers. The man could see her dilemma and sought to soothe her concerns by telling her, "Do not be afraid." He introduced himself as Sheikh Assad Kheirallah from Beirut. He said he was on a mission of mercy, looking for certain Lebanese people with relatives in America. He was on his way to Kattine to find a woman named Adela Hobeiche who had a kinsman in America.

Adela exclaimed, "I am her! Why do you seek me?"

The gentleman dismounted and went to the passenger side of the shay offering to help Adela up, telling her they could talk on the way. Adela was so surprised by the confrontation that she began to tremble but let the man help her onto the conveyance anyway.

Once the horse started his journey up the mountain path to Kattine, Sheikh Kheirallah began to quiz Adela, asking if she had relatives in America. Adela responded thatshe only had her husband, who was in a place called Cincinnati. Where it was she did not know, but he also had a cousin, Fr Toubiya Dahdah, in the same place. "Why do you want to know?"

The man said he needed to know these things if he was to discharge his duties. As the horse trudged along, Kheirallah reached into his pouch and drew out several slips of paper. He adroitly placed a monocle over his left eye and began shuffling the sheaf he had withdrawn. He singled out a page and put the rest back in the bag asking Adela who might vouch for her identity.

Adela said she had no reason to lie about her identity, and he could ask anyone. "If I could have," she added, "I would have changed my name a long time ago. Of course I am Adela Hobeiche."

Sheikh Kheirallah told her not to be offended because he had to be sure of her identification. He explained that he worked for the American Press in Beirut and was distributing moneys from relatives overseas to the unfortunate people all over Syria and Lebanon. He also told her about impostors who would take advantage of the situation. Kheirallah then stopped the buggy at the guardhouse that appeared around the bend in the road and asked the gendarme if he knew this woman.

"She is Adela Hobeiche, wife of Sheikh Namatallah Hobeiche," the guard said. Kheirallah thanked him and drove on, asking Adela just where her house was. But the puzzled woman just stared ahead as she mumbled directions to the gentleman. The road forked and wound around the valley, and soon they arrived at Adela's home.

The emissary halted his carriage and dismounted, telling her that he knew she was mystified as to what he was doing but he had a surprise for her. He then reached into a large leather wallet that he had secreted in his clothing and pulled out two twenty lira notes and handed them to Adela. He said they were only worth half what they were just the year before, but it was the best they could do. His instructions were to deliver the money with a thousand kisses.

Adela began to weep uncontrollably. The sight of the money lifted a portion of the burden off her shoulders, and she sought to kiss the hand of her unexpected benefactor.

The beneficent messenger demurred and told her there was no need for that, for he was just doing his job. He said he needed a receipt for the disbursement and handed a piece of paper to Adela showing her where to sign. She took the writing implement and scrawled her name as best she could. Kheirallah declined the hospitality that Adela offered, bid her goodbye, and embarked upon another round of finding recipients. It was a tedious job but one that provided him untold spiritual rewards.

Adela fairly skipped into the house. She wouldn't have to tell her brother-in-law about this unexpected windfall either, would she?

# 8

*Unless a crisis reaches its limit, it cannot recede.*

H OW COULD A COUNTRY GO FROM JUST MAKING ends meet to hopeless despair in less than a year? The answer lay not only with the plague of locusts but also with a plague of political persecutions as well.

The Ottoman government made several conscious decisions that were tantamount to the commission of genocide against the people of Lebanon and Syria. The Turks had been chafing under The Capitulations for a long time and now saw an opportunity to exact revenge. The Capitulations, which protected foreign nationals against potentially onerous local laws, had always been a burr under Turkey's saddle. After the outbreak of hostilities, they eagerly seized the opportunity to buck past protocols and abrogate those treaties.

It's interesting to note that the US, even after entering the war, only broke diplomatic relations with the Ottomans and never formally declared war against them. American citizens living in the Middle East continued to insist they be afforded the protections that The Capitulations offered, and most often they were successful in retaining them.

In the first of a series of catastrophic Ottoman decisions for the populations of Lebanon and Syria, they cut off all communications to the outside world, even though they knew that the people were dependent on remittances from overseas. Despite the efforts of the American Missionary Press, many people lost the income that would have sustained them during those turbulent times, and perished as a result.

The Ottomans then rapidly expanded conscription into their armed forces, in many cases taking farmers away from their lands, thus leaving crops to rot in the fields. When shortages resulted from this capricious act, the Turks then exacerbated the situation by expanding their program of confiscation to include farm animals and food stores. This was in essence a double whammy delivered on their subjects at the worst possible time.

One of the most environmentally damaging acts the Turkish Army committed was to harvest trees for wood to fuel trains or for military purposes. The huge Cedar forests of Lebanon suffered the most with over 60% being cut down in three years.

The Turkish government also confiscated any gold they could lay their hands on. This sent paper currency into immediate devaluation and caused merchants to insist on hard coin for their goods. And they refused help from all foreign institutions such as the American National Red Cross, which had established its first-ever international chapter in Beirut in 1909. The governor of Beirut claimed these people were usurping his prerogatives and interfering in civil and municipal affairs and were therefore not welcome.

Last but not least, the Empire tolerated widespread corruption that resulted in combines being formed by the wealthy class to commandeer the market in commodities such as wheat and sugar. They also let their armed forces loot shops and warehouses without recompense to the owners. This forced people to borrow money to subsist, and those who could get loans were forced to pay usurious rates, as much as 55% and more in compound interest.

Once hostilities began between Turkey and the Triple Entente (an alliance entered into by Britain, France, and Russia in 1907), ships of those nations were no longer allowed to dock in Beirut. This cut off the importation of badly needed aid from the West. In early 1915, the Entente aggravated the situation by setting up a blockade of the Syrian coastline that in turn halted the receipt of goods from ships of other nations that would ordinarily have been permitted to dock.

The farmers of Lebanon, who in addition to remittances from abroad, depended on the sale of vegetables, fruit, and silkworm production from their small farms, were totally cut of from their markets for want of transportation. Other small villages that were specialty producers of various items such as cutlery and silver filigree were also forced to close down.

Thus it was in 1916 that want and need led to starvation and disease in Syria and especially Lebanon, which suffered the most. Lebanon was in the first growing season after the ravaging locusts had done their damage, and now it faced yet another scourge. The plague that was delivered on the land the previous year reappeared when the locust larva emerged from the eggs that had been sown in the first infestation. The peasants were puzzled and everyone was enlisted in the fight against the re-emergent pestilence. Adela pressed her children into service, and they worked hard to herd the hoppers into circles, surrounding them with dry grass, which they then set afire. They cut Spanish Broom switches and used them to beat the crawling insects. All around the countryside smoke could be seen rising from similar pyres.

The only food stores that remained after the locusts came the Farmers and their families ate along with the seed that they had saved for their annual planting, a sure recipe for disaster in the coming year.

Adela's brother-in-law had faithfully produced the promised weekly allotment of wheat that sustained the family during the winter. But bad news shadowed Rashid up the Mountain to Kattine when he paid his brother's family a visit in April of 1916. Some ruffians had discovered and stolen their hoard of wheat. Not a kernel was left. And to compound the felony, the currency that was continually being devalued caused prices to rise beyond the point at which it was possible to replace the purloined stores.

Rashid said he was incredulous at what he saw on the road to Kattine. People were begging for a piece of bread from anyone who passed by. Although he couldn't help but feel pity for those wretches, he had to think of his brother's family first. He said he saw a man picking through donkey feces trying to find a few morsels of undigested grain. "Unbelievable," he said over and over as he shook his head, "Unbelievable."

Rashid quickly came to the purpose of his visit: dramatic changes would have to be made in the Hobeiche household. Safa, although not yet fourteen, would have to go to the convent at Mar Elias. Yousef would enter the Gendarmerie, the Ottoman-sanctioned paramilitary force that kept law and order in Lebanon. This, he said, was a way they might make it through the year. Two fewer mouths to feed, especially the older children, would help the household a great deal. Rashid had already made arrangements for Yousef, so the lad was sent to pack a bag and prepare to ride back to Ghazir with his uncle.

Rashid got no complaint from the boy who had just turned nineteen and was impatient to put his manhood to the test. He had grown to his adult height of six feet one inch and his body was a lean mass of muscle from his neck to his ankles. Although not handsome in the classical sense, his broad shoulders and long arms created an imposing figure, even though his hairline was already beginning to recede. His appearance, no doubt, was quite attractive to the ladies.

Adela could see that it would be useless to protest these decisions. The choice was to make changes or starve, but she wasn't certain that even these changes would prevent that from happening.

So it came to pass that Nami's left-behind family underwent substantial change, change that was designed to influence the probability of survival during the Great War, a seesaw conflict that had been raging for two years and showed no signs of abating. From that point forward, survival would be uppermost in their minds as they began each day.

# 9

*The last resort is the hangman's noose.*

T HE CHURCH BELLS RANG AND RANG AND RANG. And everybody knew why. It was at the midpoint of WWI in Lebanon, 1916, a year whose days were so often punctuated by the clamorous pealing of church bells, that the population barely took notice. The sounds echoed through the valleys and up the hilltops. Someone else had died. The peasants might take time out to bless themselves and murmur their *marhooms* (condolences), and they might even wonder who it was that had been culled from their starved and weakened population.

It wasn't that people didn't care, of course they did. But there was a more important distraction that now held their attention—staying alive! It was a time when every waking moment was spent in the pursuit of food, and there just wasn't room for mourning. People were falling dead by the roadside while traveling to scavenge sustenance, and it wasn't unusual to hear the bells toll for four or five funerals on the same day in the same town. The locusts had come and the crops had gone. It was now the beginning of summer, and hunger and sickness were exacting their toll.

It's difficult for someone who has been brought up in a land of plenty such as the United States, at least in the latter half of the twentieth century, to have an appreciation for the circumstances the Lebanese people faced. Reports from the Presbyterian missionaries of the period could not stress enough how miserable the conditions were and how no one suffered more than the Lebanese. After food, the most needed item was clothing. Garments were falling off people in tatters, and fabric to create rude clothing was also scarce. Forget modesty, protection against the harsh elements of mountain life became a primary concern.

The Hobeiches of Kattine were no better off, but geopolitical events were taking place that would exacerbate their suffering. The Young Turks, who had staged a successful bloodless coup against their Sultan eight years prior had been steadfastedly implementing their vision of pan-Islamism on the Ottoman Empire. They were vehemently opposed to any notion of Christian favoritism or recognition of any non-Turkish Muslim nationalism. In fact, the Réglement gnawed at the Young Turks, and the Empire formally abrogated the pact in July 1915. This meant that Lebanon would no longer have a Christian governor to look after their interests. Also, Ottoman troops would have a free hand to enter Lebanon to confiscate animals and foodstuffs for their army.

As a result of the burgeoning program of Turkification the Young Turks had implemented, Muslim Arabs in Syria and elsewhere in the Ottoman Empire began to feel alienated and resentful. Christian intellectuals from Lebanon, even though their goals were not totally congruent with their Muslim and Druze brethren, became leaders in an emerging Arab nationalist movement that began to gain popularity, albeit clandestinely. It was a marriage of convenience born of desperation that would ultimately fail due to the nefarious designs of the Great Powers, principally France and Great Britain.

It was near the end of April in 1916 that Adela decided to make another pilgrimage to Ghazir to confront her brother-in-law Rashid. She wanted to know if he could in any way increase help to the family. Adela's husband had been gone some seven years now, and his brother Rashid was valiantly trying to discharge his role as protector of the family.

Rashid, who had been hunched over his desk, a spectacle made all the more pronounced because of a congenital spinal deformity, admonished his sister-in-law, asking what she was thinking coming down to Ghazir. Didn't she know that travel between villages was banned and that she could be arrested? Adela said she was very careful and that the Gendarmes knew her son was now in their ranks.

"Do you hear the bells?" she asked.

Rashid didn't need Adela or the church bells to tell him that things had worsened. The Arab revolt that had begun in the Hejaz caused big problems for the non-Turkish inhabitants of the Ottoman Empire. The government in Constantinople, in its tortured thinking, had turned away all foreign aid, reasoning that since Lebanon and Syria were "Arab" countries, the revolutionaries might reconsider once they heard of the reprisals taken against their kinsmen. Rashid allowed that it might be faulty reasoning, but that was what their masters thought nonetheless. He added that the Turks' paranoia was aggravated because they knew that Lebanese loyalties lay with the French who had maintained a presence in Lebanon for nearly 200 years, ostensibly to protect the Maronite Catholics.

Rashid also mentioned that Adela should distance herself from her two first cousins, Farid and Philippe el Khazen, who had been arrested and charged with treason. He felt compelled to add that he had warned her this would happen. He called them fools for becoming involved in the nationalist movement, one that advocated the separation of Lebanon and Syria from the Ottoman Empire. The Ottomans, true to their draconian reputation, brooked no dissent and initiated a campaign of rounding up dissidents to make examples of them. Adela's cousins had drifted into the Turk crosshairs and had been arrested and imprisoned, awaiting trial.

Adela was desperate to know what was to become of the two men and asked Rashid whether he could use his connections to help them. He was a lawyer, after all, one who had appeared in Ottoman courtrooms many times. But Rashid demurred saying he could do nothing. He was not going to jeopardize his standing in the Pasha's court or risk being branded a traitor along with his sister-in-law's cousins. But he spared the woman his worst suspicions concerning their fate. Changing the subject, he dismissed Adela by saying he would do the best he could about getting more food to his brother's family.

Adela left the law office feeling deeply disconsolate. She went out into the street where people were reading copies of the *Daily Telegram*, a narrow slip of paper that was issued by the government and sold for one *bara* (approximately .001¢ *before* the war started). The propaganda sheet, as government publications are wont to do, painted a rosy picture of the war effort. The people, however, knew the party line was false because their bellies were better barometers, and their empty stomachs told them things were indeed getting worse.

As she began her journey back home, Adela saw even more women lining the streets begging for bread for their children. Occasionally when they saw an Ottoman officer ride by they would shriek at him, saying the Turks were starving them on purpose. If it were a man that had spoken up, the soldiers would not hesitate to whip him or worse, but they were hesitant to exercise their riding crops on females. Adela heard one officer turn to the crowd and say, "Have you eaten your children yet? After you do, then come to us with your complaints." The women wailed in unison, burying their heads in their hands.

As she proceeded homeward, Adela overheard a man loudly talking of things he had seen while in Beirut. The situation was so bad, he said, that even the German submarine officers could not stand what they saw. They preferred the sultry confines of their U-boats rather than listen to the cries of the starving.

The Turkish military governor of Syria and Lebanon was one of the original Young Turks, a man named Jemal Pasha. His reputation for cruelty was known far and wide and had earned him the nickname *al Saffah*, "The Butcher." Margaret McGilvary's reaction when meeting Jemal was described in her book *The Dawn of a New Era in Syria* wherein she said, "I could not be in his presence for a minute without being terrified..." The governor's reputation made Adela suspect the worst, so she took a detour to visit her church at Mar Elias to light a candle in honor of the Virgin—imploring her to intercede and spare her cousins.

So, what had Philippe and Farid been up to? Both men were reared in semi-aristocratic surroundings and had become wards of the Maronite Patriarch Johanna el Hage. As often happens in life, the well-schooled lads had a chance encounter that would reshape both their lives. Philippe met an exiled Egyptian named Mohammad Abdoo who was known as a champion for freedom from Ottoman rule. Abdoo had resettled in Lebanon where Philippe came under his tutelage.

The el Khazens, who had been publishing a newspaper in Jounieh, also began translating French documents into Arabic, documents that promoted Lebanese independence. Their thesis was that Lebanon had become an independent entity as a result of the Réglement. Philippe co-authored an article decrying Turkey's desire to amend that agreement, which also had identified Lebanon as a separate province. The offending item appeared in an Egyptian newspaper (published, interestingly enough, by a Lebanese named Habib Ferris) and word soon reached an angered Jemal Pasha. He quickly had Philippe and his co-author, Yousef Shadiach, arrested and charged with treason. Philippe reportedly said that threats didn't faze him nor would they persuade him to say he was a member of Ottoman society.

What is particularly interesting about these historical events is the circular route they often took. The Sultan of Turkey had a reputation for being very suspicious, a man who brooked no dissent. Since his subjects had no forum for airing grievances, they formed secret societies, one of which, the CUP (Committee of Union and Progress), ended up usurping his power. When the Young Turks triumvirate came to power it, in its turn, emulated the sultan's despotism—the result of which was the spawning of other secret societies. And so it goes, even to the present day.

In any event, Jamal Pasha would preside over the fate of the el Khazen brothers now lodged in the prison in Aley. The most serious charges against them came about because of the bungling of an historic figure—one Georges Picot, of the infamous Sykes-Picot-Sazanov Agreement (wherein the Great Powers got together to divvy up the spoils of war while simultaneously promising the Arabs independence for supporting their efforts).

Picot, a French bureaucrat and dedicated colonialist, was stationed in Lebanon and had been immersed in behind-the-scenes activities involving the Lebanese drive for independence. In fact, he had close relations with Philippe and Farid, whom we now know were writing and translating articles for the cause of independence. As we also know, after the war broke out all the French nationals were deported, Picot among them.

After he left, the Ottomans ransacked his residence and the French embassy offices where they found what was considered treasonous materials that Picot had foolishly left behind. The diplomat had been warned to destroy all documents but instead secreted them inside a wall of his home, which the Ottomans tore down during their search. Another account claims that Picot left the documents with the American ambassador, and the Ottomans, who were notorious for not respecting diplomatic immunity, seized the papers that ultimately implicated the el Khazen brothers. In any case, whichever method was employed, they obtained materials authored by Philippe and Farid that were construed to be conspiratorial and traitorous.

Although both men had ample opportunity to flee, the brothers chose to stay and fight for their principles. While in prison, Farid wrote to his wife claiming that, although they had no hope of redemption, they weren't being accused of helping any foreign power, and no foreign power had the right to control Lebanon. In any event, he added, it was illegal to hold a court marshal for crimes that had a six-month statute of limitations, and their writings were three years old.

All appeals went for naught—especially those made to the obdurate butcher, Jamal Pasha. A sham trial was held in which no damaging documents were ever produced. Further, all accusations were presented in Turkish with no translations into the defendants' native tongue. Afterward, the men claimed that they never fully understood the charges brought against them, but this didn't seem to matter, and the kangaroo court condemned them to death.

A final appeal was made to Jamal Pasha on the basis that it would be unusually cruel to the family to hang two brothers, but he dismissed the appeal saying, "We hanged two Muslim brothers this year so we can hang two Christians as well."

Adela heard that they had been condemned to death, and according to my mother, went around plaintively asking anyone she met, "Have they hung them yet?" On May 8, 1916, a messenger brought word to her that her cousins had been executed two days before, along with twelve others in a place that became known as Martyr's Square in Central Beirut. Seven others were also hanged in Damascus on the same day. Her grief overwhelmed her. Losing her beloved relatives was now added to the specter of starvation. She prayed to heaven and asked why this was happening to them and when they would be delivered from it all. But no answer was forthcoming.

And the church bells rang and rang and rang.

*Warrior Sheikh Yousef Hobeiche.*

# 10

*The millstones rumble after the wheat is ground.*

T HE PREVIOUS YEAR'S LOCUST PLAGUE HAD TRAVELED on capricious winds that spared much of the Bekaa, an alluvial plain on the eastern side of the Lebanon mountain range. The area had been experiencing southwestern updrafts on that fateful day, keeping the locusts to the west of the area's breadbasket. Consequently, rumors spread through the impoverished villages that food was available in the fertile Bekaa.

Private Yousef Hobeiche had completed his basic training with the Gendarmerie and was posted at a small village on the road to Zahle. His duties included the enforcement of a new law that the Ottomans had imposed forbidding travel between villages. The cruel irony of these laws was that starving people were left to die in their homes by not permitting them to journey to find food. This was but one manifestation of the paranoia of the Turkish regime. Many came to believe it was purposeful genocide against the Lebanese Christians because of their obvious French sympathies. The Ottomans believed that anyone moving from place to place did so to spy for their enemies. If caught traveling about the countryside without permission, the penalty could be death. The choice under this draconian regime often came down to death by starvation or death by the hangman's noose.

The situation was relatively good for members of the Gendarmerie, even though the country was falling apart all around them. They had food, clothing and shelter, something that was becoming scarce for much of the population. Yousef's assignments, when not patrolling the roads, took him down to Jounieh for duty at the railroad station where the six foot one inch lad, decked out in his colorful costume, presented an imposing figure. The Gendarmes' uniforms were modeled after the French Zouave forces that originated in Algeria in 1831. The first Zouaves were recruited solely from the Zouaoua tribe from whence they derived their name. Hoping that the fierce fighting tradition would follow the uniform, other countries copied the Zouave model. Even the Union forces in the American Civil War had more than fifty such Zouave regiments that saw action.

The costume was quite elaborate, and many variations of it were used with accents alternately placed on the pants, jackets, or even the caps they wore. In Lebanon the uniforms of the Gendarmes sported blue baggy pantaloons, or *chasseur* trousers, with white leggings and red bolero-style jackets. They also wrapped a wide twelve-foot long *ceinture* (sash) around the waist that was especially difficult to put on, often requiring the help of a comrade. The uniform was topped off with a red fez with a dangling black tassel.

Among Yousef's duties at the railroad station was keeping a sharp eye out for spies. Lebanon always was, and continues to be to this day, a greenhouse for sprouting undercover agents. The country is at the crossroads of East and West, and has for many centuries seen a procession of peepers pass through its portals. Even today, a tapestry of spies continues to find it relatively easy to blend into the larger fabric of the multi-racial, multi-cultural population.

If we know anything about Yousef, we have discerned that he was a man who didn't hide his feelings very well. He was often overheard carping about the kind of orders he had to follow. One such command that rankled him was patrolling the Mediterranean seashore at Byblos. He had to arrest a bather on one occasion for swimming in the ocean, an act that was strictly forbidden. The Turks claimed such people were spies signaling enemy ships.

On another occasion Yousef had heard about a messenger from the American Presbyterian mission in Tripoli who was arrested while passing through Lebanon. The hapless lad was trying to deliver a letter, which was of course written in English, to the mission in Beirut. Once Ottoman authorities saw the English script, the boy was thrown into jail. Surely it must be espionage said the Turks. Yousef said that the fools didn't really understand English (even though his was quite rudimentary at the time), so anything they saw in that foreign hand became nefarious by definition. The letter ended up causing the school in Tripoli to be ransacked and its headmaster detained. It seemed silly to Yousef that all these American missionaries could be spies, and he said so.

Because of the insatiable need for more cannon fodder, the Ottomans continued to conscript men wherever they could. The Gendarmes intensely disliked having to apprehend men who had fled conscription in Beirut or Tripoli for the comparative safety of the mountains of Lebanon. The duty meant they had to stop and examine the papers of all draft-eligible men in the area. If they found a service-avoider and he was a Maronite, his chances of being arrested were quite slim.

One young man caught up in the dragnet for draft-evaders identified himself as a *muallim* (teacher) who was unfairly due to be conscripted into the Ottoman army. He claimed he was supposed to be exempt because he was a divinity student, but the Ottomans, in their drive to fill the ranks of their armed forces, abrogated understandings they had about not inducting men of the cloth. The Protestants were first on their list, and this lad was a Presbyterian theological student.

Complicating the issue were the Maronite and Orthodox clergy who were taking in young men for religious studies who really had no intention of fulfilling a vocation. Some said that money changed hands in these spiritual enlistments, but who knows? In any event, the Protestant religious students were rounded up, and a few took to the hills of Lebanon.

The detained fugitive *muallim* began to relate his lengthy tale of woe—how the Turks would change their rules on a whim. They made them answer long lists of questions, many of them irrelevant and impertinent. They were made to make extensive charts of their church buildings and to pay the expenses of the many inspections the Ottomans performed. The officials would then claim their documents were incomplete or that the papers they required were not filled out properly.

The Turks were notorious for the development and implementation of bureaucratic procedures, and it was emblematic of their style to require reports be filled with all sorts of trivial activities. Thus, it became routine for the Gendarmes to file voluminous reports about the goings on in their country. This was a task that Yousef despised, and his reports showed it, an act about which his commanders had often chided him. This was but a precursor of the young man's behavior, one that would haunt him throughout his military career.

I must pause here to comment on the image I had in my youth about my Uncle Yousef. Mother was always poring over, and agonizing about, letters she received from him. There were so many stories about his exploits over the years that his reputation took on legendary proportions. I must admit that I scoffed at much of what I heard, perhaps because I inherited the well-known trait of Lebanese skepticism. So, when I first began trekking around those mountains, I asked people I met what they knew of Sheikh Yousef Hobeiche. I was surprised that so many of them would repeat the same stories I had heard as a youngster growing up six thousand miles away. It was as if they were talking about a Lebanese version of Paul Bunyan.

There are too many stories to present in this narrative, but one that was repeated most often was, "He killed a horse with one blow!" This story has spread far and wide in the mountains. As the tale goes, and for some unknown reason, Yousef became enraged at the horse he was riding, so he dismounted and delivered a right cross to the animal's jaw. The horse supposedly dropped dead on the spot. I have to admit I still don't believe that one, but the tale has great currency in the district of Kesrouan.

The news of Yousef's cousins' demise, although not totally unexpected, struck at the heart of the oath of loyalty he had sworn to the Empire upon receiving his appointment to the Gendarmerie. He spent a lot of time mulling over what he should do about it. Lebanon, after all, was a country with a tradition of blood feuds that were faithfully passed down to each succeeding generation. The Hobeiche clan did not shrink from that tradition, as we have seen from their history.

Yousef, of course, knew of his cousins' involvement in the independence movement. He was aware there was a plot afoot to clandestinely enlist Arabic speaking officers of the Ottoman forces into the covert *al 'Ahd* movement. This secret society, one of many that sprang up in response to the Young Turks' intransigence, aimed to convince the Ottoman rulers to give the Arabic speaking minority in their ranks equality in promotions and decision-making. Failing in that goal, they wanted to achieve decentralization with greater autonomy. The young Turks were having none of it and continued their policies of Turkification, which served to further alienate those Arabic speakers among Ottoman officer corps.

On one occasion, as I sat in the old Hobeiche homestead talking to my cousin Namatallah while he chain-smoked Marlboro cigarettes—he preferred the American brand to any of the locally manufactured kind—I asked him what he knew of the death of the el Khazen brothers during the war. "It hit the family hard," he said. It was then that he related to me the story of harassment by the Turks after the executions took place.

Because of the relatively short travel times, Yousef got to visit his mother and siblings in Kattine on a somewhat frequent basis. After the martyrdom of the two el Khazen brothers, he became concerned that the authorities knew his mother was close kin to those who were charged with treason and might be thus subject to sanctions.

On one of his visits home, Yousef saw two horses tethered outside the house. He wondered who these visitors might be. Dismounting and securing his horse a discrete distance from the house, the ever-wary Yousef proceeded on foot to get a better view of the visitors. As he drew closer, he could see that the saddles of the horses bore the insignia of the Ottoman army. Yousef stealthily made his way to the backside of the house and peeked through a window to observe the house's interior. As he edged closer, he could hear his mother's voice imploring the visitors to leave. The sight of two Turkish soldiers ransacking the house both shocked and angered the impetuous Yousef and caused him to bolt through the door demanding to know why they dared to come into this woman's house and molest her property.

The soldiers didn't look like the regular troops that Yousef had seen occasionally pass through the railroad station in Jounieh. With their disheveled uniforms and unshaven faces, they appeared to be no more than ragtag stragglers or even deserters. For their part, the soldiers were reportedly quite surprised to see a neatly decked out Lebanese Gendarme suddenly in their midst. The non-com in charge tried to quickly explain that they were ordered to question collaborators of the traitors that were hanged down in Beirut. And, given that this woman was a first cousin, they were only doing their duty.

Yousef drew his pistol and announced to the increasingly bewildered duo, "I am a cousin also!" He asked, rather sardonically, if they wished to examine him as well.

The soldiers, who had left their rifles propped against a wall while they were busy pillaging, began to fidget and stole glances at their weapons. The one closest to his rifle impetuously decided to make a dash for it while the other used the distraction to race off in the opposite direction. Just as the first man got his hand on his rifle, a shot rang out. Yousef's aim was on the mark, and the man fell mortally wounded. He then wheeled and fired again at the second man just as he was going through the doorway at the opposite side of the house. Yousef, running on adrenalin, quickly turned back and forth to ensure there was no movement from either of the wounded. Seeing no signs of life he moved in closer to inspect the bodies.

Adela was crouched in a corner and would not move until her son had finished his examination of the two dead soldiers. After he was assured that they were both lifeless, he went over to the corner and gently lifted his mother up and sat her down on the chair next to the fireplace. He consoled her with assurances that she wouldn't be bothered again.

The familiar "Ya Allah, ya Allah," (Oh God) was all the frightened Adela could muster.

Yousef then asked where his brother and sister were. Angèle had seen the Turks coming from the hilltop behind the house where she and Khalil had been frolicking and wisely decided they should stay hidden from view. After spying her older brother approach the house, and hearing the subsequent gunfire and the shrieking of her mother, the pair decided to go down for a closer look. When Yousef came outside, Angèle and Khalil ran up to the house, looked inside and saw the bodies, which had been placed together on the floor of the parlor.

Surprisingly, Angèle and her brother Khalil were wide-eyed but not frightened as the young girl said matter-of-factly, "Yousef has killed them." The war had hardened even the children to whom death was no longer a stranger.

Yousef looked at his siblings and assured them they were safe and not to worry. He said that he must hurry and dispose of the bodies before anyone came looking for them. Fortunately, the desertion rate for the Ottoman armed forces had reached epic proportions. In 1917, the number of defections totaled 1.5 million with 50% of the Arab soldiers deserting. And these two would probably be placed on those same rolls.

Yousef then carried the men outside and draped them over their horses. When they were secured for riding he retrieved his own mount, and with the reins of the intruder's horses in hand, led them up a path that was familiar only to him. After he reached a secluded spot, he dismounted and prepared a gravesite that would never be found, much less looked for. With his large hands he moved rocks, and with a spade, hollowed out a space to hold both bodies. The work took the better part of an hour, and after burying his victims and piling on enough rocks to keep the jackals away, he headed back to the house with the two horses in tow. He would bring them to the Gendarmerie station in Ghazir saying he found them grazing by the roadside. No questions would be asked.

"Yes, he killed them," Namatallah said rather dispassionately. And, just like the tale of his ancestor Sheikh Torbey before him, the story aroused no passion. If only the walls could speak to tell us what really happened.

# 11

*The day may pass but the evil thereof does not.*

THE WAR ACTUALLY ENDED FOR THE LEBANESE and Syrians with the collapse of the Ottoman government on October 1, 1918, when Sharif Hussein's troops led by his son Faysal (played by Omar Sharif in *Lawrence of Arabia*) entered Damascus. On October 7, a small French landing party from a battleship anchored in Beirut harbor entered the city. This was followed one day later by the triumphal arrival of the British forces, headed by General Sir Edmund Allenby. As the news spread, a commotion swept the mountainside with sounds of gunfire echoing through the valleys. The destitute populace began to celebrate the only way they knew how, by firing their heretofore hidden weapons into the air.

It was not until the end of the month, with the conquest of Tripoli, that the war officially ended in Lebanon. The Turks sued for peace and signed an armistice on the British ship *Agamemnon*. It was on October 31, 1918, that the Lebanese Gendarmerie was officially severed from the Ottoman Empire and made part of the emerging Lebanese Army. Yousef would serve nearly eight more years with the Gendarmerie before being transferred to the sniper unit of the Hunters of Lebanon Battalion of the Levant.

The mere fact that the war had ended didn't mean that hardship had also surrendered to the armistice. It would take the better part of a year and a half before the suffering would noticeably abate. The schools were slow to reopen, and supply lines for the goods needed to rebuild the economy were sluggishly being reestablished.

Also with the end of the war came the jockeying for position between the Great Powers. The French had an agreement with the British and Russians about the division of the spoils, and Arab nationalism was not to get in the way. The boundaries of Lebanon were changed to include the areas surrounding Tripoli, Beirut, and Sidon. The country was then given over to the French, who set about establishing their mandate and suppressing any opposition.

For the Hobeiche family, like all the other Lebanese families, things did not markedly improve with the onset of peace. They were thankful they had survived the famine and the Spanish Flu and had escaped being numbered among Lebanon's half million dead. They could now at least think about schooling for the two children—Angèle and Khalil—who were at home during the war.

One thing that did improve immediately after the armistice was the resumption of the Ottoman-curtailed mail service. The populace, nearly as hungry for communication as they were for food, returned to waiting in long lines at the post office to see if their relatives had sent them money. Soon thereafter a letter arrived for Adela postmarked from Cincinnati, Ohio. She didn't have to stand in line for it because a postal worker named Francis Nasief al Yahshushi, a friend of the family, delivered it to their home. Francis is mentioned here because he will play a part in the Hobeiche saga later on.

The Hobeiches were continually wondering what had happened to Namatallah, the titular head of the family, whom they last heard was in Cincinnati. The letter, delivered by the friendly Francis, had been postmarked two years prior but had languished in the American postal system until the war ended. Adela waited patiently as Francis opened the letter and began reading it aloud.

The postal worker's face betrayed the contents as he scanned the letter. He struggled to phrase the words as softly as possible. The missive was from Fr Toubiya Dahdah, the pastor of the Lebanese Church in Cincinnati, and the cousin that Nami traveled to after abandoning Mexico. The priest briefly explained that Adela's husband had succumbed to a heart ailment (mitral valve prolapse) and that he had just performed a requiem mass for his deceased cousin. A few people who knew Nami attended the funeral. There were several flowery words of solace, as you might imagine, along with the usual admonition of not questioning God's wisdom in these matters. Fr Dahdah also added that he was sending along the few possessions that Nami had, but none ever arrived.

One can only imagine the way the children took the news, undoubtedly with typical emotional outbursts of wailing and crying. With tears streaming down their faces they kept repeating, "He's dead. He's dead!" Sheikh Nami was fifty-three years old when he left the world, without realizing the promise of his birthright.

Adela felt her head spin as she looked down at the floor. Her life had not

84

been easy in her husband's absence, but now she felt as one thrust into a whirlpool that would drown her and her family in its swirling vortex. She was emotional and stoic at the same time. Her devout religious convictions made her think that her husband was now in heaven, a place that would be kinder to him than Earth ever was.

Francis, the bearer of ill tidings, tried to console Adela, to no avail. Her first thought was to have her eldest son back at her side, so she asked that a messenger be sent to fetch Yousef. Francis said he would take care of it and continued to offer his condolences, but Adela brushed aside the consolations and swiftly, but politely, sent the young man on his way.

The widow, somewhat uncharacteristically for a Lebanese woman, submerged the grief of this new catastrophe. Most Lebanese women in similar circumstances would moan, weep, shriek, and even beat their breasts black and blue. Adela would perform none of these rituals, and her daughter Angèle would take notice and later remark on her muted reaction.

When Angèle heard the news of her father's demise, she tore out of the house, tears pouring out on the path as she ran up the hill. When she reached the reservoir, she leaned against its wall and wondered what was to become of her.

Yousef took the news of his father's death rather quietly, muttering the obligatory phrases he had learned at similar events over the years. He would now have to officially assume the mantle as head of the household, something his uncle had been doing. It was not a responsibility that he desired at the age of twenty-one but one that he would dutifully accept, more or less, and strive to keep those duties from interfering with his penchant for living life large.

After the required period of mourning, Yousef began to think of his future. He told his mother that when he was recently in Beirut (and not being distracted by the ladies of the evening), he had made acquaintances in the occupying armies. Both British and French officers were patrons of the brothel he frequented (rumor had it that it was owned and operated by two female cousins), but Yousef spared his mother the circumstances of their congregation. Since French was his second language and English his third, his conversations were mainly with the French soldiers he met. He was particularly inquisitive about their intentions in this part of the world. It was from them that he first learned of the Sykes-Picot-Sazanov Agreement and France's designs on the Middle East.

Of course, the French claimed, they were there to protect the Christians of Lebanon, something they had been doing for nearly 200 years. Statements such as this struck a resonant chord with Yousef, and he thought these acquaintances might prove valuable to him when he sat down to seriously plot his future.

Yousef was told that the Gendarmerie would be soon absorbed into the French Mandate Forces, and one who was fluent in French could be valuable. He hadn't thought past the end of hostilities because he hadn't decided whether a military career was in his best interest. It was hard to put aside his experiences of reprimands and orders from lesser men than himself. He didn't know if he could put up with it on a steady basis. He would have to give it some thought.

Adela said she was confident that her son would do what was best, but in her heart she also knew that probably wasn't true.

# 12

*The camel's intention is one thing,*
*the camel-driver's something else.*

ANGÈLE HAPPILY WENT BACK TO SCHOOL IN THE FALL of 1919, a year after the war ended. Having been without school for four years increased her thirst for knowledge, and she quickly took up where she had left off.

Two years at school quickly passed, and the nuns could see that Angèle was now mature enough to begin giving instruction to the younger children. The school was short of teachers, and the staff scrambled to use whatever resources were available to them. Pressing older students into service was a common practice in the parochial schools. Although now only seventeen, she had progressed to the point that the nuns could use her to their advantage.

They began by having her tutor the first graders in French, which had become as much Angèle's primary language as Arabic. And Angèle loved it. She was now the boss over a group of children, a responsibility that stoked her Hobeiche appetite for a position of authority. A stickler for correct pronunciation, she dispensed discipline with unbridled enthusiasm and began to feel much more satisfied with her life. The hardships of war, the death of her father and the other villagers were necessarily shoved into the background. She was beginning another stage of life, one that began to look a bit brighter to her.

Home for the summer once more, and in an attempt to relieve the drudgery of daily living under her mother's critical eye, Angèle found herself stealing off to her hilltop refuge more often. She would carefully negotiate the torturous path through sprigs of thyme and sage, which grew between the thistles and brambles, while keeping careful watch for snakes that occasionally sunned themselves on the trail. The strong fragrances of the wild spices that were released by her footsteps were like a perfume to her, and she inhaled their odors deeply as she made her way up the hill.

87

On this particular day she had an assignation with her cousin Sheikh Edmond el Khazen from Kfar Debiane. As the story goes, a romance was developing between Angèle and her cousin Edmond, but for some unknown reason Yousef was not keen about this relationship. Edmond's family, just like the Hobeiches, had fallen on hard times, and he was without sufficient means to be considered a suitable match, cousin or not.

In that day and time, a girl was considered most marriageable between the age of sixteen and twenty. So, even Yousef had begun thinking about the day when his sister would be taking that step.

It was a long journey for Edmond to arrive at Kattine for his date but one that he was more than eager to make. He was a large lad, the same age and build as his cousin Yousef. His broad facial features, including his prominent nose, didn't make him particularly handsome however.

Angèle very much liked Edmond's company and looked forward to their furtive meetings. As they would sit next to each other on the ledge of the reservoir, Angèle could hardly conceal the happiness she felt for the attention Edmond paid her. She had spent most of her time at a girls' school or at home and was not used to having men show interest in her. Nonetheless, she took coquettish delight in the dating experience, such as it was.

Edmond was totally smitten with his cousin and often said it was fated they be together. He never failed to mention that they were of the same class and breeding, referring to the past glories of the el Khazen and Hobeiche feudal preeminence. Their families had a tradition of intermarriage, along with the Dahdahs, and he expected Angèle to follow that tradition.

To Edmond, considerations such as these were important, and persuasive. It was what he had learned at family gatherings, listening to tales of the glorious past, the same as Angèle had. It was also what he had learned at school and what he had come to cherish as the basic beliefs that shaped his character.

Angèle worried about how long they could keep their trysts secret and felt that Edmond was moving forward at a faster pace than was appropriate. She had to keep a level head because it was what she had been taught, what was expected of her. If her mother knew she was meeting Edmond up at the *jazzat*, there would be a lot of hand-wringing and remonstrations. Of that she was sure.

In any event, it prompted Angèle to keep Edmond at arm's length even though her rebellious nature inclined her to believe that what Mama thought didn't matter. At least she didn't think it did, although she still resisted her cousin's more amorous advances.

Edmond knew how Angèle's family felt, so he deferred to her wishes. But he proclaimed that it didn't change anything as far as he was concerned, and one day they would marry, of that he was sure.

Suddenly, Angèle heard her mother calling her home from down below. As noted before, one of the unique features of the mountain terrain is how easily voices carry up the hills on the gentle updrafts. People on the higher elevations can clearly and effortlessly hear conversations from below. I remember sitting on the Hobeiche veranda and listening to music cascading up from a restaurant over a mile away. Reluctantly as always, they would conclude their tryst and go their separate ways. With the breeze whistling in her ears, Angèle would hop and skip down the hill leaving Edmond to gaze at the trail after his love had disappeared.

*There is relief in changing one's place.*

The following summer, on one of his weekend visits to the homestead, Yousef called to Angèle to join him in the parlor. He was standing in the center of the room, and his mother was seated at her usual place in a chair next to the fireplace, even though it was not lit. Yousef was wearing his equestrian uniform with jodhpurs and boots, and his footsteps fell heavily on the floor as he paced back and forth. In his left hand he simultaneously held a cigarette and his ubiquitous baton while his right hand twirled a point of his handlebar mustache. He had been promoted to Sergeant a few months before, and his career was definitely on its way up.

When she came into the room, Angèle sat at the window looking out at the vast expanse before her, the majestic pines, the rocky outcropping, and the road through the valley being navigated by a mule and his rider. She acted as if she was not paying attention to her brother at all.

Yousef announced he had decided that Angèle would have to join her sister Safa, now Sr Miriam, at the Mar Elias convent. Since she had finished her schooling, the nuns would be happy to have her along with her sister Miriam. She would pay her way by serving as a teacher.

The pay Yousef received as a soldier was barely enough to keep him in the manner a sheikh required, and after a good deal of thought, he had determined that this would be the best way to relieve him of some of the family expenses. He knew his sister wouldn't take it well and she didn't. They say that history repeats itself, and there were eerie parallels between this meeting and the one that Adela's brother-in-law Rashid had convened six years earlier.

There had always been a contest of wills between the four siblings, even though Yousef was seven years older than Angèle and nine more than Khalil.

Angèle had always been quick to pass judgment on Yousef's lifestyle, as she often did on anyone else's, family or not, and to abhor his propensity for womanizing. She told him in no uncertain terms that she wouldn't go to live at the convent.

Yousef drew up his full and imposing height, looked down at his sister with his index finger twitching on his baton, drew a puff on the omnipresent fag, and firmly maintained that he would brook no objections.

Angèle appealed to her mother, to whom she quickly turned for help, just as Adela had turned to her Mother Superior for assistance those many years before, but none was forthcoming. Adela sat quietly embroidering, pulling the colored thread back and forth through the fabric without apparent distraction. She was not going to dispute Yousef's decision, for she knew this time he was right. Finally, she said simply, "Yousef knows best."

Angèle would not go willingly, mind you, for like her brother she never did anything she was ordered to do willingly. But, as always, tough times dictated stern measures.

The mulberry trees were coming back, and although Adela and other Lebanese villagers would hang on to sericulture for several years more, in reality the business was finished. The war had altered the local economic reality by opening up trade around the world. The cottage silkworm industries of Lebanon would not be able to compete with the cheaper product coming from the Far East.

Resigned to her fate, Angèle dashed off and penned a note to Edmond that her infrequent trysts with him would be coming to an end. She wondered what Edmond would say about her brother now—would he repeat what she had often heard him declare, *A thousand ladders wouldn't reach his head.* He had maintained that he would soon be earning enough money to satisfy Yousef, and he'd come for her and they would be married. Angèle was ambivalent about this because, even though she was pleased that Edmond felt he would get the better of her brother one day, she didn't think it would come to pass. Edmond, had dreams of emigrating like others among his relatives, and had talked of going to Africa where there were riches to be had. His uncles, it was rumored, had a perfume factory there and said they would take him into the business.

Angèle was acquainted with immigrants' dreams but hadn't seen them materialize. She had only to think of her father's misadventures in the New World to remind her of the harsh reality of emigration. He was going to make a fortune, too, but ended up in an unmarked grave among strangers in a strange land.

Angèle walked down the road to the convent carrying a small bag of possessions with her. The convent had been endowed by one of her Hobeiche ancestors almost three hundred years before. The Abbess of the nuns at Mar Elias met her at the door, and soon Angèle was ensconced in a tiny cell on the fourth floor.

Convent life was not dissimilar to life at boarding school, but still, Angèle found it confining. The older she got, the less prone she was to bend to the austerity required by the nuns. She thought that because of her sister, her family background, and the circumstances of her residence, Reverend Mother, who was one of the pair of her father's sisters that were nuns in the same convent, might afford her some privileges. But her circumstances didn't change much from her home life, and she would constantly be reminded of duties to be performed, just as her mother always had.

After gaining the requisite experience Angèle became a full-time French teacher, ministering to the students in the adjoining elementary school. She continued emulating her mother in manner and demeanor, and the children soon realized that they had to do their duty as well. But the reluctant convent denizen steadfastly refused all entreaties that she take the serious step to profess as a postulant and chose to remain a boarding student-teacher.

Yousef had always planned to be the architect of Angèle's destiny. He knew she didn't want to become a nun, and this secretly pleased him.

*That which is hidden is that which never takes place.*

Angèle again felt abandoned by her family, just as she had when she was trundled off to school as a child. She missed her brother Khalil and her meetings with Edmond. Now nineteen, she had been feeling the stirrings of womanhood for some time, and although she enjoyed teaching the elementary school children, she wasn't altogether happy with her circumstances. Always having to "do her duty" had constantly grated on her before, and it was no different now.

When she saw her sister, she wouldn't hesitate to complain. But Miriam was unsympathetic because she felt Angèle was old enough to carry these burdens without protest. Her only advice was always to go pray in the chapel.

If the truth were known, becoming an Antonian nun was not her sister's first choice either. Some in the family had said rather cruelly that she became a nun because she wasn't pretty enough to attract a proper suitor. In reality, although not as attractive as Angèle, she had neither dowry nor suitors with money, so it was economics that sealed her fate. Miriam didn't complain, at least not on the record.

Angèle continued to secretly communicate with Edmond and would often reread his letters that were kept in her room under her pillow. Edmond's ardor had not dimmed in the two years that had passed. He spoke to her of his inability to think of anything else, not even the business that kept him traveling the length and breadth of Lebanon. He also wrote poetry to her that spoke of the moon and the stars. His admitted goal was to make enough money to marry her, but it was not proceeding as quickly as planned. This neither surprised nor disappointed Angèle, for she was pessimistic by nature and had reservations about a long-term relationship with Edmond. His profession of undying love for her did not assuage her cynicism.

Each reading ended with an audible sigh, and Angèle folded and placed the letters in their hiding place. She then pulled a sheaf of paper from her little desk, dipped her pen into the recessed inkwell, and began to write. She told Edmond to be careful of what he wrote because her mail could get into the wrong hands, and she wouldn't want her mother or brother to hear these things. Yousef especially would say that she was encouraging Edmond and giving him false hope. He would also be angry at Edmond, and there would be alienation between the families. She filled her letters with trivial details of what she was doing and how much she liked teaching the children. Mentioned also was her increased proficiency with needlework and how her pieces garnered the highest prices at the church bazaars. She ended her letter with a lot less ardor than Edmond's, much to his dismay.

With that, Angèle placed the note in an envelope, addressed and sealed it. She would have to get a stamp from one of her teacher friends and give the letter to another friend's mother who visited her daughter on weekends, and who in turn would post it. The young girl then hurried down to the chapel for afternoon prayers. The mother superior always made sure that Angèle was accounted for.

That evening in the refectory, as she sat next to her friend, Angèle inquired if her mother were coming soon for a visit. The girl answered that her mother always came and impishly wondered if Angèle had another letter for her sweetheart. Angèle blushed and reminded her friend that everyone, even she, had secrets that they wouldn't want their mothers to know. At this rejoinder the girl also reddened and wondered just what it was her friend knew. But, Angèle would just smile.

# 13

*The beginning of a quarrel is a spark, the end is flames.*

YOUSEF WAS RAPIDLY BECOMING KNOWN AS A LIKABLE rascal, but one with whom you didn't cross swords. He drank hard, smoked a lot, and took offense at the slightest derogation. He often used the common insult *akruut* when provoked, which likened his adversaries to whores or pimps. Lebanese curses, many of which cast aspersions on one's lineage or religion, spontaneously and without contemplation cascaded from the soldier's mouth. Even his letters to his sister, as we shall see later on, contained such pejoratives. Fistfights were also not uncommon to him, but those who valued their good looks soon gave him a wide berth. He had, on occasion, harbored incipient misgivings about his country's liberators and often questioned their intentions even though he was a Francophile at heart.

When confronted, his adversaries would often look hard at Yousef and decide to ignore the insults or even assume a comedic intention. The taller Yousef's renown for sheer strength and his penchant for brawling made his opponents a bit wary of physical engagement. Although the pugnacious fellow seemed never to pass on an opportunity to add to his growing reputation, he sometimes would reluctantly take a more temperate stance in order to avoid further reprimands. Conflict with his French superiors, although deemed politically unwise, was not totally avoided, even though Yousef believed they acted prejudicially toward native-born forces, of which he was one.

An anecdote that personifies Yousef's brashness, audacity, and penchant for bawdy humor concerns an encounter he had in the course of his duties. One day, in the Christian quarter of the city of Tripoli, the soldier found himself going door to door to question residents as to the whereabouts of a missing soldier.

"Madame," he asked the matronly looking lady at one house, while showing her a photograph. "Have you seen this man?"

93

The woman replied in the negative.

"Madame, have you never seen him?"

"No," she said.

"Madame, did you know that he used to live near here?"

"Why do you keep calling me Madame?" the agitated woman answered. "I am Mademoiselle!"

Taken aback by the sudden outburst, Yousef stepped back to take the woman's measure from top to bottom. After a long pause he said in saccharine tones, "Well, I have never been between your legs to know if you are Madame or mademoiselle."

The woman recoiled, obviously not at all used to being spoken to in this manner. "How dare you!" she sputtered. "I'll report you to the commandant for this, you impertinent bastard." And she slammed the door in the grinning sheikh's face.

For a man who intended to make the military his career, the paper trail he was leaving in his records jacket was not to be envied. "Conduct unbecoming..." was a phrase used in much of the documentation.

On one of my journeys, while searching into Yousef's past, I had the good fortune to be introduced to retired General Francoise Genadry of the Lebanese Army who wintered at a chalet in the complex that cousin Désireé manages for her family. When told of my project, he volunteered to intercede with the people at the Army archives to get a look at Yousef's file. So, off we went one day to Lebanese Army Headquarters, and after passing through several layers of security, we were finally brought to the office of General Armand el Tabashi. When told of my quest, he picked up the phone, spoke a few commands, and five minutes later, an orderly appeared with a stack of records pertaining to Captain Yousef Hobeiche. I asked if we could have copies, and after a few whispered conversations and a few days, I was given facsimiles of the "complete set." It turned out not to be the complete file but was a formidable dossier of some 500 pages nonetheless.

Virtually all of the records were in French, which presented the problem of translation. Désireé and Paula Hoche helped me go through the files, and it didn't take long to verify my suspicions about Yousef's reputation. His commanders continually reminded him that non-conformance of accepted norms of conduct should make him consider a different career. It was obvious that Sheikh Yousef chafed under the command of these French officers.

Our rebellious sheikh never seemed to think he was in the wrong, and we can see from the records that he often resorted to arguing his case in writing, to little avail. At the core of his consciousness, he knew there was no career for him other than the military and that civilian job prospects in the peacetime Lebanon were not only dim, but also unattractive. He had no relatives that would take him into their business, which would never have worked anyway. He was trained and disposed to fighting and commanding other men to fight.

Another recurrent theme in Yousef's dossier was his continual need for money. Like his father before him, indebtedness was a constant companion. More than once he was threatened with legal action for failure to repay debts. That he could cajole, or perhaps intimidate, people into lending him money was more a tribute to his persuasive personality than his creditworthiness.

A soldier's lot was not a happy one in post-World War I Lebanon, but Yousef was a chap who looked for and seized opportunity whenever it presented itself. There was contentiousness afoot everywhere one looked. Often times disputes were solved without bloodshed, but much too often not. The following account gives an idea of what life was like for Yousef and his contemporaries, and how seemingly insignificant quarrels could inflame festering feuds.

One day a Christian and a Druze* were riding mules in opposite directions on a mountain road near Marjeyoun that was too narrow for both to pass. Neither would give way, and words were exchanged. The Christian lashed out at the Druze with his whip, whereupon the Druze chased him into the town of Marjeyoun where the argument continued. The villagers, after word of the encounter got round, quickly gathered in the town square, with a few even brandishing weapons. The Gendarmerie was called out to handle the situation, and Yousef and his detail hurried to the center of the town.

Yousef knew quite well what was bothering the Druze population. They felt, not without foundation, that the Maronites were unduly favored by their European masters and had too many privileges, which put the Druze at an economic disadvantage. As an example, their head taxes were higher than the Christians, and they were not given equal access to European markets for their goods. And, to spice this calamitous stew further, the Christians promoted the notion that they were socially superior to the Druze and advanced this idea at every opportunity.

Yousef was well acquainted with Druze grievances but, more importantly from a tactical viewpoint, he knew that they significantly outnumbered the

*A religious community that is an offshoot of Islam, although they are not considered Muslims by other adherents of Islam.

Maronites in Marjeyoun. He was also mindful of their well-earned reputation for being fierce fighters. Not that he minded a good fight, but he wanted it to be for more than two jackasses who were too proud to give way on a mountain road.

When the detail approached, they could hear people shouting all the way from the town square. The detachment of twelve men pulled their rifles from their saddle holsters and affixed bayonets to them. At a hand signal from Yousef, they began a measured trot toward the sounds of trouble. As they neared they could see the two disputants surrounded by a mob of shouting and gesticulating villagers. As the detail drew closer, they could easily discern from the way the crowd was dressed that they were divided along sectarian lines into two opposing groups.

I always found it interesting how the natives segregated themselves by dress in ways that only they could decode. Sergeant Sheik Yousef rode ahead into the midst of the brewing melee and signaled his men to push the two groups further apart. He wanted to create some distance between them so he could obtain a tactical advantage.

The mounted men slowly began pushing the Christians to one side of the square and the Druze to the other. The horses easily intimidated the crowd, which retreated amid shouts and curses. Once some separation was created, Yousef ordered the men to hold fast.

When confronted, the two squabblers continued to shout and point fingers at one another. The Christian said the "beggar" wouldn't give way. The Druze said he wouldn't give way to a "Christian dog" who thought he owned everything, including the roads.

This exchange poorly summed up years of contentiousness between the two sects, but through the force of arms, the mini-rebellion was quashed, and the uneasy peace was restored without bloodshed. It did, however, exemplify how small spats could easily blow up in the faces of those charged with maintaining the peace.

As the crowd dispersed, Yousef surveyed the battlefield and noticed a young woman standing in the doorway of a home across the square. This was an opportunity that he couldn't pass up, so he crossed over to the house to begin his latest romance, one that would have a rather tragic ending.

*Sister Miriam & Angèle Hobeiche.*

# 14

*He sold the bear's skin before he shot the bear.*

A NGÈLE HAD BEEN SHUTTLING BETWEEN DIFFERENT schools run by the Antonian order for two years, always boarding with the nuns in the convent next to the school. After a stint up north she was now back at Mar Elias. It was in the middle of the winter when she received the following letter from her brother.

> Beirut
> 17 February 1925
> My Dear Sister,
> Hi and how are you? I leave today to Tripoli to return tomorrow. I can't go to your place. I advise you to come join me in Jounieh tomorrow Feb. 18, at noon. If my mother wants to go with you, go by way of Kattine and bring her. That would be very good. Insist that she goes with you. You should return the coming Sunday and I will return with you. You should meet me the way I told you and my mother should if she wants, or you alone if she doesn't want. Bring with you two dresses and your coat so you can change clothes here.
> If you don't want to come I will be angry with you and will leave you forever. Do you understand? If you come, I'll buy you some nice things from Beirut that you will like. Our meeting place will be in Jounieh at Salimeh at 12. Hello to mom.
> Your Brother,
> Yousef

Angèle was wary for she wondered what her brother could possibly want this time. Well, she would just have to go to Jounieh and see. When informed of the meeting, Adela said she was not anxious to travel to Jounieh. As everyone in the family knew, she was not happy about Yousef's latest romantic adventure with that woman from Marjeyoun and was never remiss in displaying her displeasure.

Angèle told her mother the trip would be good for her to get the "air," but Adela said she liked the air in Kattine just fine. Her daughter insisted, however, because she never knew what card Yousef was going to play, having her mother with her as reinforcement would improve her hand. Adela finally weakened, and gave in to her curiosity about her son's latest schemes.

Arrangements were made for a taxi and on the next day they were on their way to Jounieh. After a forty-five minute drive, they arrived at the appointed meeting place. Following the obligatory kisses, Angèle asked her brother what the urgency was.

Yousef told them to come in and shake the dust from their shoes and have something to drink. They would, he said, then sit down and have a discussion about the future. In the meantime, Yousef turned on his considerable charm with an exchange of pleasantries, but his mother immediately began scolding him for his past inattentiveness. He hadn't written and he hadn't visited, all due to his preoccupation with his new love Dahabiya, whom he had met after the unpleasantness in Marjeyoun. (Dahabiya, whose name is derived from the word for gold, was reportedly a free-spirited member of an art colony, and would not be welcomed within the Hobeiche clan.) Adela reminded Yousef that there were other things in life besides womanizing and having fun.

Yousef demurred by suggesting there was important business to discuss and they should not begin by quarreling. Adela and Angèle took seats in the parlor while Yousef, making himself at home, found a cupboard with a bottle of *arak* and poured himself a large drink. After the milky concoction was suitably fixed, he came to the sofa, sat down with an audible sigh, and announced that he had some good news. He had found a suitor for Angèle.

This was not a complete surprise to his sister because she suspected that this was what her brother had in mind. She knew that she was the last major family asset that Yousef thought he controlled and listened as he announced that the gentleman in question would be arriving shortly. Her brother droned on about how this man came from a good family, even though, he added with a bit of condescension, not quite up to the Hobeiches.

Adela sat quietly, trying not to betray any feeling one way or the other. Angèle, on the other hand, became a bit agitated but would hold her tongue until she had heard all that Yousef had to say. She was never good at dissembling, and her dark and piercing eyes always betrayed any uneasiness.

Sheikh Yousef said he had examined the suitor's background and deemed that he would be able to afford marrying into the family. Angèle quickly and snidely accused her brother of trying to sell her off to better his own circumstances, under the pretext of caring about her and the family. Yousef refused to be drawn into a rhetorical escalation. When it came to verbal combat, only Yousef's imposing physical presence separated their abilities.

Money had become the driving force in all things for Yousef, even though it seemed to quickly trickle like grains of sand through his fingers. He told Angèle to remain calm because they all knew she was going to get married sometime, and he had found someone suitable. The sooner this happened, the better off everyone would be.

The prospective suitor was a merchant from Amioun in North Lebanon whose family owned an Oriental rug business. Being from Amioun, in the Lebanese sectarian lexicon, was a polite way of saying the suitor was a Syrian Orthodox Christian. Angèle told Yousef he was crazy if he thought she was going to marry an Orthodox man. In the Lebanese tradition of the time, intermarriage between different faiths most often required the woman to follow the man's religion.

It was good enough that he was a Christian, Yousef claimed. Adela sat quietly taking in the rapidly swelling confrontation with an uncommon reserve. She knew what her son had in mind because he was running up debts that were crimping his extravagant lifestyle. He, therefore, had been testing the market to see what considerations his sister could command. She would have no dowry, but the family name would be the currency to be used in any arrangement. That Angèle was a handsome and desirable woman only sweetened the bargain. Adela chose to wait for the proper moment to intercede and make her opinion known.

Yousef's words took on a serious tone as he cautioned that the suitor would be arriving shortly, and he wanted everyone to be civil and not embarrass the family. Angèle saw it would be useless to confront her brother head on, so she decided to say no more. Her displeasure, if it were to be unleashed, would be, like her mother, saved for a more appropriate moment.

Soon they heard a car pull up outside. A gentleman dismounted and came through the door just as Yousef was going out to greet him. The two men exchanged the usual greetings, and Yousef bade the man to come in and meet the family.

Angèle stared at the Orthodox merchant, a short man with a receding hairline who appeared to be over forty years old, and bristled internally at the notion that her brother could think that she would actually marry an older man. She remained seated as Yousef presented the man, first to his mother and then to her. The man gave a shallow bow and mouthed his *salaams* as Angèle remained mute.

Yousef offered a drink, which was declined. Some small talk ensued but the conversation, which had gotten off to a cool and stilted start, seemed

101

to have no chance of melting the ice between the prospective suitor and bride. Adela, like Angèle, was not enamored with the idea of an Orthodox union or marriage to a much older man. It wasn't that there had been no interfaith marriages in their family before, there had been. But it was always the Hobeiche men who intermarried because the women would then follow their religion. That Angèle would be expected to embrace Orthodoxy was not remotely palatable to her. But even without that constraint, she didn't think the man was attractive. He certainly didn't measure up to the likes of Sheikh Edmond el Khazen.

I couldn't help but be reminded of a similar situation that occurred in my hometown of Carthage, New York, when a young Lebanese girl became betrothed to a much older Greek man, the proprietor of a candy store. When she heard of it, Angèle was aghast—especially since the wedding was to take place in the Greek Orthodox church eighteen miles away in Watertown, meaning that the girl was converting to orthodoxy. Angèle promptly interjected herself into the fray by marching down to the candy store to let the proprietor know that this shouldn't and couldn't be. The Greek man became enraged and, after a few choice words, ordered Angèle out of his store. My somewhat chastened mother lost that battle and, of course, didn't attend the wedding.

The rug merchant tried valiantly to engage in small talk, but Angèle was unresponsive. He could see after a while that she was a headstrong young woman, and his countenance began to betray doubts that he would be up to the task of taming her. The scene recalled Shakespeare's *The Taming of the Shrew*, but this merchant was just not up to playing Petruchio to Angèle's Kate. Previous attempts at matchmaking on his behalf had resulted in women fawning over him and making him feel like a prize catch. He was not used to the kind of reception he was getting from these Hobeiche women, and he neither understood nor liked it.

He took Yousef aside and in a low voice mentioned that it appeared that his family was not interested in exploring this union. Yousef passed the whole scene off as shyness, even though the experienced soldier could see the tide of battle had turned against him. He told the suitor to give it a little time, but the merchant said he was in a hurry to get married, and there was no shortage of willing prospects. He appreciated Yousef's interest but respectfully declined any further exploration of this contract. He then turned to the seated women, bowed, and in quite unctuous tones, bade them goodbye, turned and walked out to his waiting car. Yousef followed quickly and spoke rapidly to the man, but to no avail as the rebuffed suitor quickly drove off.

Yousef stormed back into the house fuming. Angèle recoiled, thinking he was going to strike her, but her mother rose quickly from her chair and stepped between them. She told her son that he had acted hastily in a rush to augment his personal situation. He had chosen badly, she said, and he should let it pass. There would be other opportunities.

Angèle remained irritated by her brother's presumptiveness, but she decided to say nothing more, although it was unlike her to back off from a fight, especially when she felt she was the injured party. Yousef turned and stalked out without so much as a farewell to his family.

This was not the last time the issue of who would claim the bridal prize would come up. There would be many suitors, by Yousef's later recounting, and it became clear that both he and his sister would have to agree before any betrothal could be consummated.

# PART II
# The Kmeids

# 15

*A mule has to wait till the grass grows.*

"TODAY, WE GO TO BQAATOUTA,"* DÉSIREÉ announced. Soon we are on our way to visit my father's place of birth. We would continue following the ancestry trail up the slopes from Kattine past Kfar Debiane into the sleepy little village my dad called home. For this part of my journey, we will venture up to an elevation of 1,500 meters above sea level. The road is an unfaithful one because, although we can see our objective clearly across the valley, the thoroughfare sends us down and away from it. Only after several twists and turns do we climb back up toward the original objective. Such is the necessity of mountain travel, and I calculate from looking at the map that our meandering cost us four or five times the straight-line distance.

My faithful chauffeur Désireé still has no respect for the map I cradle between my knees and continues to navigate by verbal direction from pedestrians at intersections when it appears a decision has to be made. The Lebanese character does not allow them to trust authority or institutions, and even though I tell Désireé that the map wasn't made by the government, she is unimpressed.

As we near the town of Bqaatouta I tell my cousin, "This is where my father Toufic Traad Kmeid was born." The little town finally comes into view, but we know this only because of the unobtrusive sign marking its entrance. "This is a small place," Désireé remarks. There are lots of small places in Lebanon, I think, knowing from experience that these mountains are buckshot-scattered with villages like Bqaatouta. I can't even fathom the original pioneers hacking out a trail up these rugged mountains to build their

---

*The name of the town is properly pronounced Bqa·too·ta, although the local dialect would elide the "q," which made it sound as Ba·too·ta.

humble homes and construct their terraced gardens. Given the unforgiving terrain, I wondered aloud how this seemingly innate drive for independence and security could be so strong in the Lebanese people. But, once established in these mountains, you could see how the environment would actually strengthened these people's character.

My father's village is the kind of nondescript place that you could pass through without so much as a blink. Lying in the shadow of the majestic Mount Sannine, Bqaatouta swells to a summertime population of 4,500 souls, two-thirds of whom are escaping the heat of the lowland cities. The seasonal residents, in turn, give way to 1,500 hard-core inhabitants who remain during the season of *talge* (snow), a time of the year when the cold and damp weather is unpleasant no matter how romantically one tries to describe it. Mtount Sannine, with its clearly demarked timberline, serves to remind us just how high up we really are. The brownish peak pokes up through the clouds to an elevation of a little over 8,600 feet above sea level.

"Let's see if any Kmeid cousins are living here now," I say to Désireé. Since there are no pedestrians available for directional duty, we stop at a café to ask about the Kmeid family. The proprietor insists we take coffee as Désireé chats amiably about this fellow from America who is visiting his deceased father's village of Bqaatouta.

One would think that the ubiquitous ritual of imbibing coffee would be as ancient as the land itself, but in actuality, it has a rather recent genesis in Lebanon. Coffee drinking came into vogue in the latter part of the nineteenth century—as a byproduct of the economic ascendancy of the peasant class. Before that time, coffee consumption was limited to the aristocracy, for they were the only ones who could afford the expensive beans imported from Yemen. But once it became affordable, the coffee habit mimicked drug addiction as it swept through the population.

After the exchange of pleasantries, we are directed to the residence of an elderly man who turns out to be a cousin of my father. Amin Kmeid is well into his surprisingly spry seventies and greets us in the Lebanese fashion with kisses and an invitation to sit and chat. Abundantly sweet fruit, and of course, the ubiquitous Turkish coffee suddenly materialize. It is the season for cherries, and the freshly picked clusters arrayed before us are so delicious that it is hard to stop eating once you start.

"So, you are the son of Toufic Traad," Amin reiterates with a broad smile. In all the Lebanese villages, a boy is known by the conjunction of his and his father's given names, a convention that he carries throughout life. It's understandable, when you think about it, that over scores of years a surname would become profusely propagated through various branchings of a family tree. This would inevitably cause confusion whenever the same names were given to children, as often happened. The practice of conjoining the father's and the son's names seems to have developed in order to avoid misunderstandings about who was being talked about. I chuckle when I think that, had I been living there, I would have been known as Raffic Toufic. It even rhymes!

We are given a tour of the house my grandfather built after he left Ghazir in the 1860s and of the old and new Maronite churches, which define the center of town. Above the altar in the new church hangs a painting of the Blessed Virgin that, according to the affixed plaque, was the gift of my father and his first cousin, Naja. I had never heard about this gift, as my father never spoke of it, perhaps because of the falling out the two men had well before I was born. I was a bit amazed that the painting had survived the seventy-five years since its endowment.

The old house, in the spring of 1914, where the sixteen-year-old Toufic Traad did his daily laving at the cistern in the backyard, weather accommodating, stands only in my imagination. Since I saw it on my first trip, the house has been razed and replaced by a much larger and more opulent home. But I can still see him in the back of the old house getting ready for work.

It is April, and the rainy season has not yet ended, and there is a chill is in the air. He uses a small shard of a mirror placed in the crook of a branch of an apple tree, a tree that also holds his shirt and what passes for a towel. He peers into the looking glass as he meticulously parts and combs his copious mop of thick black hair. Then he carefully strops his father's sparkling, pearl-handled straight razor that will shave the thick stubble from his face. The razor had belonged to his father's father and was passed down as a family heirloom. Little things mean a lot in these mountains, and something as simple as a straight razor was a possession to be cherished.

Toufic Traad had been shaving since he was twelve, having matured early on like all the men of his clan. There he stood, with his face bursting with bristles, seeming to enjoy the process of scraping off the tough whiskers that covered his handsome face. The ritual gave him time to think and to dream, as he often did, of a better life, the life he heard was available in *Amreeka*. He also thought of simple things, such as growing a moustache and affecting the look of an older, more mature young man. He would be turning seventeen in the fall and had been promised a chance at the good life, the same life his sister and uncles were pursuing in the New World.

On these occasions the young Toufic Traad grew pensive. He was not very happy with the hardscrabble life in the mountains, a life that would not yield him even the modest future of which he dreamed. He was ambitious, but not unrealistically so because it wouldn't take much to upgrade his living standard given his humble birthright. His people depended on a bountiful Mother Nature, along with prayers for divine intercession, to take care of their basic needs. There was the weather and the water, orchards and gardens and canned and dried goods stored away for the winter. There were his father's barrels where the crushed grapes would be fermented and the pressure cooker where the mash would be distilled into *arak*, the only alcoholic drink they consumed. There were the animals, two goats and a half-dozen sheep that wintered in a stable that had been the small house where Toufic was born. In the spring the ewes would produce a lamb or two.

Life was hard and simple and worst of all, for Toufic, repetitious and boring. Perhaps this life would have satisfied him had it not been for the tales of riches garnered in *Amreeka* by those who had left his village in the preceding twenty years. It certainly didn't bother his father who was content to make do with the family's orchards and his work as a stonemason.

Even though Toufic Traad had not personally seen the tangible fruits from the American adventure, the notion beguiled him. His older sister Christine had been gone ten months, her passage having been paid, according to the SS *France's* passenger manifest, by her husband, Nebhan Abdoo Kmeid, who had preceded her. His uncles had left nearly thirteen years before, having been recruited by a smooth-talking *simsar* (steamship agent) to go to *Amreeka* where their futures awaited. The steamship company representatives regaled them with stories of wealth waiting for the taking. Some even offered to advance credit, provided the émigrés were willing to mortgage the family property as collateral. Loan sharking, probably the second oldest profession in the world, was used to pad emigration rolls the world around. These sharpies knew they would either make a handsome return on their loans, or as often happened, get the debtor's land as repayment.

So, why were these people so desperate to leave their version of paradise, the only land they had ever seen or known? There were a number of events that had ruptured the stability of rugged mountain life. The emergence of silk production in the latter half of the nineteenth century, with the consequent economic advancement of the lower classes, also had a downside. The price of silk varied from season to season due to conditions such as blight, disease, competition, and quality of production. The relative calm that had prevailed in the previous fifty years, an era that was later called "The Long Peace," was another factor. As happens in times of prolonged peace, population growth is unimpeded by the inevitable subtractions due to war. The increased number of people could no longer be fed by the available arable land. These conditions led to desperate times and desperate times called for desperate measures. Many Bqaatoutans scrimped and scraped to muster the wherewithal meet that challenge by emigrating to *Amreeka*.

Toufic went in the house for the typical breakfast that his mother Farida had prepared: yogurt, olives, cheese, and bread, along with the dark, thick coffee that was served at every meal. He picked up the lunch his mama had packed for him in the *jurab*, a goatskin bag like the one shepherds carried around their waists, and prepared to make the journey to the dusty stone quarry, some ten kilometers away. His father had gotten him the job, as he had been doing since the boy reached twelve years of age, when he didn't need his help with his masonry work or pruning apple trees.

There was always plenty of work to do, but jobs for pay were scarce, and strangely enough, even undesirable to most of the independent-minded Lebanese mountain people. The proud peasants had a list of preferred occupations and working for common wages was on the lower rung of that occupational ladder.

Toufic Traad, a more practical lad, was not one who felt that way. His Baba had taught him early on that honest labor, no matter what kind, was better than none. *He who does not drink from his own palm does not quench his thirst*, his pragmatic father had often said. Now, while the apple blossoms were blooming, the potatoes, corn, beans, chickpeas, lettuce, radishes, cucumbers, eggplant, and squash were planted, tomato seeds put in their beds and grape vines pruned, the only work was at the quarry. And Toufic was lucky to have that. He was fortified physically, if not mentally, and ready to earn his share of the family's daily bread.

His short, chubby, doting mother always told her boy to be careful after kissing him on the cheeks as he headed out the door. She had always had a special affection for her eldest son even though it was not obvious whose side of the family his features favored. His parents were cousins, after all, and looks and demeanor were much the same on both sides of the family.

Abu Toufic (Traad, the boy's father) would tell his wife not to trouble herself because the lad was strong and self-reliant. I always found it curious that his

111

father was known as Abu Toufic, the father of Toufic, going about with his son's identity, while the son, called Toufic Traad or Ibn Traad (son of Traad), went around with the father's. It wouldn't surprise me if identity problems resulted from this convention, but it certainly cemented and clarified the Lebanese family bonds.

Toufic's mother worried anyway, for she knew that her son had an impish streak. A few of his boyhood friends and a cousin had already gone to *Amreeka*, so he was continually at a loss for amusements in a town that had few to begin with. She feared that he would get into serious trouble one day.

While his mother was still voicing her concerns, the lad was out the door, shuffling down the path, away from the rude, four-room house he called home. His father had built the stone, two-story, flat-roofed house after his first son was born. He had left his father Elias' house after he married and built his first small home that now served as a stable. The latest house was unlike most other homes in the village because it was a two-story affair.

The closely spaced children, including five girls and three boys, before his sister Christine left for *Amreeka*, had fit in the upper four rooms of the house. How they all squeezed in, only they could tell. Toufic Traad and his two younger brothers' formative years were spent sleeping on thick sheepskins spread on the floor, which would be rolled up and stored away during the day. His inherited ethic was simply to work, never to complain, and to bring his meager wages home to his father. "You have to do the best you can," his father would often say, an admonition that the young and impressionable Toufic Traad carried with him and repeated to his children throughout his life.

The boy instinctively kicked pebbles and scanned the landscape as he walked down the winding path toward the main road. There was his friend Amin Sabbagh's home, Uncle Seghaan's house, and the house where his Uncle Nasif and cousin Naja had lived, all of whom were now in *Amreeka*. The boisterous, self-confident Naja, only nine at the time, had gone to the States with his mother to join his dad eight years before. Amin had gone to the US to be united with his father just two years prior, at the age of eleven, and Toufic Traad hadn't heard a word from either of them, or his uncles, since. The lad could only wonder what the pair were doing, and if they were picking gold off trees as was rumored. Ah, if only he could shake the dust from his shoes and join them.

When walking down the path from Toufic Traad's house, you can't see the roads leading to the other houses. The hilly terrain is deceptive in that the streets are not visible until you are practically on top of them. It reminds me of the landscape in the North Hills of Pittsburgh where the houses look as if they are randomly pasted onto the hillsides, a striking view that is often captured in landscape paintings.

At the main road Toufic hitched a ride in a wagon pulled by a tired-looking mule that was on its way to pick up a load of limestone at the Faitroun quarry. The wagon bed was covered with a thick layer of straw upon which the workers reclined, mildly easing the jarring and jostling from the bumpy, rutted road. The men of varying ages didn't seem to mind the rough ride, for they were just happy they didn't have to walk all the way to the stone quarry.

Young girls strolling along the roadside would call to Toufic as the wagon passed, causing the boy to blush and the older men to tease him. Although only five-and-a-half feet tall—his family on both sides were generally short in stature—Toufic Traad was a popular boy. He had caught many a young girl's eye down at the fountain in the town's square. His broad, square face, pleasant nose, tightly placed ears, thick black hair, and overall good looks were attractive to the opposite sex. (I always thought, from his early pictures, that he bore a striking resemblance to a young Omar Sharif.) But he had acquired a reputation of being aloof in matters of the heart. By all accounts he was a pleasant, easy-going, fun-loving, hard-working chap, and one who was slow to anger, but when stirred up, his rage ran long and deep.

In a small town like Bqaatouta, everyone knew, or thought they knew, everybody else's business. Amin Kmeid related to me an incident that occurred in the month prior to Toufic Traad's last days in Bqaatouta. It was a confrontation that set tongues wagging because the boy seemed too young to be involved in fisticuffs with an older man.

Toufic Traad had come to the defense of his widowed cousin's children, who had been slapped around by the proprietor of the local bakery. As the story went, the man didn't want the kids, who were naturally attracted to the aroma of freshly baked bread and pastries, hanging around his shop. They had stood in front of the shop with their tongues hanging out and mouths drooling, hoping the owner would give them a sample. But he shooed them off, not once but three times. Finally, the exasperated man administered the slaps that, when he heard about it, caused Toufic to fly into a rage. He marched down to the shop and confronted the man, and when words began to fly, fists soon followed. Had he not been pulled off by bystanders, Toufic probably would have ended up in jail instead of riding a wagon to the quarry in Faitroun. His cousin Amin could still chuckle about it all those years later.

One of the boys walking on the roadside called out to Toufic Traad as the wagon ambled by, asking if he had heard about the meeting later that night. Toufic was aware of the two visitors from *Amreeka* who would be holding court down at Khalil's coffee house. A large crowd would be there for sure to hear about the wonders of *Amreeka*, and Toufic also wanted to hear about the country he dreamed of, the land of riches.

Riding bumpily along in the wagon, Toufic Traad would absentmindedly rub the back of his left hand while deep in dreams of the Promised Land. It was as if he were subconsciously trying to erase the tattoo that had been rudely etched there when he was but twelve years old. It was part of an initiation rite for a group of young boys who, like himself, needed the excitement and entertainment that a gang could provide. Chaffing under the idea of Ottoman rule, even though they only knew their oppressors through stories they heard or the taxes their fathers grumbled about, caused them to incessantly curse those "goddamned Turks."

The gang, as young boys often do, had created an initiation ritual for inclusion into their group. They made a bond to each other by putting a pinch of salt on the tip of their knives and offering it to each other in a rite that mimicked an ancient shepherds' compact. This offering signified that their weapons would never be used against one another. It's a wonder that they didn't also hang wolf bones around their necks to ward off their enemies as shepherds did with their sheep. They would, somewhat ridiculously I thought for their age, swear allegiance and secrecy to each other under penalty of death.

The tattoo was painfully applied by a Bedouin on his annual journey through Bqaatouta, and came out large and clear. A scimitar hung menacingly between the wrist and knuckles of his hand, surrounded by the Arabic letters that spelled out the gang's motto, "Together We Are Strong."

Older men would often inquire if he was proud of belonging to a gang of ruffians, and this would cause Toufic to bristle. He didn't like having to defend his actions and would exasperatingly reply that it happened when he was just a kid. He would also be reminded that he was the same kid that was always disturbing the peace by ringing the church bell at all hours of the night, and he didn't like that either.

Toufic Traad could see, when he thought about it, that these people might have a justifiable complaint, but his jaw would tighten anyway as his flashing brown eyes would darken and glare back at his inquisitors. It was a demeanor that I became familiar with while growing up, and it always reminded me of a coiled snake ready to strike. I quickly learned to get the hell out of harm's way at that point. But Toufic felt that he and his buddies had to stand up to those Turk bastards and not behave like sheep. He wondered, as adolescents often do, why the older folks seemed so satisfied with the status quo. If the

114

younger generation had their way, things would certainly change, or so he thought. It caused me to think that if adults were honest with themselves and could accurately remember how they felt in their youth, they'd admit that that they also believed the older generation had compromised itself in one way or another.

Toufic Traad's feelings were a bit surprising because respecting your elders, as any child brought up in the Lebanese tradition knows, is a cultural given ingrained from birth. In spite of this, he and his gang members often spoke of letting the adults know that they were not going to put up with this crap forever, but it was mostly just talk.

Toufic Traad returned to his reveries of *Amreeka* until the quarry came into sight around a jagged bend in the road. Another day at the arduous quarry wasn't what he wanted for his life, but…it had to do for now.

It was late when he got home from his day's labor. He was dusty and dirty and went to clean up in the backyard. Looking down at his rough, callused hands, he shook his head and told himself that he soon would be finished with hard labor. He went inside, and along with all six of his remaining siblings, crowded around the rough-hewn table for a dinner that might have included stuffed grape leaves or squash, yogurt and fresh vegetables coupled with copious amounts of *marqooq* (flat mountain bread) that his mother would have baked that day. Although tired from all the tugging and lifting of stones, he decided he had to go down to the coffee shop to see those men who had returned from *Amreeka*. His two younger brothers wanted to tag along, but Toufic told them their time would come later.

# 16

*If you wish to tell lies, be far away from those you lie about.*

THE COFFEE HOUSES IN LEBANON TODAY ARE QUITE different from those
of my father's time. With the advent of electricity, refrigeration, and tiled
floors, they sparkle with the whiteness of a 1950s American ice cream parlor.
Their menus have expanded to serve a wide variety of pastries in a somewhat
westernized fashion. When Désireé and I sat down for our afternoon break,
we were offered some of those pastries along with omnipresent thick Turkish
coffee. "This is not the same as I remember on my first trip," I reminisced,
recalling twenty years earlier when the coffee was made in a miniature brass
pot, brought to a boil four or five times, and delivered to my table before
being poured into my cup. The clash of antiquity with modernity in Lebanon
is seen even in a simple cup of coffee that is now made in an espresso-like
machine.

In my father's time, the coffee house was the center of social activity for a
village, a place where men would exchange gossip while playing backgammon
until the wee hours. It was also used for small gatherings such as the one he
attended on that April evening in 1914.

*People tell lies when it concerns wealth.*

Half of the large crowd had taken all the available chairs, and Toufic joined
the group that was jostling for standing-room-only positions. The group was
abuzz while pointing at the two well-dressed men, standing at the back of the
shop. One of the older standees told Toufic Traad that these men had come
from New York in *Amreeka*.

Toufic looked with barely concealed wonder at the prosperously dressed
gentlemen who wore shimmering western garb, clothes the likes of which he
had never seen before. He wondered if everybody in *Amreeka* wore silk suits.

It is not hard for me to imagine the impact such a display would have made on the poor villagers of Bqaatouta. Traveling Americans are easily recognizable wherever they go. I remember being singled out in Italy by salesmen looking to sell land in Florida to American tourists and by shoeshine boys on the streets of Beirut. No matter how hard I tried to blend in, it was to no avail.

The two peacocks, one with a prominent gold front tooth and the other with an immaculately waxed handlebar moustache, rustled their feathers while basking in the adulation from the receptive audience. When the coffee shop could hold no more, Gold Tooth bade the crowd to be still, and everyone hushed to listen. He began to extol *Amreeka* as a wonderful place with riches beyond their wildest dreams. As if to cement that notion in their minds, he reached into a leather pouch that he had been holding and withdrew a fistful of coins. With a grand gesture he held them up, and with a long sweep of his arm, threw the money into the air. As the treasure hit the earthen floor, young and old alike dove, tumbling over each other to retrieve the coins. Some even tried to wrest coins from the grasp of their neighbors.

The two expats were laughing uproariously at the reaction they had touched off. And when all the coins had been scooped up, the crowd settled back to give their benefactors renewed attention, waiting with even broader smiles for more coins to be tossed. There would be no more coins because the two men had gotten the attention they wanted, so they launched into their sales pitch.

Moustache extolled the weather in *Amreeka* but cautioned that it changed quickly. He said it was cold in the winter but not as cold as in the mountains of Lebanon. It was warm in summer but not warm as Beirut. He added that often, after a hot day in the summer, rain would fall and cool things off. The crowd gasped in unbelieving unison, knowing that rain in Lebanon in the summer months was unheard of.

I can give testimony to this belief because on one of my summer visits I noticed that my chauffeur had removed the windshield wipers from his car. When I asked why, he said they were for rain, and there was no rain in the summertime.

Gold Tooth nodded affirmation and added that there were very tall buildings in New York and trolley cars running everywhere. Why, in New York there was a great river spanned by a long bridge, and cars traveled across the bridge while boats plied the waters underneath. And if that wasn't startling enough, in a tunnel under the river, trains transported people back and forth to work. One man shouted that he believed all that, but rain in the summertime? He didn't believe that!

Moustache was undeterred and added that the most important thing was the availability of work for everyone. The audience's enthusiasm was accented by their palpable breathing, and they began asking questions about the kind of work that was available, how much they could earn, and how they would get started. There were so many questions, in fact, that the two recruiters had to use vigorous hand gestures to calm down the crowd.

When the din subsided, the two men took turns explaining how they were recruited to peddle goods such as underwear, socks, scarves, and notions. After four years of peddling they had opened their own store to become suppliers to other peddlers. They needed more people to come and ply the peddling trade to other areas of the country. The country was big and growing, with new factories and more and more workers to sell to. They continually emphasized what a great opportunity this was.

There was, of course, the question of passage to this world of opportunity, and Gold Tooth said that money could be borrowed if you owned property. They could get a loan with their land used as collateral.

These people, whose rough hands and tanned faces betrayed their relationship with Mother Earth, had no experience in the mercantile world. This detail was ignored as Moustache launched into a soliloquy about the riches to be made in the peddling business, reemphasizing that the profits were lucrative. Given that these people averaged two piasters (about 10¢) a day for work in Lebanon, the notion that in *Amreeka* they could make ten or twenty times that in a day was indeed appealing. And the two men beamed broadly, for they could see in the faces of their audience that they had struck the right chords.

One might wonder, as I did, what it was in the Lebanese psyche that made entrepreneurship so attractive? It seems to come down to a fundamental yearning for independence. Historically, a man with a plot of land and a few animals felt unfettered and was loath to surrender that way of life. Even when silk factories came to the mountains of Lebanon, the owners found it difficult to find men willing to work in them and thus hired women almost exclusively. So, the peddling trade, for those who desired to emigrate, would hold a certain attraction, for they could be their own bosses and would not be working for wages.

My father understood these urges but was skeptical. The few letters from his uncles and Christine, as told through their priest, spoke of jobs, but also described a lot of hardship. Several lived together in a house, in order to save money, and they had to be very frugal. Remittances to their families, although most welcome, were not so large that you'd believe there was gold on trees. But he decided to shove any reservations he might have out of his mind's back door. There was no need to spoil the mood of the moment for the rest of his fellow Bqaatoutans.

The visitors enjoyed their exalted prominence with the "old country" folks and regaled them with even more stories of the New World. One of the things they talked about was the maple tree with sap so sweet you could make sugar from it. The murmuring crowd was skeptical, just as they were with rain in the summertime. But the salesmen were undeterred, explaining how they mixed the syrup with *tahini* (ground, hulled sesame seeds) and had it at breakfast. The people were salivating at the thought because they loved *tahini* sauce mixed with *dibs* (grape molasses).

Talk of food led to the description of *Amreeka* as a land of plenty, with vegetables and fruit in such profusion they would never go hungry. They pointed out that the people over there didn't have to import any food, referring of course to the shortages in Lebanon caused by the stampede to sericulture and the subsequent use of the land for mulberry trees.

The men also gave a short course on how to behave in the New World, both en route and after arriving. They warned about people all along the way who would try to take advantage of them. Unmarried women had to be accompanied by a relative and this added to the mystery of why Christine's ship's manifest stated her fare was paid by her husband, even though the family never mentioned she was married at the time.

Boys under the age of nineteen also were not allowed to travel alone. It wasn't said aloud, but the inference was that boys should lie about their ages if needed. They were told they would have to endure a physical exam both in France, before boarding ship, and in New York after debarking. And they had to bring with them a letter from the village sheikh certifying that they were not wanted for any crime and had permission to leave the country. Last but not least, they had to have money and clothing to carry with them. In 1914, the cash requirement upon entry in *Amreeka*, which had fluctuated from year to year, and seemingly was never rigidly enforced, was $50.

At the end of the sales pitch, the duo told the crowd they would take names and help arrange passage for them to the New World. People began talking with each other about where they could borrow money or what property they might mortgage. Toufic shook his head because, although he could empathize with the crowd's eagerness, he also understood those who had somber faces and shoulders hunched with disappointment. Those with greatest need to emigrate, ironically were the ones least able to manage it. Toufic Traad conceded that it was indeed difficult not to become enthusiastic about *Amreeka*, something he had been dreaming of for quite a while.

His hopes were pinned on his sister (and perhaps her husband) sending him the fare, even though he didn't know if she could manage it.

Little did he know his hopes were about to be realized.

*Young Toufic Kmeid.*

# 17

*The kindred of the spade are easily recognizable.*

After the Young Turks gained power in 1908, they began implementing drastic changes that affected personal decisions being made throughout Lebanon. The people of Bqaatouta were hearing rumors, and taking notice. The covenants adopted in 1863 were being challenged by the new regime, taxes had been increased, and there was talk of conscripting Lebanese into the Ottoman armies. Their forces were always engaged in battle somewhere in the far-flung empire and they continually needed replacements. Stories of conscripts going off to remote places, never to be seen or heard from again were rife. Those, who like Toufic Traad wished to emigrate, were getting worried and more anxious. Talk of war had increased, and economic pressures were building. Silk prices had plummeted, and the scant work for wages was becoming even scarcer. Toufic's days at the stone quarry, not that he really minded, were numbered.

Two months after the visit from Gold Tooth and Moustache, Toufic came home from the quarry to find the parish priest, Fr Tanoury, sitting with his parents. "A letter has arrived from your sister," the priest said. Shukrullah Mobark, the scribe of Christine's village of Carthage, New York, had penned a note for her, and the local priest was summoned to translate.

The priest told Toufic Traad that he was in luck, for his sister Christine had arranged passage for him to America, along with instructions on what to do once he got there. The priest added that she had sent something called a voucher that he would have to exchange it at the port for a ticket. It was good for any available ship on the White Star Line. The expatriates had learned quickly about theft in the mails and sharpies defrauding passengers trying to buy steamship tickets at the port. It was rumored that many seeking passage to *Amreeka* were put on ships going to other places, such as Africa. So, the

Lebanese quickly became familiar with bank drafts and vouchers, and they exercised caution in sending money home. In Toufic's case, Christine had sent a bank draft for five liras (about $25) for expenses and a voucher for steamship passage on the White Star Line. He would be able to cash the draft at the *baladia* (government house) in Jounieh.

Toufic, surprising everyone with his haste, immediately went to start packing, even though he didn't have very many possessions to pack. His father wondered aloud if he couldn't wait until the harvest was brought in, but Toufic said that there was plenty of help, including his younger brothers Rafic and Chafic. He also pointed out that the sooner he left, the sooner he'd start sending money back.

There was no stopping Toufic ("I ran for the boat," he would say with a smile in later years), and he knew that the prospect of financial aid would assuage any misgivings his father had. It would be down to Jounieh on the morrow to get a passport. No more stone quarry, no more planting or pruning apple trees, no more hoeing the garden, and no more picking apples. He was going to the land of opportunity.

News traveled fast in the village, and that evening, as was the custom, a crowd gathered about his house to wish the traveler well. Among them were Afifi, a first cousin and close friend of Toufic's, and her father Mansour. The girl was misty eyed and tried to edge closer to Toufic without being obvious. As the evening wore on and the *arak* flowed, Toufic meandered outside at the back of the house where Afifi had headed a few minutes earlier.

The girl could scarcely hold back the tears as she asked Toufic why he had to leave so soon. Toufic answered that the sooner he left, the sooner he'd be back. Afifi then asked if he wanted her to wait for him.

According to the customs of the day, romancing by kids that age was greatly frowned upon. The families and village sheikh would arrange all such liaisons. But, boys and girls will be boys and girls the world around, and there had been surreptitious meetings that took place down by the town's fountain and in the apple orchards. As forbidden and exciting as those trysts were, Toufic knew they were coming to an end. Afifi, a nice-looking girl of fifteen and barely five feet tall, was rapidly growing into womanhood. In those surroundings, as noted before, a girl was considered marriageable at sixteen, and more often than not, would be wed by the time she reached twenty.

Afifi's long black hair hung in ringlets, and her dark brown eyes flashed in the moonlight as Toufic told her that he couldn't ask her to wait because he didn't know when he'd be coming back. He was ambivalent because their acquaintanceship had never gotten past the occasional holding of hands, mostly due to fear of discovery and the resulting opprobrium. That, coupled with the feeling that he was not ready to get seriously involved, prevented the budding romance from proceeding into dangerous territory.

Afifi said she'd wait if he would say the word, but Toufic was not ready to make a serious commitment. Oh, he had genuine affection for Afifi but had great difficulty in expressing it. His family, her family, his lack of property, his abiding need to gain some wealth and independence were all stumbling blocks that he couldn't avoid tripping over. To relieve his discomfort, he suggested that they had better get back to the party before her father missed her.

Afifi quickly dabbed the tears that swelled in her eyes with the tiny cloth that had been tucked into the sleeve of her dress. She came closer to Toufic, put her arms around his neck, reached up and kissed him full on the lips. After finally ending the embrace, she said she wanted to remind him what would be waiting for him when he came back. Turning quickly, she returned to the party.

Toufic remained outside until the emotional and physical jolt that Afifi sent through his body had abated. He basked in the blush of the passionate moment, and finally, when the glow had receded, he also returned to the party. Afifi had already left.

The next morning, just as the cock crowed, Toufic was up and ready to leave. He had never been to the city of Beirut, although he had spent the last four winters planting olive trees in Baabda. (Olives and dates were the only commodities that would not grow in the altitude of Bqaatouta. Many villagers, like nomadic tribesmen, took their livestock to winter down to the lower elevations, and also to work there.) Although now considered a suburb of sprawling Beirut, Baabda was then too far away for Toufic to walk there, although he had been tempted. But now he would, out of necessity, see it for the first time.

His mother Farida said her tearful goodbyes after she finished packing his *jurab* with enough food to last him until he got aboard ship. He was reminded to give their love to Christine and all of their relatives that had gone to *Amreeka*.

His father hated to lose his eldest and hardest working boy, the one who never complained and gladly remitted whatever he earned. He knew it was inevitable that Toufic would have to go because they needed the money he could remit and they didn't want to chance his being caught up in the ever-widening Ottoman conscription net. His eyes misted over as he told the boy to take care of himself while giving him a kiss on each cheek. He thereupon handed Toufic the straight razor that his father had given him. Toufic started to protest, but his father reached for one of his omnipresent proverbs, *The hand that takes not, gives not.* Exchanging gifts was a time-honored custom, and one had to accept or risk insulting the giver.

Toufic tried valiantly to stanch the tears that forced their way down his cheeks as he thanked his father. Anxious as he was to go, the scene stirred misgivings that the young man didn't know lurked beneath his carefree demeanor. Homesickness was a new and strange emotion for him, one he would revisit many times, both during his journey and after he arrived in *Amreeka.*

Toufic's voice brimmed with confidence when he announced that he'd be coming back as soon as he made a lot of money. Little did he know he would never see his family again.

On the first leg of his journey, he had to walk to Jounieh to obtain his passport. The long trek on the mountain road had one saving grace—it was all downhill. By the time Toufic reached the government offices in Jounieh, six hours later, it was two in the afternoon. There were long lines of people waiting to conduct business, almost all of which concerned emigration.

Toufic was disappointed as he could see that getting his passport was going to take a long time. Nonetheless he took up a position at the end of the line to wait his turn while listening to the chatter of people talking about where they were going: America, Canada, Cuba, Brazil, and Argentina. The man in line in front of Toufic turned and asked him where he was going, and he proudly replied—*Amreeka!*

The gentleman seemed to be an experienced traveler and told Toufic that it was going to take several hours to get through the lines. They would probably have to stay overnight and offered to share a room with him at the *khan* (hotel).

Toufic, remembering the warnings he had been given about people trying to take advantage of him on the way to *Amreeka,* quickly demurred. He said that he'd be all right even though the man proposed to split the cost. The boy had slept in the open many times in his young life and could do it again. Besides, he wanted to be up early to get to the head of the line, and he might need the money a room would have cost.

Promptly at 5:00 PM, a clerk appeared and announced that the offices were closed. The large metal doors to the building banged shut, and the remaining crowd grumbled and shuffled off. Toufic fingered his food-filled *jurab* and felt all he needed was to find some water and a place where he could rest his head.

He learned that the seashore lay a few blocks to the south of the government building, so he headed there to eat his meal and spend the night. He picked a flat rock that was far enough from the water to avoid the splash of the breakers, spread his coat and sat down to eat. As he looked westward, watching the waves lick the shore, his thoughts again turned to *Amreeka* and what it must be like.

After consuming his modest supper, Toufic laid back to watch the sun set. The flaming orb descended slowly in the west, burning a hole in the sea as it disappeared for another day. Toufic had seen many a sunset in the mountains overlooking the bay of Jounieh, but they did not seem as brilliant as this one. His body quickly harmonized with the rhythms of the waves, and an aura of peace settled upon him as he fell asleep. His slumber was filled with strange dreams wherein he found himself swimming across the ocean, barely touching the surface of the water, heading toward *Amreeka*. This was a strange dream indeed because the lad couldn't swim a stroke.

Up at first light, Toufic shook off the stiffness caused by his hard bed and prepared to hurry back into line at the government house. The strange calming effect of the previous night had worn off, and apprehensiveness again overtook him. His air of decided confidence had been penetrated by sharp pangs of homesickness even though he was fewer than twenty miles into his journey. And he still had 6,000 miles to go.

At the government offices he saw that several people from the previous day were sleeping on the entrance steps. He took a position in front of the large metal doors and was first in line when the office opened two hours later.

I remember the first time I saw the building that houses the *baladia*. It is still mainly the way my father saw it, and I felt a little giddy as I walked up the same steps he had climbed some eighty-five years before. The only changes to the original building were repairs made from the shelling it had suffered during the recent civil war. After you pass through the front gate, you enter a large atrium in the center of the building with offices all around its perimeter. I could see the lines winding around to go up the steps to the second floor where the necessary paperwork would be completed. There are marble plaques on the walls of the stairwell commemorating the building's opening in the latter part of the nineteenth century. It's mind boggling just to imagine the thousands of Lebanese émigrés that passed through these same portals to obtain their visas and passports.

Upon entering the main salon, Toufic surely was dazzled by the room's ornate oriental design with its high arched columns and the scrolled bas-relief decorations. The ancient architecture along with the granite counters, barred cages, and officious looking clerks stationed behind them was a bit intimidating to the average Lebanese peasant. But Toufic marched up determinedly to the first cage on the second floor and showed his vouchers to the clerk. The man peered over the top of his delicate pince-nez glasses at the eager young man before him, cashed the bank draft, and handed Toufic a few bills and coins. Then he pulled out a little blue book, opened it, and began asking the applicant questions: Where were you born? How old are you? What are your father and mother's names? The information would be taken down in Arabic and duplicated in French.

Toufic promptly answered all that was asked of him and was then told the passport would cost ten piasters. The lad produced one of the small coins he had been given, a *nus-Majidi*, which he fingered tightly before proffering it for payment. After taking the money, the clerk wet an officious looking stamp with a sponge and affixed it on a page of the little blue book before handing it back. He was told to take the train to the port because it was very fast and cost only five piasters. The clerk could see by the puzzled expression that Toufic had never been on a train before. It amused him, as it always did, to see the look on the faces of the many innocent peasants that passed before him.

He was told to wait and follow the next person in line because everyone was going to the same place. The older man in line behind Toufic told him he could go with him as he was also going to the port to board a ship.

Toufic, although still harboring a suspicion that this man could also be one of the grifters he had been warned about, felt he didn't have much choice.

Unfortunately, the trains have been discontinued in Lebanon, but one can still see the tracks that are reminders of the days when immigrants took that conveyance to the port. It's a great loss, especially to the commuter, as anyone who has braved the clogged highways of Lebanon can attest.

The train ride was an experience in itself. Toufic had never before traveled so fast in his life. As it chugged down the tracks, the bewildering, noisy contraption belched a column of thick black smoke that occasionally penetrated the passenger cars. The smoky odor of coal was foreign to him because the people of his village burned only wood or charcoal. Soon he was at the port where the long train, with its many cars and gleaming windows, disgorged hordes of people who immediately rushed toward the terminal area. The port of Beirut was a hub of activity that made Toufic's head spin—so many people in such close proximity with one another. The harbor was also teeming with boats of all descriptions. All the larger boats, both steamships and those with sails, were anchored out in the bay.

The port has undergone many changes over the years, as one might imagine. Beirut had become the gateway for goods being imported to

Damascus and beyond, and expansion was needed to facilitate the increased freight tonnage.

Toufic was astonished at the number of people clogging the passageway. His newfound friend said they were all like him, trying to get out of the country. The young man took his place in line along with the ragtag army of émigrés. It would be two hours before he even got inside the building. The place resembled the government building in Jounieh. It had similar ornate decorations and cages with clerks manning them. Finally, when it was his turn, he proffered his voucher and said he wanted to go to *Amreeka*.

The harried ticket agent turned to the long lists that contained booking information on all ships leaving Beirut. There was a boat leaving that evening that would take him to Marseilles by way of Alexandria and Naples, Italy, and once in France, he would take a train to Cherbourg to catch a ship to New York.

The anxious passenger, even though he knew not of the places the clerk mentioned, was elated that he could sail on the same day. When asked, he presented his passport and the other papers to the clerk. The ticket agent began writing and stamping on a sheaf of tickets, also printed in both French and Arabic.

The Beirut harbor was a bit of a mess due to an altercation between Italy and the Ottomans that had spilled over into Beirut two years before. The dispute arose over Italy's adventures in Ottoman-occupied Libya, and the Italians, in a show of force, sank Turkey's torpedo boat *Angora* and gunboat *Aunullah* as they lay at anchor in Beirut harbor. Because of the resultant clutter of wreckage, passengers had to be ferried to their ships waiting out in the bay. (The wrecks would remain in the harbor until they were cleared in 1920.)

The rain-canvas draped ferries could hold as many as twenty passengers, and Toufic hopped aboard the next available one. It wasn't long before the ferryman had rowed his boat to Toufic's ship and the young lad scurried up the gangplank to start his journey to *Amreeka*.

# 18

*A man is worth what his clothes are.*

THE STAY AT THE PORT OF ALEXANDRIA, EGYPT, was short and the voyage to Naples uneventful. Toufic spent much of his time looking out to sea wherever he could get a glimpse. He was amazed at the size of the boat with its different levels, most of which were blocked off to him. Those in third class were crowded into a dormitory setting, living and sleeping close to one another. All of the men were older than Toufic and were also on their way somewhere to strike it rich. They regaled each other with optimistic stories of how their relatives or men they knew had made their fortunes in the New World, and each successive story vied to top the previous one.

Toufic listened, but soon began to regard some of the tales with a healthy dose of skepticism. He knew, after all, a little bit about how hard things were for the immigrants. His sister scrimped and saved to help meet his passage fee. Many years later he would say with a chuckle as he recalled those emigrants, "They all thought they were going to sweep gold up in the streets!"

Time weighed heavily on Toufic, and he paced the confined area incessantly. He was impatient for *Amreeka*. His reading skills were next to nil, so reading books or newspapers wasn't an option for passing the time. Staring out to sea and dreaming of how he was going to fare in *Amreeka* became his consuming pastime. His aspiration of becoming a businessman, despite his past experiences, was increasing with the distance traveled from home. Like the vast majority of Lebanese immigrants, when queried, he would confess to immigration authorities that he was a laborer, even though that occupation wasn't his ambition.

The ship finally docked for a one-day layover in Naples. Of course Toufic, being in third class, could not leave the ship. He spent the time loitering around the deck, all the while being accosted by an incessant parade of vendors selling food and religious trinkets. The ship took on many Italians who were

131

also going to the New World, and he heard many of them excitedly talking about some event that had happened, but of course, he couldn't understand what they were saying.

Unable to contain his curiosity, he asked one of his Lebanese compatriots what all the excitement was about and was told there had been an earthquake in Sicily where nearly 200 people had died. He began wondering if they had earthquakes in *Amreeka* and was informed that they happened only in the western part of the country. Another man added that just a few years before there was a big one in a place called San Francisco. Toufic wondered if that was near New York but was assured that it was quite a distance from there. Earthquakes were a new phenomenon to him since the last notable seismic activity in Lebanon had occurred several hundred years before.

Toufic stayed on the periphery of a ring of people buzzing about various events and rumors, and he pieced together news about a passenger ship that had sunk someplace in Canada. It was *The Empress of Ireland* that was rammed by another ship carrying coal, and over a thousand people lost their lives. This news fueled Toufic's thoughts about his own safety. He had never learned to swim, even though that skill wouldn't have helped much on the enormous expanse of the Mediterranean Sea.

After arriving in Marseilles and passing through customs as a transiting passenger, he was shepherded to the railroad station to catch the train to Cherbourg, where he boarded the RMS *Oceanic* of the White Star Line. Joining him in third class, besides the thirty-three others from "Syria," (all Lebanese in that time period were classified as coming from either Syria or Turkey) was an eclectic group from all over Europe and even South America. There were passengers from Germany, France, Spain, Portugal, Albania, Armenia, Bulgaria, Serbia, Switzerland, and North and South Italy (they were segregated back then). Added to this mix were people from San Salvador, Nicaragua, Brazil, and Canada. Finally, the *Oceanic* set sail for Southampton, England, on July 22, 1914.

It was a relatively short hop of five hours across the English Channel to Southampton to board additional passengers from northern and eastern Europe who had congregated there for the final leg of their journey to New York. The liner stopped just long enough to pick up those who had come from Austria, Poland, Hungary, Russia, Romania, Croatia, Sweden, Finland, Denmark, Belgium, and even Wales and Scotland. Strangely, there were a few passengers from Japan and the West Indies. The ship's surgeon listed some forty-six different races or nationalities on his affidavit.

The *Oceanic* then made an overnight trip around the southern tip of

England to the western port of Queenstown where several Irish and English travelers awaited. According to the ship's manifest, the steerage enrollment now numbered 664, which was just two-thirds of the third class capacity. The compartment took on a Tower of Babel atmosphere, and if one could differentiate, he would hear at least two-dozen different languages. In all, thirty countries were represented, which would have made a decent start for a mini United Nations.

Travelers in "steerage" owe that classification to being housed on a deck just above the steering mechanism of the ship. It is hot and noisy, and there is no privacy. The odors prevalent in close quarters, coupled with limited sanitary facilities, increase proportionately with the miles traveled. The stench would ultimately numb the passengers' sense of smell, but this was a price they willingly paid to escape their economic circumstances.

Although conditions in steerage class had improved in recent years, they were still poor by any measure. Luckily Toufic was on an English ship, for their accommodations were reputedly much better than those of German registry. The crews were more disciplined and courteous. He was also fortunate that his deck was only two-thirds full. Had it been filled to capacity, he and his shipmates would have been packed together like seeds in a pomegranate. The marginal food was served from large pots into mess kits provided by the White Star Line. But Toufic got used to it fairly quickly because the only thing on his mind was getting to *Amreeka.*

Shortly after the final leg of the journey got underway, a call went out for a lifeboat drill, a procedure that had been instituted only after the tragic sinking of the *Titanic* two years prior. Toufic was first in line and paid rapt attention while the crew took the passengers through the donning of life vests and making lifeboat assignments. He was mindful of the tales of disaster he had heard and would be ready to dash to his assigned dinghy should anything untoward occur.

Toufic and his shipmates were now on the Atlantic Ocean headed to the Promised Land. Having acquired his sea legs, Toufic began to relax. There were ten Arabic-speaking men over the age of eighteen in steerage. Several of them had serious bouts of *mal de mer*, which strangely enough, Toufic proudly remembered, did not affect him. In between their continual running for nearby slop pots, he listened to them talk of things he never knew, and he absorbed it all. One had worked in South Africa peddling goods to diamond miners, and the other had furnished pots and pans to workers on rubber plantations in Brazil. They told wild stories of the natives in these foreign lands, headhunters, cannibals, and pygmies with poison darts. The tales fascinated Toufic, and he asked many questions while wondering what the natives in America were like.

When they were about halfway to New York, another commotion arose that swept over the ship like a tidal wave. The news concerned Archduke Ferdinand and his wife being assassinated in Serbia, which caused some to speculate that this act was a precursor to war. Toufic had never heard of these people, and it didn't occur to him that such an event would have any repercussions in his homeland.

People were talking about the Austrians, Germans, and the Turks being allied against the French, British, and Russians. Rumors crossed from language to language and spread throughout the steerage compartment. This made time pass more quickly, if uneasily, as people tried to make sense of what they were hearing. Rumors begat rumors, and by the time they were mistranslated into the various tongues, they would bear no resemblance to the original story.

Toufic also eavesdropped on passengers as they were reading bulletins aloud as soon as they were posted on the deck's message board. Once he heard someone say there was work in a place called Detroit and that a man named Henry Ford was paying wages of five dollars a day.

He wondered who Henry Ford was and how much five dollars was in piasters. When he was told its worth, he calculated that it would take a month to earn that at the stone quarry, which then caused him to wonder where Detroit was.

The trip from Queenstown to New York took only five days, and soon the ship dropped anchor in the Narrows of New York Harbor. An announcement was made that the boat had been placed in quarantine for a medical inspection, and they would have to wait until cleared by examiners before they could dock in New York Harbor.

Once again rumors took wing like a flock of vultures casting ominous shadows over the ship. Many of the passengers had experienced the rule of oppressive governments and had good reason to be distrustful of authorities. Some fretted aloud that they would not be allowed to land, or worse, be sent back to their countries of origin.

A launch soon pulled up alongside the ship, and a group of six medical personnel in white lab coats came aboard. The passengers were lined up and made to pass before the medics, who gave each traveler a cursory glance, looking for any obvious signs of contagious disease. Everyone tried to look robust by standing up straight, throwing out their chests, and flashing broad smiles. It took less than three hours for the quarantine to be lifted and the boat allowed to proceed into New York Harbor to sighs of relief from the huddled masses.

The New York skyline dwarfed anything Toufic had seen of Beirut, Naples, or even Cherbourg. After the boat docked, the steerage passengers were still not allowed to leave their quarters. Stewards called out names from the ship's manifest as they pinned nametags on the clothing of each third class passenger. Since it was too late to take them through immigration, they would have to stay on board another night. The grapevine again began to circulate rumors among the émigrés. It was speculated that many would be rejected for medical reasons or they would have to pay a bribe to gain entry, a practice they were all too familiar with in their homelands. These thoughts made for a restless night for everyone, especially Toufic, who didn't really understand what the commotion was about but could sense the anxiety.

The morning came none too soon for the passengers who were offloaded onto ferries that took them across the Hudson River to Ellis Island. Toufic took one last look at the RMS *Oceanic* as the ferry departed, not suspecting that the ship would never carry another passenger. World War I had begun, and the liner was immediately ordered back to England to be outfitted as a British troop carrier. It ran aground and sank off the Shetland Islands just two months later.

After docking at the Ellis Island Immigration Station, the new arrivals were escorted off the ferries and taken to the first floor of the main building where their belongings were taken from them in exchange for a baggage receipt. Most were apprehensive as they watched the entirety of their earthly possessions rise into a mountain of suitcases, trunks, and satchels lining the far wall.

When I took the same journey on a visit to Ellis Island, I couldn't help but feel an apprehension that must have been similar to the feelings of these immigrants as I stood in front of the display of piled up luggage. I tried to imagine being funneled from place to place, not knowing what was going to happen next and always anticipating the worst. The angst must have hung heavy in the air.

The group then negotiated the long set of stairs that led up to the impressive Great Hall where registration and examinations took place. Toufic was in awe of the size of the room, which was 200 feet long by 100 feet wide with a ceiling nearly sixty feet in height. Seven ships had docked on the same day and along with the *Oceanic* there were three ships from Germany and one each from Greece, Russia, Italy, and Liverpool, England. At any given moment more than a thousand people were waiting in line to be processed.

Relatively few of the arrivals could decipher the writing inscribed on the tags attached to their clothing. Toufic's group was ushered to the medical section for what would be their third physical, the sole purpose of which was to weed out undesirables. America was only for those who were healthy enough to work, be productive, and not become wards of the state. A look down the throat, gaze into the eyes, another check for infectious diseases. The examiners took pride in being able to spot the undesirables with but a cursory glance. It was said that a doctor could identify medical conditions ranging from anemia to goiters to varicose veins without even touching the anxious immigrant. Life and death decisions were being made on an average of every six seconds.

Surprisingly, only two or three out of every hundred were singled out as being defective and were sent to the quarantine section to await clearance or transport back to the shipping line that brought them. Although the rejections were a small percentage of the total, they had actually slipped through the screenings performed by the carriers. The shipping lines had an incentive to be selective as they would be responsible for the return passage if one were deemed unwelcome.

One of Toufic's shipmates was told he had trachoma, a highly infectious eye disease, a common malady in the Middle East. The doctor made a chalk mark on the back of his jacket denoting that the man would have to be quarantined or sent back to his point of origin. As sometimes happened, the next available ship he would be put on would be heading south, thus providing him an opportunity to get off at a port of call in the Caribbean or South America.

The Immigration Station personnel grouped passengers by arriving ship so they could match them to the manifests that had been filled out by the ship's bursar. For the *Oceanic*, Master Harry Smith signed as the commanding officer. They also had the affidavit of the ship's surgeon, in Toufic's case a Dr L Adamson, which attested that these immigrants had been examined and were to the best of their knowledge mentally and physically fit.

After a few hours of standing in the long, snaking line, Toufic reached the principal inspector. An interpreter, a former immigrant from Lebanon himself, had been provided, and he questioned the young man and translated the answers to the clerks. Many were the same questions he had been asked when he boarded the RMS *Oceanic*, and the US Immigration Service would verify the answers that appeared on the ship's log by inserting a check mark alongside the passenger's name.

These are the entries taken from the RMS *Oceanic's* manifest for Toufic.

- *How old are you?* 20. [He would turn 17 in October of that year.]
- *Married or Single?* Single.
- *Occupation?* Laborer.
- *Able to read and write?* No.
- *Race or nationality?* Syrian. [Not what he answered but the designation that was used for all Lebanese.]
  - *Last residence?* Baatouta. [Bqaatouta is the correct spelling.]
  - *Name and address of nearest relative in country where from?* Father, Traad Elias, Baatouta.
  - *Who paid passage?* Self. [Interesting response because he would later tell me it was his sister who footed the bill.]
  - *Do you possess $50, if not how much?* $16. [The *Oceanic's* bursar had left this column blank and the translator converted foreign currency into American dollars. Even though $50 was the law at the time, Toufic's shipmates were being allowed in with as little a $6 in their pockets, and if they didn't have that, others would "lend" them the money for as long as it took to pass the inspection.]
  - *Address for relative or friend where going?* 57 State St., Carthage. [The Maroun brothers' address that appeared frequently on manifests for people from Bqaatouta going to Carthage, New York.]
  - *Ever in prison, an institution or supported by a charity?* No. [They were trying to weed out criminals, mental defectives, and people on the dole.]
- *Are you a polygamist?* No.
- *Are you an anarchist?* No. [This concept had to be explained by the translator.]
- *Are you indentured to anyone?* No. [The question was more convoluted but this is what was meant.]
  - *Condition of health?* Healthy.
  - *Height?* 5'3". [His passport said 5'7" and he was actually 5'6".]
- *Complexion?* White.

The one outstanding fact about these ship manifests, as demonstrated above, is that they are not accurate—a problem I ran into several times in my research. First of all, my father was listed on the manifest as Toufic Traad (his father's given name), not Kmeid. He would rectify this as soon as permissible by taking the surname Ellis, as had his Uncle Nasief who was listed as Nasief Elias (his father's and Toufic's grandfather's given name) when he arrived thirteen years before. Ellis became the Anglicized equivalent of Elias.

After the examination was finished, the newly admitted immigrant returned to the ground floor where he reclaimed his satchel and exchanged his remaining four Turkish liras for American currency. The moneychanger gave Toufic $4.25 for each of his liras. This was 20 cents below the posted exchange rate, but the difference was the agio extracted for the trader. He was directed toward a railroad ticket counter where passengers going to other parts of the country could get train tickets on either the New York Central or

Pennsylvania Railroads. Toufic redeemed his voucher for a ticket to Carthage and went to the wharf to await a ferry that would take him back to the mainland. Vendors lined the way, selling fruit and sandwiches to the hungry immigrants. Toufic pointed at a ham sandwich and a banana and offered the man one of the coins he had received in the money exchange. The meal, including the first banana he'd ever seen, cost a dime. It was so memorable for the young lad that he would relate the experience years afterward to his grandchildren.

After the ferry docked, Toufic followed the hustling crowd to a trolley car that was going to Grand Central Station. Soon he was inside yet another large building and again was struck by the size, even bigger than what he'd seen at Ellis Island! The main concourse was over twice as large as the Reception Center where his initial processing took place. He never imagined buildings so large, and all those people crisscrossing the concourse made it even more confusing. Between the boat, Ellis Island, and Grand Central, Toufic reckoned he'd seen more people than there were in all the little villages of Lebanon. And he was probably right.

At the center of the main concourse, Toufic showed a uniformed man his ticket and was directed to the appropriate gate. What sights and smells he experienced walking through the tunnel to his train! The experience was so foreign to him that his brain couldn't process, much less catalog, it all.

Once on the train Toufic breathed a sigh of relief. As tired as he was, the young man was so excited about being in America and taking his second train ride that he couldn't sleep. Even the rhythmic clack of the wheels against the rails didn't make him doze off. It was late at night, and there wasn't much to see, but he peered out into the darkness anyway. Occasionally he would glimpse a boat with its running lights on plowing its way up or down the mighty Hudson River. The train would take the better part of six hours, counting stops, to reach Utica. The weary traveler finally went to sleep, rather fitfully, after the train left the Albany station.

At six in the morning, the conductor called out, "Utica! Station Utica!" and tapped Toufic on the shoulder, motioning him to get off. He grabbed his satchel, detrained, and went into the station. He had completed the first leg of the land journey that would take him to his final destination.

I've been in the Utica station a few times, but the most memorable one was when my mother took me along to visit friends in the large Lebanese community there. The reason I remember my visit to the Utica station was because my mom, not wanting to let me out of her sight, insisted I come into the ladies room with her. I was eight at the time and quite reluctant to follow.

As you might have learned by now, my mother could be quite demanding, but luckily the stationmaster intervened and told her that I was way too old to be going in there with her. I breathed a sigh of relief as mother reluctantly allowed me to sit on the nearest bench outside the ladies room until she came out.

The Utica station was hot, even for that time of morning, and Toufic's white shirt bore the sweat stains of several days wear. His rumpled clothes, along with his unshaven face, gave him an undeniable immigrant look. As he stood at the center of the station concourse, a stranger with a familiar face approached and asked if he was Toufic Kmeid. The weary traveler was so happy to hear his native tongue spoken again that he answered with a resounding yes.

The man was Peter Tanoury, a cousin of the priest from Bqaatouta, who told Toufic, "Christine sent me to make sure that you got on the right train for Carthage." Tanoury had been watching for him for two days, and since the train taking him to Carthage wasn't due for a couple of hours, guided the boy to the restaurant to get some breakfast.

Toufic was happy to have someone that he could freely communicate with. They talked of news from Lebanon, of which the lad didn't have much. He wasn't exactly on intimate terms with newspapers, and the only news he could offer was that things were getting more difficult at home. He also imparted what he'd heard on the boat about the Turks getting into a big war soon. Some people were saying that America would be helping out against the Ottomans. But Tanoury politely dismissed that idea saying, "Americans don't want any part of a war with Turkey or anyone else," echoing the prevailing isolationist sentiment in America.

When it was time for his train, Tanoury led Toufic to the gate and bid him goodbye and good luck as the boy embarked on the final leg of his journey. The tired traveler caught a glimpse of his escort out of the corner of his eye, shaking his head and smiling as he turned to walk away.

At 11:05 AM the train arrived in Carthage, the bustling little papermaking town nestled in the foothills of the Adirondack Mountains. Toufic could see his sister waiting on the station platform. He gathered his satchel and quickly descended the coach's steps, into Christine's waiting arms. His sister hugged and kissed him, murmuring praises to God. She'd been waiting for two days, and now that he had finally arrived, she wasn't going let go for a while.

139

# 19

*Carthago delenda est.*

ONE OF THE THINGS THAT PUZZLED ME, EVEN IN my youth, was the question why those Lebanese immigrants chose Carthage, New York, as their final destination? I'm always amazed at how millions of lives were affected by the simple choices their ancestors made many years before. I found the selection of Carthage a bit ironic because 2,500 years before, another group of people also left that same Phoenician port of Beirut to reside in that fabled city-state called Carthage on the northern coast of Africa.

As we know, Phoenicia eventually became Lebanon, and it is interesting to note that recent genetic studies have verified a DNA link between those ancient Phoenicians and the modern day inhabitants of Lebanon. The geneticists tell us that the Y chromosome genetic marker is passed down only from the male progenitor. What is also known is that haplogroup J2 (M172) is the point of reference for Phoenician ancestry. Haplogroup J2 is found frequently in Lebanon, Greece, Turkey (aboriginal not Seljuk), Italy, and the Caucus region, all points visited by the Phoenician fleets. I was quite surprised that my DNA profile was also haplogroup J2 (M172) because my father was descended from mountain people, as opposed to those from the coastal region, where the Phoenicians resided. Intrigued, I sent a kit to my male first cousin, Namatallah Hobeiche, on my mother's side of the family. I expected the same result but it was not so. It turns out that the Hobeiche DNA fell into haplogroup J (12f2.1). Further investigation revealed that Phoenicians *descended* from this group. So, what can we make of all this? Probably that we really are all related if one goes back far enough.

Today, there are many towns and cities around the globe named after the fabled and ill-fated city of Carthage. How or why the New York Carthage got its name is not recorded. It seems that those who were in charge of such matters in the first half of the nineteenth century were smitten with that period in history. A glance at a map of New York reveals other historic names from the Mediterranean, such as Troy, Rome, Utica, and Syracuse, as well as Athens, Ithaca, Sparta, and Massena (Messina in the ancient spelling)—along with Carthage.

At its height, the Lebanese population of Carthage would number nearly thirty families, all from the same village in Lebanon. The early arrivals began life in America as peddlers, and most ended up as shopkeepers such as grocers, haberdashers, barkeeps, or vendors of produce, fruit, liquor, tobacco, ice cream, candy, and notions. Although little Carthage's population by 1930 numbered fewer than 4,500, the Lebanese immigrants found fertile ground for their entrepreneurial aspirations. They arrived in an era when virtually everyone traveled on foot or by horse-drawn carriage to buy their weekly provisions. Thus, as many as ten Lebanese families in that small town owned neighborhood corner grocery stores at the same time, some less than a block apart. The village of Carthage and its institutions, mainly the St. James Catholic Church and the Augustinian Academy parochial school, have an interesting history of their own, and they played an important part in the lives of the transplanted Lebanese.

Ancient Carthage was immortalized by violence—namely the Roman conquest that overtook and destroyed it in 146 BC at the end of the Third Punic War. The disaster for those ancient Carthaginians was a direct result of instigation by Roman statesman and moralist, Cato the Elder. Cato (there is also a New York State town named after him) had fought in the Second Punic War and in his later years was said to despise the sybaritic lifestyle he saw in Carthage. He thereupon took to ending every speech he made with a Latin phrase that meant, "Carthage must be destroyed."

And, so it was that every Carthaginian house was destroyed, the people sold into slavery, the city plowed under, and by some accounts, the ground sown with salt. That, however, seems to be one of those apocryphal tales that somehow became confused with history because it would have required an enormous amount of the then precious commodity, which was actually being used as currency at the time.

It is interesting that Carthage's demise began with its intercession in a dispute between Messina and Syracuse, an act that gave Rome an excuse to join the fray. Intriguingly, in New York State, Carthage is at the center of a circle with a radius of approximately seventy miles that encompasses all four of these same namesake towns and cities.

Some 2,030 years later, in the year 1884, eleven years before any modern day Lebanese was to set foot in the town, the sleepy New York village of Carthage awoke to a balmy October Indian summer morn with no hint of what lay in store for it. The economic outlook was bright, and preparations for the winter had been made with stores of coal in the cellars and cordwood piled in the backyards. Add a bright fall day to this tranquil scene and it would seem that the Lord had indeed blessed this little northern New York enclave, one that had seen its share of ups and downs over its eighty years of existence.

Across the river from Carthage lay its twin sister village of West Carthage. Half the size of its sibling, West Carthage was composed of a few residences and mills that lined the western bank of the Black River. At 10:30 that morning, the engineer at Eaton's Sash and Blind, as he had done hundreds of times before, shoveled hot ashes from the wood kiln out into the mill yard. But, what was not usual that day was the wind that blew down the river from the south carrying sparks from the ash pile to a nearby heap of wood shavings, the natural waste from making the factory's product. The bone-dry shavings immediately roared up into a hot fire, sending one of the men scurrying to inform the West Carthage Fire Department that they could not control the blaze. At 11:10 AM, Carthaginians could hear the fire bells tolling from across the river, and the Carthage firemen rushed to their aid.

It wasn't long after that the fire bells began ringing on the east side of the river as well. The Carthage volunteer firemen, who had raced across the Black River Bridge, could soon see that airborne blazing embers had carried the fire to their side of the river.

Fear and panic gripped the residents as a distress signal went up and down the railroad tracks in both directions by phone and telegraph. Bells rang from schools, churches, and the fire hall. Every vehicle with wheels was pressed into service to carry precious household possessions to safety. The streets became arteries clogged with humans and material cargo, rushing in different directions as neighbors appealed to each other for help in saving their prized possessions.

Even after aid from surrounding communities arrived, the blaze continued to burn out of control for the better part of seven hours. When things finally died down, residents could see that the inferno had consumed some seventy-five acres of factories, stores, churches, and homes.

Cato the Elder would have been proud—Carthage had indeed been destroyed... again, even though a sybaritic lifestyle had nothing to do with it.

*From the ashes the Phoenix rises.*

But the tiny town of Carthage refused to die and slowly but surely began the process of rebuilding. The St. James Roman Catholic Church, which sat on the crest of three insulating acres, was spared any damage from the fire. In fact, the edifice looked so majestic, towering above the ruins, that a legend was passed to future generations that, "The whole town burned down except for the Catholic Church." This was not quite true but made wide-eyed tales of the disaster far more interesting, especially to the Catholics who could impute some divine intervention on their behalf.

The New York Carthage nearing the end of the nineteenth century was beginning to experience a significant growth spurt and was becoming established as a papermaking center. By 1898 six small papermakers had appeared on the scene, and larger firms such as Crown Zellerbach, Champion, and St. Regis would follow them.

Of course, whenever word got out that such an expansion was taking place, people flocked to the area seeking jobs or to start businesses that supported those workers. Emigrants from Southern and Eastern Europe—Italians, Poles, Germans, Ukrainians, and Serbs—came to supply the manpower for constructing and running these mills. As a result, the population of Carthage grew an astonishing 85% (over 1,500 people) from 1880 to 1910.

Several Lebanese who landed in New York City made their way upstate and formed a colony in Utica, New York. Among those who left Beirut at the end of 1894 and arrived in Utica, curiously enough on a ship named the *Phoenicia*, was a young man who called himself Abdoo Maroun, a man who would play a significant role in the settlement of Lebanese to Carthage, New York. He gave his age as eighteen years, as he was told to do by his relatives in Utica who had preceded him. In fact, young Abdoo had not yet reached his sixteenth birthday. And his family name wasn't Maroun either—it was Kmeid.

But, as we have seen, many Kmeids ventured forth to *Amreeka* from the little town of Bqaatouta. In order to avoid confusion in their new environment, most took their grandfather's or father's given name as their surname. In America, the custom of using given names as surnames among Lebanese families proliferated. Names such as Anthony, Joseph, Jacob, Thomas, George, Andre, Michaels, Charles, Moses, etcetera, became common. Many also have family names that were transliterated phonetically from original Arabic given names such as Amin, Maroun, Ferris, Boulos, Ablan, Abdullah, and so on. Thus, Abdoo Maroun used his grandfather's first name, Maroun, as his family name. In Carthage, there would reside Kmeids with the surnames of Maroun, Abdoo, Hannah, and Ellis, as well as Kamide (the Americanized spelling of the primary family name).

Meanwhile, the suppliers to the itinerant peddlers, ever vigilant for opportunities to expand their markets, kept their ears to the ground as they mapped out routes for the Lebanese newcomers. It hadn't taken them long in the Utica hub to digest the news of growth in Carthage and to send peddlers in that direction.

Although the census records show a half-dozen Lebanese peddlers in Carthage in 1900, the first one who actually settled and remained there was young Abdoo Maroun. He had served his apprenticeship in Utica where he became familiar with his new trade before setting his cap to the northwest. With a large peddler's rig on his back that towered a foot over his short stature, he began a journey that eventually landed him in Carthage in late 1895. Four years later his brother Scander (Arabic for Alexander) joined him, and virtually all the subsequent Lebanese immigrants to Carthage would owe their arrival in that village to the sponsorship of these two brothers. That is why we saw Toufic use 57 State Street, the Maroun brothers' address at the time, as his final destination.

The congregation of these people from the same village into the same town in America was by no means a seamless or harmonious one. This was a time of rapidly rising immigration, and the indigenous population of English, Irish, and French who had preceded them by a generation or more did not exactly open their arms to the newcomers. And, as usually happens on America's social ladder, the newcomers would take their place on the lowest rung. Stratification of class seems to be more pronounced and therefore more obvious in small towns such as Carthage. I'm reminded of that old adage, "God made the country, man made the city, but the devil made the small town."

However, the Lebanese peddlers of that era had a way about them that, if not totally endearing, certainly allowed them to do business with the "*Amirkaan*" (Americans) they solicited (to the Lebanese immigrants, all the natives regardless of origin, with the exception of those on the same social strata such as Italians, Poles, and Greeks, were "*Amirkaan*"). They wheedled sales and a place to sleep from reluctant farmers as they traveled on foot through the countryside selling their wares. Summer, winter, spring, or fall they walked the landscape selling all manner of goods carried on their backs. Their backpacks weighed as much as 300 pounds, and the straps dug into their shoulders, scarring some for life. They slept under the stars or with the animals in the farmer's barn.

The peddlers were seldom known by their actual names, as Americans gave them Anglicized names, whether they liked it or not, that they could remember and pronounce. This practice gained favor because the Arabic language has a few consonants that are virtually impossible for Westerners to pronounce. The most notable are the guttural sounding "kh," "gh," and the vocal fricative "hah." Their alphabet is also missing a couple of letters—*p* and *v*, for which the newcomers compensated with the substitution of *b* and *f*.

The transliterations took on a comic opera effect in Carthage as one Toufic became Charley and another became John; Amin also became Charley; Najib became Jimmy; Seghaan became Tommy; Khillu became Tony; and Shikary became Jake. But the Lebanese didn't seem to mind because they sincerely wanted to be accepted in their new country, so much so that they began to address each other with their Anglicized names (which I always thought to be truly comical).*

So, this was the environment in which Toufic began his American adventure in 1914—a bit overwhelming, to say the least.

---

*This would be a good time to clarfiy my own given name. For most of my adult life I've used a truncated version of my given name, which is Raffee. It was a name I despised as a youth because no one seemed able to pronounce it correctly, and it made me stand out from my fellow Americans. I remember complaining at age seven to my mother, telling her in a fit of pique, "I'd rather you had called me Banana!" My name, which means comrade or good friend, has been transliterated into English as Rafic, Rafik, Rafiq, or Rafique, all the different ways I've seen it spelled. The way my folks and the country people of Lebanon voiced it was with a glottal wind stop at the end, thus eliding the final consonant. This peculiarity is evidenced in the spelling my mother chose for my birth certificate, Raffee. I mention this so the reader will not be confused later on when I refer to my given name with different spellings.

*Christine with husband Rebhan Abdoo Kmeid.*

# 20

*His tongue fails when it comes to his own praise.*

As Toufic surveyed the bustling scene with the small, neat-looking New York Central railroad station in the background, he had no idea of the history that had preceded him. All he cared about was how he would earn his fortune. Christine took him by the hand to the house at 308 Furnace Street, right around the corner from the station. It was a narrow, gray-painted, two-story structure perched on a rise and nestled between two tall maple trees. It had a steep set of stairs leading up to the front porch, a porch that was as wide as the gingerbread-latticed house.

Christine, an unabashed free spirit throughout life, wasn't ashamed of showing her emotions or saying whatever came to mind. She was one of those slender people who looked much taller than her actual height and had an incredible way with animals. Her brother fully expected to see her house inhabited by birds or a goat or two in the backyard. I used to spend summers at Aunt Christine's home in Tupper Lake, New York, and became acquainted with many of her non-traditional pets. Even much later in life she continued this inclination and once had a pair of birds that she had somehow taught to sleep under a miniature sheet in a straw basket. (My kids still talk about that.) Another time she had a couple of goats that would run into the house through the back door whenever she called "*ta, ta,*" just like a shepherd in the hills of Lebanon. Christine was the Doctor Doolittle of her time.

The house Toufic now entered was large by his standards. It was also home to Christine's husband Rebhan, Aunt Sadie, Uncles Seghaan and Nasief, along with his wife Marta and son Naja. Toufic was assigned to sleep in Naja's room.

After the family group returned home from their day of peddling, wherever their goods could be sold, they sat down to dinner. Toufic asked where Naja was and was told that the young man was out with friends and would be home later. Toufic thought this was strange because family etiquette dictated that he should have been there to greet him, not out with "friends." The next question was how he should go about getting work and whether he could go into business with one of them. He was taken aback when he found all of them reluctant to employ him.

Seghaan, always ready to invoke one of the many Lebanese proverbs he'd committed to memory, said to Toufic, "*Two men can't dance on one rope.*" He added that his one-man business made just enough for himself. The boy was disappointed in his uncle, who had come to the "Promised Land" in 1901, wasn't married, didn't have his own store, and worst of all, didn't have a job for him.

The relationship between Toufic and Seghaan over the years proved to be an uneasy one. His uncle was a short, stubby man who sported a handlebar moustache. He had a light complexion, and as he aged, his hair and moustache turned snow white. His affability seemed limited to his customers, for I never recalled him being jocular with any of his relatives.

It was difficult for Toufic to reconcile his sister finding the wherewithal to send him passage after only one year of residence in the States when his uncle couldn't manage it after thirteen. The confirmed bachelor (whom Lebanese kids called Captain Marvel after the comic book character, who invoked his powers with the word "Shazzam!") always lived alone or boarded with relatives.

As for Uncle Nasief, he had his son Naja working with him, so he couldn't use Toufic either. This compounded the lad's disappointment so he asked about this Henry Ford he'd heard about where people were making $5 a day.

Detroit was a long way from Carthage, they said, and many people had gone there from other parts of the country, especially the South. The consensus was he probably wouldn't be able to get a job even if he found his way there.

Christine advised that he could find work in one of the paper mills, which would permit him to remain in Carthage with his extended family. Although the notion of laboring for wages wasn't foreign to him, it conjured up his stone quarry days, the memories of which were not among his most pleasant. So it came to pass that Toufic reluctantly applied for a job at the Crown Zellerbach mill.

What followed for Toufic was a succession of jobs in paper mills—working in Carthage and Harrisville, eighteen miles further north, during summers and quitting during winters. His main complaint was the freezing temperatures, which often dropped to 10° below zero. His job was usually in the mill yard where he got 25¢ a cord for splitting and piling logs for the groundwood operation. Remember, a cord measures 128 cubic feet—a formidable pile that is four feet high by four feet deep by eight feet wide. The young man just couldn't abide those conditions—compounded by the fact that, at most, he could split and pile just three cords a day, for a grand total of 75¢. Although quite a bit more than he would earn in Lebanon, not up to his expected American standard.

Christine, as always, was concerned about her younger brother, but Uncle Seghaan didn't appear very sympathetic and more than once glanced at his nephew with a disappointing look. Finally the uncle agreed that the lad could go peddling with him, even though he doubted they could make enough for two people. But, it would give his nephew a chance to learn the peddling trade. He would take the boy with him to the adjacent towns of Herrings and Deferiet, about six miles west of Carthage, where Seghaan had developed a loyal clientele.

The uncle had graduated from the backpack to a pushcart, which was favored by city peddlers because it could carry more than twice as many goods and was physically easier on the body. A backpack could hold 200 to 300 pounds of wares at most, while a cart could easily double that. Toufic would push the cart, and the uncle agreed to give him a quarter of the profits.

So, off they went down the road to Herrings, with Toufic struggling with the cart laden with underwear, overalls, shirts, socks, gloves, bolts of cloth, pots, pans, and a variety of notions such as needles and thread, which were kept in a small case called a *kashishi*.. The usually snow-packed road, although a bit slick, would offer little resistance to the cart. And, before he got the hang of it, Toufic would slip and fall, often to the chuckles of his uncle.

It would take the pair nearly an hour-and-a-half to get to Herrings, where they would quickly begin knocking on doors. The saving grace for Toufic was the short respites he got inside warm houses while Seghaan was displaying their wares. Most of the people were actually glad to see the two men, as they had no means to go to town, and they seldom got visitors.

In the beginning, Toufic was relegated to listening to his uncle's fractured English sales spiel and running back and forth to the cart to fetch the desired goods. The exercise helped to keep him from freezing, and the pair was able to service more customers than Seghaan ever could by himself.

When hungry, they ate from their packed lunch in between sales calls, wiping their dripping noses on the sleeves of their coats as steamy breath gushed from their nostrils—not unlike the horses that occasionally trudged by. But Toufic felt warmer on the road selling wares than chopping wood in the yard at the paper mill, even though he sometimes wasn't sure if he still had feeling in his toes. He didn't complain, however, because his share of the profits already began to exceed the amount he would have made splitting and piling wood at the mill. It did occur to him though, that he could make a lot more with a bigger share of the profits.

The duo would then trudge on to Deferiet, two miles farther down the road, pausing at a few farmhouses on the way. The customers at the next town were immigrants like themselves, mostly from Italy, Poland, and the Balkans. An innate empathy existed between these immigrants and the peddlers since they were all strangers in a strange land. A few would even invite the two men to come inside and warm themselves by their pot-bellied stoves.

Toufic wondered why there always seemed to be men present in the households during the day. He soon found that it was because the mill operated three shifts and having non-family member boarders was the rule of the day for immigrants, including the Lebanese of Carthage. Between families and boarders sharing the same cramped quarters, the men joked about never having to sleep in a cold bed.

Toufic listened to the whispered conversations and once thought he heard a women say, "*Syriani*," while apparently talking about him and his uncle. Once in a while he would bristle when he heard them mutter, "Turks." He was always sensitive to the various labels he would be given over the years, always maintaining that he was Lebanese.

The weather in America was a lot like his native Lebanon, where the winters were bitter and cold. The only difference was that winters in the Carthage area were dry, and as a result, his lips began to chap. He never liked the cold weather at home, and he didn't like it in America either.

Toufic worked hard and saved some money but became frustrated that his labors didn't yield more profits. His English improved slowly, and when he spoke, it became less and less accented. As mentioned before, a problem endemic to all Arabic speakers concerned the letters *p* and *v*, which were non-existent in his native tongue. They seemed to Lebanese immigrants, however, to be plentiful in the English language. A lot of times his transliterations of those letters into *b* and *f* went unnoticed because America during that period was awash with fractured English speakers.

Back in Carthage, the Lebanese men of the town had gotten together to rent a room for a social club, on the third floor of the Bones Building on State Street. They would gather there in the evenings to smoke, drink *arak*, play cards, and talk about news from home. The only literate man in the group was

Shukrullah Mobark, who also subscribed to an Arabic newspaper, *al Hoda*, published in Brooklyn. Shukrullah was a distinguished looking gentleman of medium height, ruddy complexion, and sported a closely clipped moustache. He had been in the country the same length of time that Seghaan had, and his English had become fairly polished, mainly due to the innate Lebanese aptitude for language and his association with Americans through various failed business enterprises. He spoke in attention-demanding, stentorian tones, for he relished his position as a spokesman for the Lebanese community. Even though he wasn't very successful as a businessman, his friends indulged him this position because of his age and education.

Shukrullah would usually bring his weekly Arabic newspaper to the club and read aloud to the others. He would tell his friends the news from Lebanon, such as the plague that was raging in Beirut and the city being placed under quarantine. The paper failed to mention exactly what kind of plague it was.

Mobark also would read items about the war that was raging in Europe and how the Turks were beating the English badly. The British had been chased off the Gallipolis Peninsula and forced to surrender in Mesopotamia. He also noted that the Allies were hoping America would enter the war while Germany feared she would. The Kaiser didn't want to provoke the Americans any more than he had already and announced there wouldn't be any more sinking of American merchant ships—even though he knew they were carrying supplies to Germany's enemies.

As always, there was good news and bad news. The Lebanese men agreed that Turkey gaining the upper hand was bad news indeed. But the good news was that America was prospering under wartime conditions. Unemployment was practically nonexistent, and wages were high. There was plenty of work, and people were spending as never before. And the Lebanese peddlers and merchants capitalized on these conditions by working hard, saving their money, and continuing to learn the language of their adopted land.

Toufic would take Shukrullah's weekly Arabic newspaper home with him to study. In this way he would eventually learn to read and passably write his native language. He was one of the few non-literates who seemed to have a desire to do this.

Letters sent to relatives in Lebanon that were returned undelivered, alerted the community that the Turks had curtailed mail service. This created a great deal of anguish because immigrants knew the families back home were dependent on remittances they had been sending.

One day Shukrullah came across an important announcement in *al Hoda*. He looked at the ad placed by the Presbyterian Mission Board more closely

153

and informed the group of the board's offer to act as middleman for the transmission of remittances. The ever-suspicious Lebanese wondered aloud if the missionaries could be trusted to actually deliver the money to their relatives. Mobark said with a chuckle that he didn't think the Presbyterians would steal, because they also ran the Syrian Protestant College in Beirut (later renamed American University of Beirut) where Maronites and Orthodox Christians, Muslims, and Jews attended. Their offer to be a conduit for remittances claimed to be independent of denomination.

After some discussion, the group decided they would gather some money to be sent, and Shukrullah would transmit it to New York with the names of the recipients and amounts they were to receive. They could not have known that these small sums would spell the difference between life and death for some of their relatives. At a gathering the following week, the group presented Shukrullah a total of $220 to be sent to the Presbyterian Board of Missions in New York. It averaged a little less than $10 per family, but for their relatives, it would be a godsend.

As we saw, 1916 was a very bad year back in Lebanon with Sheik Namattalh Hobeiche's passing. It seems that tragedy did not spare the Kmeids in Carthage either. In trying to verify Christine's marriage, I went to the St James Church to examine the death records for Rebhan Abdoo (the surname he and his brother Nebhan had chosen). I had found a tombstone in their cemetary for Rebhan, showing that he had passed away in June 1916 (the tombstone had his name as Rapan Abdoo). I thought that his death record, kept at the church, would reveal the names of survivors but, alas, it did not even note the cause of death. The only way I was able to verify this union was through the picture that started this chapter. At first glance, everyone in the family believed that the man was Toufic. But upon extremely close inspection, involving enlarging, measuring, and comparing, it became apparent that this was not Toufic. Also, the pose with the woman's hand on the shoulder was typical of husband and wife photographs of that period. So we are certain that the ship manifest was correct and that Christine was indeed married to Rebhan Abdoo. The resemblance to Toufic is easily explained by the fact that the two men were first cousins.

I don't think anyone alive among Christine's family or friends knows about this first marriage.

# 21

*The sky was dark, but they knew not the storm.*

WHEN I WENT TO LEBANON IN 1999, DÉSIREÉ AND I again stopped to visit with Amin Kmeid in Bqaatouta. He was quite glad to see us, and after serving refreshments and engaging in the usual amenities, he volunteered to drive me around to get a closer glimpse of Mt. Sannine. It is indeed a majestic sight. But what happened next was totally unexpected and would qualify for a story in *National Geographic*.

Harris Kmeid and his two sons were walking out of their apple orchard when Amin exclaimed, "Look, there are some of your cousins!" Harris was a short man, as were almost all my father's relatives, but the turban he wore added some six inches to his height. The headdress had a certain antiquity about it; a wrap made with two types of cloth, a gray felt one topping a traditional cotton *kafiya*. I got out of the car to be introduced to my dad's ninety-five-year-old first cousin. When Harris heard my father's name, he began to weep, murmuring, "*Marhoom*, (condolences) *marhoom*, Toufic," between hugs and kisses.

Harris recalled my father's death some seven years before. The news had quickly traveled across the ocean and up the mountain to his village. Although my dad's junior by seven years, Harris vividly remembered his cousin as a boy when they romped together and played a game similar to marbles but using pebbles instead.

The incredibly spry Harris eschewed my assistance as I tried to help him step up into Amin's automobile. Later, over Turkish coffee in the house that my great-grandfather Elias had built some 135 years before, I had a chance to study more closely his weather-creased face, searching for clues to his longevity. I finally asked to what he owed his long life, and before he could answer, Amin blurted, "He never was with a woman until he was fifty years old! That's his secret!" Apparently Harris hadn't married until that ripe age but still managed to sire a large family. He was a remarkable specimen considering that he had lived through two world wars and countless other hostilities in his long life.

When he doffed his turban, I expected a bald head to emerge, but instead a full crop of thick silvery hair was revealed that many a younger man would kill for, myself included. It turned out that he was not only spry of body but alert of mind as well. His memories were vivid, and when prodded about life in these mountains he became quite animated.

This was exactly what I was after—a chance to understand what life was like all those years ago for my ancestors. I had extensively researched one important incident that I wanted to ask cousin Harris about. "Do you remember the invasion of the locusts?"

"The *jarrod!*" he exclaimed. "Oh yes, I remember them well." He shrugged when I asked if he knew why they had come, and although he knew not their origins, he knew all too well the effect they had. On that fateful April day in 1915 when the locusts first came, eleven-year-old Harris had been tending the few sheep the family owned, grazing them on the rocky slopes near his home. He carried with him a long staff to prod or spank any of the ewes that strayed too far from the herd in search of food.

It had been only six months since the Ottoman Empire entered the "war to end all wars" in an alliance with other countries known as the Central Powers. But for Harris this was not a great concern. Everyone talked of war, but the people in the little town of Bqaatouta had not yet felt its impact. Until the war began, the Turks had pretty much let the Christians and Druze who inhabited the mountains govern themselves.

In fact, Harris had never even seen a Turkish soldier before the war started, but caught glimpses of them now and then, as they came to confiscate foodstuffs and animals to support their war effort. When he spied them coming, he would herd the sheep into a secluded recess in the mountainside, just as his father had instructed. Their mountain isolation, which had been a refuge from interference by the Turks or clashes with the Druze, was now being regularly violated, but with typical Lebanese ingenuity they found ways to conduct their lives pretty much as usual.

The family had celebrated their meager Christmas of 1914 some four months prior, and they certainly were not aware of events taking place a thousand miles away. While Harris was still basking in the joys of the holiday celebration, torrential rains were pelting the western coast of the Arabian Peninsula and the Red Sea shoreline of Egypt. The sudden downpour caused vegetation to burst forth in a carpet of greenery, while billions of Desert

Locust eggs that lurked close to the surface were waiting patiently for the moisture needed to hatch. And, hatch they did!

On January 10, 1915, the first stage wingless nymph hordes emerged from the ground as if on a sorcerer's command. The genetically gregarious (entomologically called *Schistocerca gregaria)* insects began forming large hopper bands, leaping and crawling over the verdant countryside, munching on every blade of grass in sight. From a distance it looked like a grass fire without the smoke. The hungry horde gorged on the vegetation for the next month, passing through five separate developmental stages, shedding their skin each time, before actually sprouting wings. The burgeoning population then spent two more months becoming mature adults up to three inches long. A report from Presbyterian missionary George H. Scherer, stationed in Syria at the time said, "Unless one has actually seen them in their various stages, he cannot believe any description to be true."

Abruptly, on the morning of April 11, the sun-drenched desert floor became so hot that strong updrafts formed, and almost in unison, the locusts were lifted by thermals into the strong upper air currents that would carry them wherever the whimsical winds were going. Before long the sky was black with huge clouds of winged creatures, with as many as 130 million per square mile. The insects were swept up on a one-way trip north, the direction of the air stream on that day. The journey, which would take the better part of three days and cover a thousand miles, abruptly ended on April 14. The combination of mountain altitudes and cooler temperatures plunged the multitude of insects down upon the unsuspecting inhabitants of Lebanon, Syria, and southern Turkey.

It was four in the afternoon, and Harris was lazily prodding his sheep around the mountainside. He noticed that the brisk southerly breeze that had been blowing most of the day had suddenly died down. "The sky became black!" he exclaimed, thinking he would be caught in one of those violent mountain thunderstorms, complete with darting lightning bolts. Then he heard a high-pitched roaring din that echoed through the valley, and his anxiety turned to fear. Other farmers working their lands were also frightened.

Harris looked skyward, unable to fathom what was happening. Suddenly he, along with the sheep and the ground as far as he could see, was covered with hungry yellow insects. "I tried to kill them but there were too many!" he exclaimed. The invaders had been without food for three days and they were voraciously hungry. But Harris knew nothing of the entomology of these creatures. He didn't know that an adult locust would consume its own two-gram weight in vegetation each day. The boy had no choice but to run home, leaving the sheep to fend for themselves. His mother, between wringing her hands and incantations to the Virgin, lit candles so they could see well enough to kill the insects that had infiltrated the house. There was nothing to do but sweep up bugs and look out the windows to watch as the locusts did what locusts do.

In the morning light, Harris and his family went out to survey the damage. They were awestruck by the utter devastation. "Everything, everything was gone! They ate everything," he exclaimed as his flickering brown eyes played the newsreel over in his mind. Mulberry trees, whose leaves were the staple of the silkworms they cultivated, were denuded, standing bare as if they had suddenly died. Tiny budded fruit stood out on branches of apple trees that were stripped naked of their greenery. Vegetable gardens were undressed to the bare earth, gardens that would have sustained them through the summer months and provided preserves for winter. They didn't think about starvation then but would be forced to in the coming months.

What Harris also did not know was that a female locust would lay a pod of eighty eggs in each of the next three months of its life. It would be mid-July before the locust plague abated, and up to 80,000 eggs per square meter would litter the mountainside in their wake, awaiting the next warm-weather rainfall.

In the coastal areas the government hired poor people, of which there were now an increasing number, to gather up these eggs to be destroyed. But it was a losing battle because there were billions of them, and not all were in plain sight. The locust is an adaptive species, and the pattern of development for one generation may be altered for the next if environmental conditions change. The people had become weary in their battle with the insects and most simply resigned themselves to watch as the enemy marched up and down the mountain, practicing a scorched earth policy.

"And the next year they came again, this time out of the ground," Harris recalled, "and they had no wings!" With the coming of spring in 1916, when the weather warmed and the rain continued to moisten the landscape, the peasants were puzzled by the emergence of large bands of crawling, hopping worms. Recalling this event some eighty-three years later, Harris still did not understand that this was but the first stage of locust development. The insatiable insects attacked Mt. Lebanon once again, and the residents dutifully beat them with switches, burned and stomped on them, to little avail.

The world war, the increased taxation, the confiscation of foodstuffs and animals by Ottoman soldiers, the locusts, the ensuing food shortages, and finally the Spanish Flu would scheme against the vulnerable Lebanese population. Plagues of typhus, dysentery, cholera, small pox, and malignant malaria would sweet the country. "The people would walk to Zahle where they heard there was food, even though travel was forbidden," Harris said, "but many died on the road from the 'yellow wind.'"* Harris could not hold back the tears as he recounted the many friends and family he had lost by the time the war ended.

"But not until the locusts came, did conditions become serious," continued the Presbyterian missionary Mr Scherer in his report. "The appearance of them is as the appearance of horses; and as horsemen so do they run," he added, quoting from the biblical Book of Joel.

Harris Kmeid, one of the few remaining witnesses of the great plague, died two years after giving his oral account to me, at the age of ninety-seven. His death was the result of complications from simple hernia surgery.

*The name was derived from the dusty yellow breeze that travelers encountered, and thought caused the disease cholera.

# 22

*The world sides with he who is left standing.*

WAR INEVITABLY BRINGS BOOM TIMES, AND Carthage was no different. Because of labor shortages, women were pressed into service in the paper mills, and arduous, unskilled jobs were plentiful. Carthage was a beehive of papermaking activity, which required, and utilized the abundant supply of spruce logs from the nearby Adirondack Mountains. The mills also obtained cheap power from the flow of the Black River, which, like the spruce logs, made its westerly journey from the Adirondacks, passing by each of the many paper mills on its way to Lake Ontario.

By 1918 most of the Lebanese had graduated from peddling to shop keeping, which left Toufic, his uncle, and a few of the women relatively free to ply their trade wherever it was most profitable. Uncle Seghaan decided that they would continue to peddle to the villages where the paper mills were working three shifts a day, seven days a week. Often times he would let Toufic make the trek to Deferiet by himself, and the lad actually began enjoying it, for there he had social contact with a number of girls of other nationalities, without coming under the watchful eye of his uncle. This poor man's version of Omar Sharif attracted the young ladies' glances at many of the houses he visited, and while running back and forth to the peddler's cart.

One evening Toufic told his sister that he was disappointed with the way things were going. They weren't getting any letters from home, and he didn't know if the money they were sending was getting to their relatives. And he'd been in the States almost three years and was barely making ends meet. What little he'd saved wasn't enough, he said.

Even in their later years, when I could observe the relationship between the two, I saw how solicitous Christine was of her younger brother Toufic. She counseled him to take his time because he was doing as well as could be expected, and there were people who were worse off.

Still, it wasn't what he'd anticipated because the work was hard and the pay was low. He yearned to open his own store. His countrymen now operated a total of eight stores in the village, and Toufic had become a bit envious. Most retailed groceries while a few sold dry goods, and one ran a meat market.

Soon the tides of war began showing signs of turning in favor of the Allies. Germany broke its promise and declared all-out submarine warfare against any and all shipping, an act of desperation that would end up as the *causus belli* for the US to enter the war.

One evening at the Lebanese club Shukrullah announced that the Germans had sunk the Cunard Line's *Lanconia*, and the United States had broken off relations as a result. It looked as though America couldn't avoid war now, and sure enough, a little more than a month later, the US declared war against Germany.

Successive meetings of the Lebanese Club became more spirited as the men wondered what these developments meant to Lebanon and when America would declare war against Turkey. What they didn't know was that a behind-the-scenes political arrangement had been made.

Washington broke off diplomatic relations with the Ottomans but avoided a declaration of hostilities, primarily because of the activities of Cleveland Dodge, an American trustee of Roberts College in Constantinople, Turkey (also founded by the Presbyterians). Dodge was a good friend of President Wilson and had made a special trip to Washington to implore the president not to go to war with Turkey. He convinced Wilson that the numerous American missions operating in Syria and Turkey would be closed and their personnel expelled, imprisoned, or worse, if hostilities were formalized. Wilson agreed, although no public policy announcement was made. The members of the Lebanese Club would lament this puzzling development right up to the end of the war.

The Réglement, which exempted Lebanese Christians from forced military service, was perhaps one of the reason that conscription was a hated concept for the Lebanese. However, once in America they came to look at this requirement differently. This was a country where everybody was treated equally, or so the immigrants understood, and most agreed they owed service as repayment to the country that took them in.

Another month passed before the United States Congress passed the Selective Draft Act, which stipulated that all men from twenty-one to thirty years of age would have to register for the draft. There were several exceptions in the law, with one specifying that aliens who didn't speak English would be exempt.

Toufic was still under the age limit—only nineteen even though his passport fib would have made him twenty-three. However, if the government lowered the age or decided that you didn't have to be an American citizen, he would indeed be subject to the draft.

As an example of the newfound patriotism of the Lebanese, Christine volunteered her services to the Red Cross and spent her free time making up bandage rolls and performing whatever other chores she was assigned. She was proud to do her bit for the war effort.

*Dead are my people.*

November 11, 1918, soon came and with it the Armistice that ended World War I. Within a month letters began arriving in Carthage from Lebanon, and shortly before Christmas, one came addressed to Toufic. Christine was recovering from the Spanish Flu, the influenza outbreak that killed 18 million people across the US, Europe, Lebanon, and the rest of the world. She fingered the letter and could see that it was from home, even though she couldn't read it. Eagerly, she awaited Toufic's return home to spill out its contents.

Toufic also became excited when he saw it was from his cousin Malik in Bqaatouta. He quickly opened the envelope and began to carefully make out the message. In the letter Malik described the sadness that had overtaken their little town with the deaths of nearly half of the population due to starvation and disease. He said he was heartbroken to report that only Toufic's sister Emiline from his family had survived. Toufic and Christine's father, mother, three sisters, and two brothers had perished, all victims of a virulent form of the Spanish Flu.

When Toufic finished reading the letter, both he and Christine, still mourning the loss of her husband two years prior, were weeping uncontrollably. The young man's grief was exacerbated by the thought that he had come all this distance to help his parents and now they were gone. Guilt overwhelmed him, for he felt he should have stayed in Lebanon and perhaps could have saved his family. He also felt ashamed as he recalled the good time he was having in America while his loved ones were suffering and dying. The magnitude of his grief was never overcome as evidenced by the number of times Toufic recalled it over the rest of his life.

He had been in America for a little over four years and had put away little money. He worked hard for low wages but now, with no reason to send money back home, he began to lose interest in news from the old country. He no longer cared that the Turks had been defeated soundly and the Ottoman Empire dismembered. He withdrew into himself and became focused on his innate Lebanese drive to achieve financial independence. That was all that was left for him now.

The young man threw himself into peddling and began to think only of himself and the pleasures that a single male his age could enjoy. He would encounter girls on his route, whether Polish or Italian, that caught his eye, something that was not unnoticed by his Uncle Seghaan. His uncle began to ask him if he liked Italian girls, to which Toufic replied that he liked all kinds of girls. He saw no real difference between himself and the immigrant girls since they all came to America on the same boats under the same circumstances.

His uncle would often remind him that he'd have to find a good Lebanese girl, like his sister. But Toufic said he hadn't seen any Lebanese girls in this country that he'd want to marry.

Christine asked her brother if the rumors she heard were true about this or that *Italyaniya* (an Italian girl). Toufic became annoyed at his uncle, knowing that he was the one spreading this gossip. Christine, whose lack of guile was often incorrectly interpreted as tactlessness, was a straightforward person— what you saw was exactly what you got. Even though her uncle cautioned her not to say anything, it was her nature to blurt out such secrets. Noticing how angry Toufic had gotten, she told him there must be something to it.

It was a different time and people had different ideas, as that old song went, about love and marriage. It irritated Toufic that he couldn't talk to a girl without people getting him married off. His sister maintained that she wasn't worried because she knew he was going to marry a nice Lebanese girl.

*If you take a partner, let him be an emir.*

It didn't take long for Seghaan, the ever-astute businessman, to notice that the peddling business was becoming a victim of post-war prosperity. The only ones that seemed to be able to make a decent living from the peddling trade were women like Aunt Sadie and Christine. The farmers seemed to take pity on women peddlers, and were more receptive to them. People also had fewer reservations about letting women come into their houses to stay the night, which peddlers often did.

They were going to have to open up a store, Seghaan said to his nephew one day. He had his eye on the small candy store adjoining the Hippodrome Theater and had talked to the fellow that owned it. The man was planning to go back home to Greece and wanted to sell the shop.

A little known fact about the immigration pattern in the early twentieth century was that many of the newcomers opted to return to their native countries once the Great War was over. One study maintains that upwards of 25% of the Lebanese immigrants returned home after cessation of hostilities. Their savings would go much further there than in America. But, in Toufic's case, there was no reason or desire to return. For others, desires faded over time and dissolved into dreams that would never materialize.

Seghaan agreed on a price of $1,200 with Mr Gergeadis for his candy store. He told Toufic he would make him a junior partner for $500, a sum his nephew didn't have, and would put up the remainder and own the store's fixtures. But Aunt Sadie, upon hearing of Toufic's predicament, said she would lend him the money. Toufic was, of course, ecstatic.

Now one may wonder, as I did, how Sadie, who was supporting a husband in the old country, could have saved enough money to stake her nephew in business, while his unencumbered uncle, working in America for eighteen years, offered no financial assistance. Sadie was a short, frail-looking waif of a woman who, all the years I observed her, dressed in black, perhaps in mourning over the death of her husband. Sadie had developed a loyal clientele and made a decent margin on cloth and notions that were her specialty. I could never imagine anyone turning her away from their door because she projected an image of someone to be pitied. Sadie continued peddling her wares into the 1940's when she was past sixty years of age.

Seghaan and Toufic consummated the deal with the Greek storeowner, and after the agreement was finalized, organized a list of wholesalers who would provide the merchandise they needed. They would sell newspapers, magazines, and tobacco products, along with the main staple of candy. They also discussed getting a popcorn machine for the movie patrons. Seghaan felt they should also put in a shoeshine stand since there were none were available on the street.

Toufic expressed a worry that their kinsmen would look down on them for shining shoes, and he was mindful that in the old country anything connected with shoes was considered low class and dirty. As an example, showing someone the soles of your shoes is still considered extremely rude and insulting by Middle Easterners. One of the many Lebanese ways of insulting a person was to call him a shoe.

But Seghaan felt that America was a country where no honest work was beneath them. A good profit could be had in shoe shining. They would charge 5¢ for a shine and use less than a penny's worth of material. If one wanted to make money, he would shine shoes his uncle said.

The concept of immigrants easily abandoning long-held traditions was always interesting to me. They engaged in occupations that they normally wouldn't dream of performing back in Lebanon. Surely they didn't want their relatives back home to know they engaged in such work in America. It made eminent good sense to me because I knew from personal experience that there were a lot of old-fashioned ideas in the old country. The people back home might not approve, but they would take the money and wouldn't care where it came from.

Toufic was excited about the new enterprise. No more working in the mill yard in the cold for him. No more pushing the peddler's cart through the snow. He would now be a businessman.

# 23

*He who experiences the good should expect the better.*

A FTER THE BOYS CAME MARCHING HOME FROM THE war, the job that
Christine had taken in the tissue mill was eliminated and she went
back to peddling. Wanting to put her bad experience in Carthage behind
her, she traveled with a pack on her back to visit friends in Utica. It was
amazing how much she could tote in the contrivance that towered
above her head while also holding on to her *kashishi*. After a short stay
in Utica she peddled north to Tupper Lake, finally taking up residence
there among the large contingent of Lebanese that were serving the
lumber camps in the area. She would stop at farmhouses along the way,
selling needles here and a spool of thread there. The farmers' wives were
starved for company and often times offered her sleeping quarters, if
not in the house, in their barn along with the cows and chickens.

Hanna & Ellis opened for business on Independence Day, 1919, at 271
State Street. (The 1920 census listed the business as a shoeshine parlor.) The
combination of location and the steadily improving economy in what was
to become the "Roaring Twenties" served to create a surfeit of customers
for the newfound business. The motion picture craze was in full swing, and
people from Carthage and the surrounding area flocked to the Hippodrome,
stopping to buy candy, popcorn, and cigarettes from the little shop adjacent
to the theater. The piano music that accompanied the silent flicks could be
heard in the store and when it stopped, it signaled that the show was over.
There were times before performances began and shortly after they ended
when it took all that both men could do to keep up with the trade.

No longer burdened with his remittance obligations to Lebanon, Toufic
began saving with parsimonious zeal. He opened an account at the First
National Bank of Carthage and deposited money there a couple of times a
week. He denied himself the simple pleasures of life and worked at the store

seven days a week from eight in the morning until the last film showing finished at around 11:00 PM. At this point in his work, he didn't have time to indulge in the many diversions offered a young single man. There wasn't even time to go to the Lebanese Club, even though it was just across the street from the store. The club was slowly dying and eventually closed because most of its members were keeping long hours in their shops. Toufic didn't even have time to consider the girls that had occupied his thoughts when he was peddling. When things were slack in the store he would peruse newspapers or an occasional magazine, which helped him improve his language skills.

Language was something that often preoccupied the Lebanese immigrants. There were a number of humorous linguistic faux pas that both Toufic and Seghaan recalled in their later years, incidents that were no doubt repeated with other nationalities. One story that the usually droll Seghaan told concerned a Lebanese man inquiring of a stranger what time it was. In Arabic when one asks for the time, he literally says, "How much is the clock?" So, Seghaan said, the Lebanese man asked the chap, "How much is the watch?" "Oh, you can get one for as little as $1 or $2," the fellow replied. Seghaan found this faux pas quite amusing, one of the few times I saw him display even a modest sense of humor.

Seghaan was not a social animal but was always curious about what his partner was doing in the time he was away from the store. He wanted to know if he was running around with his cousin Naja who had earned a reputation as a gambler and carouser, something Seghaan thoroughly disapproved of. Naja had come with his mother to America at the age of nine, and his English was more accomplished than Toufic's due to his public schooling. Along the way he had acquired an affable Americanized manner and had taken to calling himself Nelson and told people that his father's name was Nathaniel, not Nasief. Toufic enjoyed Naja's company and would cruise around the countryside with his cousin in his twelve-cylinder Packard.

When he was not needed in the store and wasn't enjoying the idle pursuits of an unattached single man, Toufic decided to try his hand at distilling *arak* as he had done with his father back home. *Arak* is quite similar to the Greek ouzo and Turkish *raki* and was not commercially available in Carthage. His thinking was that this would be a good pastime during the cold winter months when there wasn't much else to do with his free time.

Toufic soon collected the materials needed to construct a still. He had found a fabricator who would fashion a twenty gallon copper pot with a brass screw-on lid for him. He also acquired a coil of copper tubing that would be attached and immersed in an old ice cream churn that would be filled with water and serve as the condenser for the distillate. He also acquired an old beer barrel that would be used to ferment the mash, made from grapes, if available, or raisins if not. The beer barrel with West End Brg. Co. visibly etched into its side still resides in the cellar of the final Ellis homestead. Toufic set up the apparatus in the basement of the house on Furnace Street and eagerly went about making his first batch of home brew.

A flood of quite vivid memories rush in whenever I think of my experiences with the *arak*-making enterprise. Pop, as all his children called him, would bring home boxes of large Muscatel raisins and set up a hand-cranked meat grinder at the kitchen table. Dutifully, my brother and I would take turns grinding the raisins, a muscle-building chore to say the least.

Finally, when the last raisin had been ground, the mess would be transported to the cellar and dumped into the old beer barrel, filled with water and covered. From there nature would do the job of fermentation—the anaerobic conversion of sugar to carbon dioxide and alcohol. Pop would stir the boiling mash with a hardwood stick every so often, and after about a week to ten days, he would announce it was ready for distillation. One time I asked him how he knew when it was ready. "When you can see your face in it," he replied as he lifted the lid from the barrel and stared down into the calm dark pool to see his mirror image.

After the fermentation had stopped, the liquid was poured into the still and a cloth sack full of anise seeds was thrown in with it. The brass cap was affixed and the tubing, that led from the still into the cylindrical cooling tower, was attached. The copper cauldron sat atop a kerosene stove, and the cooling tower had a garden hose continually running cold water through it to force condensation of the finished product as it bubbled its way through the contraption.

My dad would fire up the stove and patiently wait for the mash to come to a boil. He didn't dare leave the still untended because, if it clogged up for some reason, it would become a ticking time bomb. There was no pressure relief valve attached to the still so he had to take notice if the liquid suddenly ceased dripping. If it did, he would quickly remove heat from the mixture and abort the process. He said his father hadn't been vigilant enough one time, and the anise seeds clogged up the tubing causing the still to explode with a deafening blast.

Finally, the *arak* would complete its drooling from the bottom of the cooling tower into a gallon jug placed below the spout. The potent "white lightning" resembled vodka or gin, as it was totally colorless. Toufic would then take a shot glass of the distilled product, open the furnace door, and splash it on the red-hot coals. When this action was greeted with just the right flash of flame, known only to him, he would announce that the *arak* was ready. It would have been simpler if he had a spirit hydrometer, but like pressure valves, he didn't know such devices existed.

After three or four gallons of the product had been distilled, the liquid coming out of the cooling tower would turn milky in color. That was the signal that the batch was finished. Our diligent moonshiner would then mix the contents of all the gallon jugs together to even out the potency, which I came to learn later was around 100 proof. The jugs would then be set aside to cool. Often he would distill the *arak* a second or third time—hence the label "triple distilled" that is seen on some commercially available Lebanese produced *arak*.

The process that Toufic brought with him from Lebanon made him quite popular with his compatriots. There was a ready market for whatever remained after reserving enough to provide him with an occasional drink at Sunday dinner.

A short time after Toufic had made his first batch of *arak*, he was surprised to read that a law had been passed banning all liquor sales. It had been rumored for some time that this was being considered, but until it was actually passed, most people didn't take it seriously.

Toufic perused the six-column headline, "Volstead Act Becomes Law," in the New York City newspapers at his store. The articles went on to say that by the next day, people who had liquor stored in warehouses, safes, or deposit vaults must move the contraband to their private residences. A companion article announced that New York Alderman Fiorello LaGuardia was extremely skeptical about the law, saying that it would take 250,000 police to enforce it in New York City alone and an equal number to police the police. Toufic couldn't imagine people going without their liquor. It was quite the topic in the store for several days thereafter.

The Lebanese community, (and I'm sure the Italians, as well) thought these Americans were crazy to even think of banning booze. In the old country, they said if the politicians tried to do that they would be shot. Even Christ changed water into wine, they said. How could these people think they were better than Christ?

*Toufic and his 1923 Buick Roadster.*

# 24

*A lover of his money has no lover.*

T HINGS WERE FINALLY TURNING OUT WELL FOR Toufic in his adopted
America. He was saving money and had amassed, by his standards
at least, a small fortune. It was more money than he had ever dreamed of
having. Uncle Nasief and cousin Naja had moved to Tupper Lake and opened
a grocery store. Toufic, in a move of economic convenience, was now sharing
an apartment with his Uncle Seghaan above the Hippodrome Theater.

After a few years had passed, he began thinking it was time for him to
own a car, and a 1923 Buick roadster caught his eye. He imagined himself
in such a car, tooling down the road to clandestine meetings with the Italian
or Polish girls he had met on his peddling route. Yes, a Buick would be the
ticket!

His uncle was expectedly unhappy with the lad's choices, for he
considered expenditures such as a car to be profligate and cavorting with
girls of different nationalities intemperate. Toufic had already paid back
the loan to Aunt Sadie, had no debts, and money in the bank. What more
could he ask for?

When his uncle asked how much the car cost, Toufic demurred because
he thought it wasn't any of his uncle's business. No matter how much
the price tag, Seghaan would have thought it was too much. His uncle
was more than frugal, he was a deep-rooted miser, saving his money for
what, nobody knew. He was a confirmed bachelor, never having shown the
slightest interest in women, all of which Toufic couldn't understand. He
also had never owned or learned to drive a car. We can only assume that he
was sending his money back to relatives in Lebanon, although we have no
evidence of that either.

I remember the uncle only after he had retired and came round to my dad's
store to pass the time. He used a cane to steady his gait but still sported the

gray handlebar moustache now yellowing around the edges. His hands had a palsied shake that was noticeable when he raised a finger to make a point or give unsolicited advice, usually about saving money and not having big ideas. I knew he'd struggled hard in life, but did he have to worship the god of money?

On the rare occasions that I saw him open his billfold, I noticed that the bills were crisp and carefully sorted. I suspected that he ironed his money to keep the bills so tidy. My dad obviously unconsciously learned some of his habits from Uncle Seghaan. He would always put older bills on the outside of the wad he carried in his pocket so they would be used first, that is if he had to spend any at all. When someone came into his store and gave him a new bill, he would immediately exchange it for an older one in his pocket. If he pulled out some money to pay for a purchase, he always snapped the bills to make sure there weren't two stuck together, the way newly minted ones often did. I find myself doing the same thing. I guess the apple doesn't fall far from the tree.

It's not often that children get to examine or even discuss their parents' amorous history, particularly prior to marriage. My father certainly never discussed any romances he had, but my mother occasionally alluded to women that my father knew prior to her arrival. Even afterwards, she grudgingly showed concern that some of those same ladies continued to come to the store to chat him up.

At weddings our family attended when I was boy, I recall my father's contemporaries kidding him about the old days, giving me the impression that he was quite the lady's man. As a single man about town I have to assume that the young virile Toufic didn't go around behaving like a celibate monk. I also heard similar stories about his first cousin and sometime companion Naja. So, it isn't a stretch to believe that Toufic had an affair or two as a single man about town. It was, after all, the Roaring Twenties, with speakeasies, flappers, and cars with rumble seats.

It also has to be noted that relationships outside of one's ethnic group in those days were somewhat rare and generally frowned upon by one's tribe. When an immigrant man's thoughts turned to serious romance that might lead to marriage, he most often sought out his own kind, arranged or otherwise. I suspect this was partially due to the fact that the language of love is much better whispered in one's native tongue.

In those early immigrant days, the quantity of eligible males vastly outnumbered the supply of eligible women. Why else would there have been such a business as mail-order brides? The number of single women who came along with their families, or the young girls who grew to womanhood after their families arrived, were not of sufficient quantity to meet the pent-up demand. And, due to changes in the immigration laws, it was next to impossible for immigrants without immediate relatives in America to enter the country. Because of these social and demographic pressures, immigrants of all nationalities trekked back to their homelands to marry.

Toufic was really no different, even though he often expressed a belief in the equality of all immigrant nationalities. The girls who caught his eye while he worked in the store would serve as passing fancies and nothing more. His cousin Naja had a string of girls that he romanced, and he would include Toufic on double dates. Inevitably, as often happened, romance would bring into question the basic societal values they both held dear, much more so than they realized.

More than once Toufic told himself that he couldn't get serious about a girl because Lebanese marry Lebanese women, and for that matter, Italians marry Italians, Poles marry Poles, and so forth. In the event of an inter-ethnic romance, the men made themselves believe that the girls didn't really expect it to lead to marriage either. Certainly some of the women hoped against hope that these boys would buck the conventions of their culture and wed them, but they didn't realize how deep those proscriptions ran.

*Put one foot in ploughed ground and the other in fallow.*

Cousin Naja's sojourn in Tupper Lake at his father's grocery store was short lived because he found it too tame for his tastes. He returned to Carthage with the idea that he and Toufic should cast their lot together and open a dry goods business. Naja had his eye on a store across the street and down the block from Hanna & Ellis, at 236 State Street, that had come vacant and told Toufic that they could make a lot more money than he was making in his "shoeshine parlor." The hours would be shorter, and Toufic, now twenty-seven would have more time to think about marriage and starting a family.

His uncle, of course, told him he should go back to the old country to find a bride. But, all the girls Toufic had known over there, including Afifi, who had wed and was now in Argentina, were already married or had died during the war. Rushing into an arranged marriage didn't appeal to him because he said he would need to know a woman before he married

175

her. He wasn't ready to go back to Lebanon because he hadn't as yet attained American citizenship. He didn't want to take the chance that US Immigration, with its ever-changing laws, wouldn't let him back into the country. He felt he was fortunate to get in when he did and decided to stay put until his citizenship was confirmed.

*He who eats garlic smells of garlic.*

The prospect of a new business tantalized Toufic, and getting out from under his uncle's scrutiny only sweetened the deal. But Seghaan, as was to be expected, was genuinely wary. He neither approved of Naja nor the company he kept. And, in typical Lebanese fashion, told his nephew, "*When you shake hands with him, you better count your fingers.*" That was one saying that Toufic would regretfully recall later on.

Out of ingrained respect for his elders, Toufic valiantly suppressed his irritation with his uncle who was twenty-six years his senior and typically never had anything good to say about the younger generation, especially somebody like Naja, whom he saw as a drinking, gambling, American playboy who had a lot of "big ideas." Having "big ideas" was the kiss of death as far as he was concerned.

Toufic made light of his uncle's reservations even though Naja's attempts at striking it rich had resulted in a series of failed ventures. After leaving his father's grocery store in Tupper Lake, he tried to start a wholesale produce business with one of his mother's relatives in Fulton, New York, but that hadn't worked out either. "*If he traded in hats, people would be born without heads,*" Seghaan said.

Toufic was amused at his uncle's quaint humor, but having an innately optimistic nature, he felt that he could have a positive influence over Naja, whom he knew to be a great salesman. He said Naja could sell a pair of shoes to a one-legged man. Of course his cousin liked to play around, but Toufic felt that down deep they both had the same ingrained Lebanese values.

Seghaan was a modern day Polonious, (he of *Hamlet* fame), who felt he had to give his nephew some parting advice. He admonished him to neither borrow nor lend, just as he hadn't loaned to him when they went into business. He warned against reckless spending because he'd seen some bad signs what with a new car, girls, and hanging around with characters he didn't approve of. He just didn't see a good conclusion to it at all.

Finally, Toufic and his uncle came to an agreement that Seghaan would hold his nephew's share in the business until they saw how things worked out. If the new business succeeded, then they would agree on a buyout. Seghaan said he could get Joseph Solomon, one of the other Lebanese immigrants, to work in the store with him while Toufic's new business, with the impressive name of the Boston Sales Company, got started.

What Toufic failed to tell his uncle was that it was largely his money that was financing the dry goods venture. He had loaned Naja $2,500, which left him a little less than $2,000 in savings. It wouldn't have been a good idea to tell Seghaan about that.

Toufic, who now planned on staying in America permanently, felt that citizenship had become a priority. He attended night classes with other immigrants, learned the requisite American history, and continued improving his language skills. His written English, although somewhat scrawly and permeated with misspellings, was passable. Other Lebanese who were also trying to attain naturalization would quiz each other to pass the time. "What is the capital of New York?" one would ask. "Who was the father of our country?" was another. ("Georgie Wash" was the answer Khillu Ferris gave.) And so it went until the time came to appear before a special term of the Supreme Court of New York State held at the Watertown courthouse.

Although he was nervous, Toufic passed the examination, and along with a group of thirty-four others, was administered the oath of citizenship. The judge concluded with his congratulations and an admonition about the awesome responsibility that citizenship entailed. The newly Americanized subjects looked at each other with wide smiles, shook hands, and patted each other on the back. A linguistic revolution suddenly broke out, with clashing consonants and vowels marching forth to form an army of incomprehensible syllables and phrases, compounded by salvos of mispronunciations in various accents. None of the new citizens seemed to care because becoming an American was the fulfillment of a dream for all of them.

Toufic became a citizen of the United States on November 22, 1924, ten years and five months after he had arrived in the country. One of the requirements for American citizenship was the renouncing of any allegiance to a foreign power, including those of previous citizenship. This posed no problem for Toufic because he intended to live nowhere but in the United States of America.

It was much later that we realized how much Toufic treasured his citizenship certificate. He kept it safely stored in a locked box with all his other important papers, including passports, visas, and letters of recommendation. By the care he took in preserving these documents, I believe he felt his decision to come to America was the most important one he made in his entire life.

And you can't imagine how many times I've personally given thanks for that decision.

# 25

*The homeland yearns for its sons.*

O N June 19, 1925, Toufic boarded ship in New York Harbor to return to Lebanon after a decade plus in America, along with two companions from Carthage, Amin Abbass and Aziz Elhage. The trip to their ultimate destination had taken thirty-seven days because of the trio's traipsing across Europe and a stop in Egypt.

As their ship was preparing to enter Beirut harbor, the dapper Toufic, who had been up since dawn, was nervously pacing the deck. Peering into the early morning fog, smoothing the lapels of his cream-colored, linen suit, and adjusting the chain that looped through the buttonholes of his vest, Toufic was visibly anxious. He withdrew his watch and saw that it was still an hour before they were scheduled to dock. As his anxiety rose, his celluloid collar, which topped the silk shirt and tie he had labored over to get just right, seemed a bit tight. He wanted to look his best and as far removed as possible from his appearance when he first left Lebanon. The rude shirt and trousers he wore then had quickly been consigned to a rag peddler, and he felt his acquaintances from those bygone days would hardly recognize him in his straw hat and highly polished, spats-clad, wingtip shoes. He couldn't wait for them to see him.

Yes, he definitely was a changed man from the anxious teenager that had run for the boat to America. Why, the gold cuff links he had on were alone worth a hundred times more than everything he possessed back then. Yes sir, he was now a successful businessman, on a triumphant return home. His pride and excitement could barely be concealed.

Toufic Tarrod Kmeid Ellis, along with his two companions, was now a world traveler. He had crossed the ocean twice, visited the European continent, seen the famous cathedral at Reims (even though he remarked that it was still in ruins from the previous world war), the Eiffel Tower in Paris, the Alps

179

from the Orient Express, the Leaning Tower of Pisa, the catacombs of Rome, and the pyramids of Egypt. While visiting St. Peter's at Vatican City, Pope Pious XI made a public appearance and ritually sprinkled the crowd with holy water. Toufic was standing right under the balcony when a single drop of the sacred fluid landed on his forehead, right above the bridge of his nose! It was the capstone of his long journey from poverty to prosperity. It certainly gave him a lot to think about as he impatiently walked the deck of his ship, the Italian registered SS *Esperia*.

As the landscape abruptly rose out of the mist, Toufic could see the majestic Mount Sannine in the distance, still standing guard over the place where he was born. It was the first landmark he would see as the boat steamed toward Beirut harbor. Suddenly, gripped with uncharacteristic emotion, tears came to his eyes and began to trickle down his cheeks. A handkerchief was quickly pulled from his breast pocket to keep the drops from staining his linen suit. He was not one who was easily brought to tears, and on those rare occasions when he was, he rapidly retreated from view. Nonetheless, he was surprised at his spontaneous display of sentimentality.

He was impatient for the ship to dock, and his eyes turned to the skyline of the looming city of Beirut. He imagined himself touring the city and countryside, things he was never able to do in his youth. When his appetite for adventure was sated, he'd be on that winding road taking him to his ancestral home in Bqaatouta. He nostalgically envisioned the low-hanging clouds and morning mist that often bathed the mountains. It was July, the nicest time of the year to be in the upper regions.

The stevedores were looping the thick hawsers around the piers as Toufic went off to his quarters to retrieve his two friends along with their hand luggage. After debarking, he presented his papers to the customs agents who were much more courteous to him this time around. He thought back to the rude way he was treated when he first left the country. Why, now he would even tip the porters, something he wouldn't and couldn't afford to do back then. A man of property had to act the part.

Amin, one of his traveling companions, was only eleven years of age when he first arrived in the US, and he was the first to remark how things had changed since he saw Lebanon thirteen years before. The country had indeed changed and these nouveau Three Musketeers were eager to experience the sights of their homeland, both new and old. There would be archaeological digs to visit, nightclubs to enjoy, and restaurants to savor. They engaged an obsequious taxi driver to commandeer their suitcases, load them onto the back and top of the cab, and head to the Grand Hotel D'Orient, one of Beirut's finest.

After registering and being shown to the room they would share, the travelers went down to the expansive patio, sat at a table, and ordered drinks. Their lodgings were right on the Mediterranean, and the three men not only enjoyed the view but also the deference they were shown by the hotel staff. The lapping of the waves on the rocks was positively mesmerizing as they sipped the tall coolers the waiter had brought them. Toufic, who had become a photography aficionado, would take a lot of pictures to document where he had been and what he had seen. The trio then put their heads together to plan their itinerary.

They talked of seeing Damascus, going to the north of Lebanon to see the cedars and the Roman ruins at Baalbek and to stop at cafés in Zahle where babbling brooks coursed through the middle of the restaurants. In the meantime they would tour the city of Beirut and make a time of it. Amin, who had been a spoilsport by balking at going down into the Italian catacombs and then complaining that it was too hot in Egypt, had forced the trio to cut short their visit there. Both Toufic and Aziz never ceased needling him about it.

Their plans to go to Damascus to see the great mosque, the one that had a sarcophagus reportedly containing the head of John the Baptist had to be abandoned. They had unluckily returned to Lebanon at a time when a Druze insurrection was in progress, one that would last for a year. Traveling to Syria would be too hazardous as the road went through Druze territory. Even without that conflict, the unrest had also spread to Damascus, further complicating any travel to Syria. The revolutionaries had captured the citadel and most of the rest of the city. The French replied to the insurrection with a 48-hour bombardment of Damascus using both artillery and aircraft. The remaining revolutionaries in the city were forced to surrender. The root of the strife was French plans to change the way in which they administered the territories in question and French authorities amended their plans as a result of the native reaction. The trio would have to forego visiting the great *souk* (marketplace) where Damascene merchants would have assailed them with bargains they couldn't possibly refuse. They went about touring nightclubs, Baalbek, the cedars, and whatever other sites struck their fancy.

When their touring was done they hired a car to go up the mountains to Bqaatouta. The trio piled into the back seat, and the driver regaled them with a non-stop stream of conversation that is a trademark of Lebanese taxi drivers. They were now ready for the villagers to finally get a look at them. It was time to show them that they too had "made it" in *Amreeka*, just like Gold Tooth and Moustache before them.

*To him who has enough money, a princess is his bride.*

It wasn't long before word spread through the district that a rich and handsome expatriate from Bqaatouta, Toufic Traad Kmeid, had come home to find a bride. The story, which was embellished with each repetition, told of how he had left as a pauper, and in a decade, had become a "rich" and successful businessman. It was a tale that was certainly far from unique, as many expatriates had returned with trumped-up reputations, just as he had. "Rich" was an extremely relative term and many returnees reputed to be prosperous by the Lebanese peasant's standards were actually a bit less than middle class in America.

Toufic's friends and relatives began teasing him about bridal prospects, saying he could have his pick of the girls in the village. But he wasn't looking for just any village girl and told his cousin Malik that he was going to take his time because he didn't want to make a mistake.

Malik laughed because he said a man could mold a woman to his tastes. Toufic told him that things were different in America because once there a woman acquired all kinds of "fancy ideas." He thought it best to take his time. "Fancy ideas," like "big ideas," were suspect in the Lebanese male mindset. I wondered when growing up amongst these people whether any ideas that didn't conform to their age-old norms were acceptable to them.

When Amin was queried about his intentions, he humorously replied that he wanted to marry a girl "that knew how to walk on sidewalks." In any event, he was already engaged to a Lebanese girl from Shenandoah, Pennsylvania, who was born in America (and certainly knew how to perambulate sidewalks). Amin was also returning to America in a couple of weeks because he didn't want to leave his business unattended any longer than needed. He was successful in his own right, having acquired his first store, a small neighborhood grocery, when he was only sixteen years old.

Aziz on the other hand, as the story goes, was ready for the matrimonial step and spied a beauty in a tree picking apples shortly after arriving in Bqaatouta. The village was famous for its apples and a sixteen-year-old lass named Victoria was harvesting some of them. Aziz was so taken with the girl that he immediately proposed. He soon married and hurried back to Carthage with his bride.

Toufic, however, was in no rush, knowing that his affairs were in good hands back in the States. He had resolved to stay as long as needed to find the right girl.

Many matchmakers appeared on the scene and were persistent in their entreaties to Toufic, who kept insisting he was in no hurry. He wanted time to savor his newfound role as a man of property and leisure. When someone told him his handlebar moustache made him look older, he promptly shaved it off. There was, no doubt, a touch of youthful vanity present in the man, but that symbol of masculinity would appear and disappear throughout his life. I remember once asking my father, who hadn't sported facial hair for a long time, why he didn't grow another moustache. He exclaimed that he tried but it came in all white. "So I shaved it off," he announced. This was when he was seventy-five years old!

Toufic's time in Lebanon passed quickly, and although his traveling companions had been gone for a while, he betrayed no impatience for returning to the States. He was, however, disappointed with the marriage prospects in his hometown. Peasant girls could no longer compare to the cosmopolitan ideal he now fancied in a mate, not that Carthage was a cosmopolitan Mecca. But, compared to Bqaatouta it might have seemed that way to him.

He had been in the country for nine months when, while at a local coffee house watching the men play *towla* (backgammon), a stranger approached him and announced, "I am Sheikh Wadih Hobeiche, and I have the perfect woman for you." Toufic was a bit taken aback to be confronted by a sheikh from the Hobeiche family, but he listened as the man continued, "My cousin Angèle, who is teaching school in Beirut would be perfect for you. Believe me, she's a prize to behold."

Toufic was intrigued, of course, and listened intently. He certainly knew the family name and replied that the Hobeiches wouldn't want to take someone like him into their family.

Wadih related that the girl's brother was the head of the family, and he knew that Sheikh Yousef loved money more than the trappings of class. He told Toufic to think about it and for the usual stipend he'd work on it for him.

Toufic remembered thinking, *Does someone buy a fish while it is still in the sea?* He found the practice of paying money for a bride repugnant. Sheikh Wadih was undeterred and said he'd make inquiries anyway. Toufic, the more he thought about it, begrudgingly found the notion intriguing. Many people had approached him about this girl or that, but he always feigned disinterest because it was a buyer's market after all, and he wanted to examine all the merchandise available.

Toufic was also wary because there were many scams making the rounds. It crossed his mind that this might be another swindle, like the man who told him he could find his two brothers, whom he knew had perished during the war. "You think they are dead?" said the man who came knocking at his hotel room door in Baskinta (a larger town to the south of Bqaatouta). "They ran away before the plague hit here. They were in an orphanage. I can help you find them," he said.

"Find them? Where?" an agitated Toufic replied as he began rapidly questioning the fellow. The con man soon withered under Toufic's questioning and began contradicting himself. Toufic flew at him in a rage and in the process raised such a ruckus that people came running up the steps to see what was happening. The crowd quickly separated the two men, who were rolling on the floor, before Toufic could do any serious damage. The charlatan, as soon as he was able, beat a hasty retreat down the stairs. Toufic, enraged that his two dead siblings would be used in a con game, shouted after the swindler that he would kill him if he saw him again. No one tried that particular scam on him again, but Toufic remained wary nonetheless.

As time passed, the notion of finding the right bride began to look futile for Toufic. None of the many candidates had struck his fancy, and there had been several to pick from. Some were fawning, some were eager, and the rest just weren't good looking enough. None of the prospects could read or write. No, he decided he would hold out for the right one. Maybe this fellow Wadih was genuine. He had to find out.

Before the war the notables were already in decline, even though class remained important to them. The war and the plagues that ensued may have delivered the final blow to the aristocracy. Eating was much more important than titles. Perhaps they really wouldn't care how a man had become successful, just that he was.

Wadih continued to cultivate Toufic over several meetings. He related how the girl's brother Yousef had previously failed in arranging matches for her, how the girl, named Angèle, had rejected a rich Orthodox rug merchant and all the others that were offered. Sheikh Yousef had to be more careful now, and Wadih said when he mentioned Toufic to him, he immediately became interested. He wanted to know everything his cousin could tell him about this young man.

Toufic became hopeful—things could possibly be moving in the right direction. And Wadih encouraged him with embellished stories of meetings with his cousin Yousef, reinforcing his enthusiasm for the proposed match. He had told his cousin all about Toufic and his family. But, in fact, all he could really relate to Yousef was that Toufic was rich, looking for a bride, and his family were all dead.

Wadih said that Yousef was definitely interested and wanted to know specifics such as age and appearance. Still smarting over Angèle's encounter with the older rug merchant, Yousef felt he had to find someone who was closer to his sister's age. Wadih told him that Toufic was young, handsome, healthy, and quite strong too. He had emphasized the latter because he knew that Yousef placed a premium on physical strength and did not tolerate weaklings, no matter what their station in life.

Wadih finally arranged a meeting between the prospective brothers-in-law. He was happy because there was no telling how much this rich *Amreekani* would be willing to pay for a sheikha.

The first meeting took place at a coffee house in the Bourge section of Beirut. Toufic and Wadih arrived before Yousef and sat down to have tea while they waited. Toufic loved the way they served tea in Lebanon. It was poured into a glass, and although he didn't know why, it tasted much better than in a china cup.

After about ten minutes, Yousef arrived with a flourish, decked out in his resplendent uniform complete with the medals he had earned for his skirmishes in South Lebanon. Almost everyone in the café greeted him, much like the way his father was welcomed on that fateful day thirty-two years before, when Sheikh Nami first encountered Adela, at the el Khazen hostel in Kfar Debiane. He smiled broadly and stopped at each table to exchange a few pleasantries. He spied Wadih seated in the rear of the establishment with a stranger, whom he assumed to be the prospective groom, and took his time making his way over to their table.

Wadih rose to make the introduction of Toufic, who also stood to greet the imposing man. As they shook hands, Toufic tried not to be intimidated by this giant who stood a half-foot taller than he. They sat down and Yousef ordered Turkish coffee, which was quickly brought by a fawning waiter.

To Toufic's surprise, the meeting took on an extremely cordial tone. He had expected a grilling by the sheikh because when he enquired about Yousef in Bqaatouta, he was told many stories, most of which concerned his hot temper and feats of physical prowess.

Yousef was very interested in *Amreeka* and asked Toufic many questions, whereupon the young man launched into the monologue that he could repeat on cue, having performed it so many times since his return to Lebanon. Yousef listened intently to the recitation about going to America, starting two businesses, becoming a citizen, and returning to find a wife.

Sheikh Yousef seemed genuinely impressed because the whole story reeked of success, which in turn spelled money. Yes, he thought, this man might do nicely. After an hour of animated conversation, Yousef got up to go and parted with the statement that he would be seeing his sister soon and would be discussing this matter with her. Wadih would let him know what, if any, the next steps would be. With the exchanging of salaams all around, Toufic was relieved that the get-together was concluded. He felt he had done very well and could indeed comport himself in the company of the sheikhs.

This, he thought, could be the start of something big. Little did he know how big.

# PART III
## The Hobeiche—Kmeid Union

# 26

*Ask your heart and it will tell you what to do.*

A NGÈLE WAS ENJOYING HER LATEST POSTING IN BEIRUT, even though she still resided at the adjoining convent. The children had done well under her tutelage, and their parents often showed their appreciation with small gifts. She had found a career that suited her temperament and intelligence. The hardships of war, although not forgotten, were relegated to family reminiscences. The trouble that was brewing in the Shouf, a primarily Druze district of Lebanon, was irksome, but she was sure the French would protect them.

Things were going well until the day she received a letter from her brother Yousef. In her last communication with him that she had saved, he instructed her to go to a meeting in Jounieh for that disastrous encounter with the rug merchant from Amioun. She had vowed not to let this happen again. Yousef never wrote, of course, unless he wanted something, and if he were suggesting a similar meeting, she just wouldn't go. He told her simply, that he and cousin Wadih from Bqaatouta would be coming for a visit the following Sunday. Angèle thought this was strange because cousin Wadih had never visited her before.

The nuns, always gracious and ready to receive Angèle's visitors, had been treating the teacher as one of their equals for some time as a valued, if unprofessed, member of their community.

Sunday, promptly at three in the afternoon, a car pulled up to the convent, and a loud knock on the convent door soon followed. The young postulant, who answered the knock, ushered Yousef and Wadih into the parlor. Tea and sweets were soon served, and Angèle was summoned. She gave both her brother and cousin the obligatory three kisses, while voicing her curiosity about the visit.

Yousef affected an unusually obsequious manner while telling Angèle to listen carefully to what he had to say. He proceeded to relate that he had become acquainted, through Wadih, with a gentleman who had recently returned to Lebanon from *Amreeka*, looking for a wife. The young man was originally from Bqaatouta and was well known to cousin Wadih. Yousef said that the man might make a suitable match for her. But, because of past missteps, Yousef's gentle approach was no doubt designed to put Angèle in a receptive mood.

Yousef proceeded to explain that he had already met with the prospective suitor a few times and believed he was a good and hard-working fellow, one she should seriously consider. He was twenty-eight and had been in Lebanon for several months looking for the right woman. And, although he had been offered several prospects, he had not yet found the right match.

Wadih, not to be shut out of his role in the affair, interjected that the man was also handsome and rich, and it was he who had discovered him in Bqaatouta. He came from a good family, almost all of whom had tragically perished during the war, but the man's roots were still in Lebanon.

When Angèle heard the word *Amreeka*, she was immediately intrigued. She could hardly contain her curiosity about a young, rich, good-looking Lebanese man who lived in the United States, a place she had read and heard so many stories about. She often wondered what it would be like to actually go there. Deciding to listen to more about this prospect was an easy choice.

"When do I meet him?" Angèle asked. It was then she found that the duo had actually brought the suitor with them. He was waiting outside. Angèle went to the window and looked out to see a well-dressed man leaning against the hired car with his foot resting on the running board. Wadih went to fetch him.

Angèle was confident that this man, no matter who he was, would be taken with her. It just remained to be seen whether she would like him or not. Her self-esteem had always been buttressed by the fact that she was, after all, a sheikha. Although this attitude bordered on arrogance, she had experienced nothing in her life that would persuade her to modify this posture.

Yousef was relieved as a grinning Wadih reappeared with Toufic in tow and led the young man over to the uncharacteristically beaming Angèle to make the introduction.

Angèle's first thoughts, as she related later, was that Toufic was quite handsome. It was eerily similar to the thoughts that her mother had when she first laid eyes on Sheikh Nami at the hostel in the Mazzrat. This man also appeared well mannered, not at all what she expected of the son of a stonemason from Bqaatouta. She allowed that he was certainly a much better prospect than the rug merchant from Amioun.

The duo engaged in polite conversation about Angèle's teaching and Toufic's business, as they had no mutual friends to talk about. Toufic was a trifle uncomfortable but hid it by only talking when he had to. Angèle, not noticing the young man's uneasiness, was positively ebullient, conversing in rapid sequences and occasionally lapsing into French to get just the right phrasing. When she saw that her suitor didn't understand, she apologized and redoubled her efforts to correct the affectation that had become second nature to her.

After an hour of listening to small talk, Yousef was bored. There was no conversation of politics or war, no bawdy inferences, nothing that would be standard fare in his typical social intercourse. At an appropriate point he interjected that they resolve to continue these discussions in the coming weeks. He would arrange an outing where the couple could get to know each other better.

Everyone said their goodbyes and the meeting concluded without an awkward moment, all of which pleased Toufic. He was attracted to this woman, but felt it wise to act blasé.

*On the first day they sang to him, on the second they begged.*

The three men proceeded in their hired car to *Kahwa el Azaz,* a coffee shop in downtown Beirut, to continue their discussions. After they were seated comfortably, Yousef began to regale Toufic about how his sister was treasured in their family as a precious jewel and how she had many suitors but had rejected them all. He suggested that Toufic should meet his mother, Adela, who would not easily give up her prized daughter. It was then that Toufic began to suspect that he had gotten into something deeper than he had first suspected. The ritual was becoming a bit exaggerated, but he decided it was one that had to be performed according to Lebanese custom. In America, he had been conditioned to get down to business and quickly say what was on his mind. In Lebanon, he soon remembered, it would be insulting to be so direct. He had come to like and prefer the American way.

Yousef droned on about "considerations," and that he must be sure that a suitor could take care of Angèle in the manner her station dictated. Toufic answered that this was not a problem and he had banking references, which he would be happy to provide. He mentioned his business again and asked what else Yousef required.

Finally, Yousef broached what had always been on his mind, the matter of compensation. "The loss of his mother's daughter and wage earner would require some compensation, didn't he agree?"

There it was, out on the table. Toufic had been coached by Wadih, so he expected it, and was therefore undaunted by the indelicately proposed question. He wondered aloud what Yousef had in mind.

Yousef had taken an extremely circuitous route around the problem of establishing the price. He was not selling a cow or any other chattel, this was his sister after all, his flesh and blood, and matters such as these had to be handled delicately and discreetly. When he thought that he had danced around the subject adequately, Yousef said that he thought $2,500 American should adequately compensate the family for their loss.

Toufic would later admit he was taken aback but masked his shock with a smile. This was certainly more than he had expected, and at first he didn't know how to respond. He kept smiling as he ran the number through his head to see if it would make financial sense. He would have to call in his loan from Naja, sell his partnership back to Uncle Seghaan, pay for the rest of his trip and any other unplanned expenses, but he should have enough to get home and get things in order. And there would be the profits from his business while he'd been gone. Bottom line, he thought he could manage it. Although it was a steep price, he was getting a sheikha, after all, and no price could really be put on that.

Toufic was adamantly determined not to look cheap by quibbling about something so personal as marriage. Having determined that it was a figure he could work with, he demurred, saying he thought they were rushing things. Before going any further, he wanted to know if Yousef's sister was agreeable.

Yousef said confidently that he saw no problem, as Angèle betrayed her interest by agreeing to take the next step, something she had not done before. But he understood Toufic's concerns, so they agreed to talk again after the couple's next meeting. Following the usual, elaborate goodbyes, the car dropped Toufic off at his hotel where he was soon overtaken by buyer's remorse, a sickening feeling one often gets after committing to a large purchase, and it nagged him for several days.

On my first trip to Lebanon in 1971, I had occasion to meet the matchmaker Wadih in the very same coffee shop, the *Kahwa el Azaz*, where the fateful meeting took place. I had been out touring with my cousin Namatallah and we stopped at the café to meet his father Yousef, who regularly held court there. The two cousins were sitting, sipping coffee, and when I was introduced as Angèle's son, Wadih beamed and proudly announced that it was he who arranged the marriage between my parents. "So you're the son of a bitch who's responsible for that!" I instinctively blurted. Namatallah was aghast. He whispered for me to keep quiet because Wadih understood a little English and could possibly understand what I was saying. I told him it was OK because I did, after all, say it with a smile.

Later, when Angèle told her sister about the developments, Miriam brought up Edmond and wondered how he would react to the news. She thought Angèle and he had an understanding but, surprisingly, Angèle said she hadn't really thought about Edmond. After all, it was he, not her, who thought the groom's shoes would be worn by him. Miriam was certain that Edmond would be angry and disappointed when news of the courtship reached him. But Angèle defensively responded that Yousef didn't approve of Edmond and insisted that she consider this match instead.

Miriam felt compelled, and a bit delighted, to remind Angèle about comments she'd made about never letting Yousef dictate her life. But Angèle replied that *Amreeka* was a long way off, and going there just might be a good way to get out from under her brother's thumb.

*Toufic & Angèle on their wedding day.*

# 27

*He who wants to eat honey should bear the stings of bees.*

AFTER THE COUPLE'S FIRST MEETING AT THE convent, a traditional chaperoned courtship began, one that was still de rigueur in Lebanon. Chaperone duties alternated between Wadih and an aunt and her husband. With the escorts trailing at a discreet distance, the couple took slow walks along the boulevard by the sea not far from Angèle's school. Numerous street vendors that cruised the Corniche continually assailed them, offering a glass of *sousse,* a licorice-tamarind drink, or *jellab,* a mixture of carob, molasses and ice. While sipping these delightful delicacies, the couple would sit on a bench in view of the Grotte aux Pigeons and talk, with Angèle asking unceasing questions about *Amreeka*. She found Toufic to be reserved, even shy, and she liked that because it was a refreshing change from the men in the Hobeiche and el Khazen clans. After three such meetings, their engagement was announced.

Upon hearing the news, a procession of friends and family arrived at the convent seeking an audience with Angèle, trying to dissuade her from consummating this marriage. There were so many, Angèle recalled, that she actually felt badly about the inconvenience to the nuns. The news of her betrothal had spread among the clans, and not surprisingly, had caused a great deal of consternation, mostly among her mother's relatives. Even though somewhat flattered, Angèle politely told them that she was committed to the marriage and couldn't back out.

Wadih could not conceal his glee at being the one who had arranged the union, and broadcast the news far and wide in the district of Kesrouan. As Sr Miriam predicted, Sheikh Edmond exploded when he heard of it, loudly proclaiming that this could not and would not be. He vowed to quickly put a stop to this foolishness.

Soon afterward Sheikh Edmond arrived at the convent without warning and insisted upon seeing his cousin. Angèle became apprehensive as soon as she was alerted to Edmond's arrival. She entered the parlor to see an obviously agitated, red-faced Edmond rapidly pacing the floor. Trying her best to be blasé, she fatuously asked him why he had come.

"You know very well why I'm here," he thundered. "I want to hear from your lips that your betrothal to this peasant is not true." Edmond told her he knew in his heart that she was being forced into this arrangement and she didn't have to go through with it. She couldn't possibly want to marry this man who was totally beneath her.

There was no way for Angèle to spare Edmond's feelings. It was true that she was engaged to this expatriate from America. Her brother Yousef had approved of the marriage, and it was to take place a week from Sunday in the Patriarchal Chapel in Bekerke, the town where the Maronite Patriarchy is located.

He'd heard of these plans but he had a plan of his own to foil this marriage. He told Angèle how he and his cousins would have two cars waiting on the road to Bekerke from Kattine. At the bend in the road five kilometers from the church, one car would block the road to Bekerke while the other would be headed back down the mountain. When her automobile stopped, she would jump out and get into the waiting vehicle with him. From there they would speed down to Jounieh and get married by an el Khazen priest, with whom he had already made arrangements. After that there was nothing anyone, not even her brother, could do about it.

Angèle was stunned, flattered, and amused by Edmond's resolve, so much so that she could not answer immediately. After staring at her cousin for a few minutes, she said she didn't think she could do it. Her family would never forgive her and would disown her, and she would never be able to go home again.

Edmond persisted and said her family would forget in time. In fact, all the families would forgive and forget because everyone knew they were of the same blood, and it was understood that they would be married. The very idea that she would marry some nondescript peasant was preposterous.

Angèle began to fear that Edmond's persistence might change her mind. She thought of her brother and how he might just kill her in a rage if she abandoned this engagement, even though the tradition of kidnapping brides was certainly not unknown to their families. She had only to point to her mother as an example. Then she thought of Toufic, the shy, good looking, well-to-do man who wanted to take her to *Amreeka*. She would say later that she was quite dazzled by it all.

196

Finally, she told Edmond that, although they had been dear friends for a long time and she was very fond of him, it was too late, and there was nothing she could do. She was sorry but that was how it had to be.

Edmond was crushed but gave the appearance of resignation. His pride was wounded, and he told his love that, if this was her final answer, then there was no more to say except goodbye. His last words were, "One day, my dear Angèle, you'll regret this!"

Angèle sat for a while in the parlor, plagued by doubts. Was she doing the right thing? Was this man beneath her as Edmond had said? Would she regret this? She truly didn't know.

After a time, Angèle arose and went to her room to compose a letter to Edmond. She read it over, then tore it up and threw it into the wastebasket.

*The bride was dressed but did not know whom she was to wed.*

The wedding took place on the sunny Sunday of May 16, 1926, just two short months after the initial introductions. There was no abduction on the road to Bekerke. The bridegroom was at least spared that embarrassment, and Yousef would not be provided with an opportunity to display his temper or exercise his physical prowess.

It was not just any wedding, of course, for a sheikha had to be properly betrothed. It had to be in the right church attended by prominent notables and performed by ranking clergy. Bishop Feghali would preside at the service in the Patriarchal Chapel in Bekerke. The bride's gown was a simple, two-piece affair, with a long-sleeved jacket over a silk dress whose hem extended down to mid-calf. Her dark hair, combed into a chignon, was partially revealed by the long lace veil that flowed from her head down to the floor. The groom wore a dark blue, pinstriped suit, vest, and trousers with pegged cuffs. Even though their passports would say there was a two-inch height difference in favor of Toufic, in their wedding picture the bride, in heels, looks to be two inches taller than the groom. Although the custom of the time when being photographed was to affect a somber demeanor, looking at their wedding picture I think Angèle overdid it a bit.

The ceremony was a religious tour de force, a high mass with a lot of echoic chanting accompanied by the odor of incense and fragrant roses wafting throughout the church. The celebrant, a bishop who was a friend of the Hobeiche family, performed exquisitely, singing with an inspired flourish that some said was reserved only for special occasions.

After the ceremony, a noisy procession, with a train of automobiles tooting their horns and flying makeshift streamers and banners, found its way to the open-air restaurant on the road to Kattine, where the reception was held. The couple detoured to the photographer's studio to record a wedding photograph for posterity. The newlyweds then motored to the reception to find that the attendees had gotten off to a rousing start without them. Their appearance caused another round of cheering and toasts.

Toufic spared no expense in providing a lavish feast for his bride and her family. Copious quantities of food were served, and consumed, as a seemingly inexhaustible supply of *arak* was poured from the attentive waiters' flasks. The potent liquid served to lubricate the vocal chords of most of the men well into the next morning. When the mood of the group became sufficiently uninhibited, even the attending clergy joined in dancing the traditional *debke* (Lebanese folk dance). Toufic actually reveled in the extravagance, although given to occasional moments of remorse that his parents were not there to see their first-born son get married.

A two-week honeymoon in the north of the country among the cedars followed. As was common among inexperienced brides of the period, no amount of verbal instruction had prepared Angèle for the physical encounter with a member of the opposite sex. The attempts at serious intimacy were clumsy, but Toufic was very patient, a characteristic that would be called upon throughout his life.

*Zakia (far left), Emily (second from left), & Angèle (far right) in Marseilles.*

# 28

*When an object is kept from the eyes, the heart forgets it.*

THE HONEYMOON PASSED, AND THE BRIDEGROOM's thoughts drifted to the return trip home and his business. The couple went to apply for visas at the American Consulate in Beirut. The consul advised Toufic that he had a better chance for a visa for his bride in France. The United States was now limiting immigration to 3% of the nationalities represented in the 1910 US census, which recorded a very small Syrian (including Lebanese) population.

American Consuls in countries such as Lebanon, which now had an extremely low quota, were issuing visas only to US citizens. Northern and western Europeans, a decided majority of residents in the States, were most favored under the new, post-WWI regulations. Thus, going to France where the quota was higher offered a better chance for the new bride. However, even as the wife of an American citizen, Angèle was not guaranteed quick entry. The American Vice Consul stamped Toufic's visa with the official designation of Beirut, Syria, even though that city had been incorporated into Lebanon in 1920, some six years before. (Another example of the uphill fight the Lebanese had in trying to achieve their own identity.)

On May 31, Angèle received her passport from the high commissioner of the Republic of France, and two days later the French Consul of Lebanon stamped it with a visa for entry to Canada. The prevailing thought was, if all else failed, that she would go to Canada and then her husband would spirit her over the border into the US. This was apparently was a ruse that many Lebanese had used to bypass the more restrictive American immigration laws. The Lebanese, as well as other nationalities, were running an underground railroad of sorts by sending their relatives to Canada and then smuggling them across the porous northern border into the US.

Toufic's sister Emily (the only member of the family to survive the plague in Lebanon), who had become fast friends with Angèle's family, pleaded with her brother to take her with them to *Amreeka*. Toufic was opposed to the idea, but Emily's persistence and uncontrollable weeping moved Angèle to intervene and persuade Toufic that this would be the proper thing to do.

Emily also obtained a visa to Canada, and the trio left Beirut on June 2, 1926. They stopped in Egypt for four days of additional honeymooning where they saw the pyramids and the Sphinx before departing to Marseilles. They arrived in France on June 10, hoping to complete Angèle's American visa requirements.

Thus began a bureaucratic nightmare for the couple. Xenophobia was rampant in the US, and new laws were continually being enacted to curtail immigration. To overcome these new restrictions, hopeful travelers were continually devising new and resourceful ruses besides the Canadian gambit. There was, of course—as there has no doubt been throughout history—white slavery trafficking, and unscrupulous men were importing prostitutes by posing them as their wives. Immigration authorities soon caught on to this maneuver, and in order to thwart such poseurs, insisted upon documented proof that a couple was indeed married. The world was changing, and the need to have "papers" was becoming more and more acute.

The word "papers" was anathema for the Lebanese who associated such requirements with governmental intrusion and a loss of independence. Many blamed the Turks, who were infamous as the reputed originators of the paperwork legacy. Even though the Ottomans had long since been deposed, their procedures lived on.

Arriving in Marseilles, the newlyweds found a large colony of in-transit Lebanese residing there. A group of their enterprising countrymen had set up a profitable infrastructure to assist those that passed through the French portal on their way westward. These Lebanese entrepreneurs offered language assistance, advice, food, and lodging, all for a price of course. Young boys were waiting at the docks to hawk these services to the new arrivals—in both French and Arabic.

The trio put up in one of the Lebanese-owned hotels where the atmosphere took on the air of a get-together back home. With so many like-minded, co-religionist countrymen congregated there, they were made to feel as if they were still in Lebanon.

Attempts to secure a visa for Angèle at the American Consulate in

Marseilles were futile, and the couple was told they would have to go to Paris. They soon boarded a train to that city and found their way to the American Embassy where they stood in line with a horde of others also trying to obtain visas for the Promised Land. When their turn came, the first thing they were asked was to see their marriage certificate and letter of recommendation. They had no such documents with them, a serious oversight, for which Angèle would subsequently and incessantly blame her spouse.

No amount of pleading by Angèle in her accomplished French swayed the consul. They brandished their wedding bands but were told that anyone could acquire rings and pretend marriage, and many often did. Since their case was not going to be acted upon favorably, the couple returned to Marseilles.

Both Angèle and Toufic undertook a letter writing campaign to the Hobeiche family, informing them of their difficulties and their need for "papers." The couple had been in France for three weeks when the first of what would be a string of missives arrived. It was obvious that Toufic had mentioned Angèle's frustration and her increasingly irritable demeanor to his in-laws. The first letter they received was addressed to him from his mother-in-law, wherein she attributed any such problems to Angèle's homesickness.

27 June 1926
Our Beloved Son-in-law,
    We kiss your cheeks and ask about you and Angèle and Emily. We are in good health. We have received your letter and thanked God that you are in good health but we are upset to hear that your matters did not work out. We hope this will not take long and as soon as you receive our letter we will hear a good piece of news from you.
    Concerning Angèle, please take it easy with her because she is alone there and has no one from her family, even though you are closer to her than family. But you well know it is natural for one to miss her family.
    We received a letter from Yousef on the same day we received yours. He is in good health and asked if you have written to us. We sent him a letter and enclosed your letter in it. Always write to us and tell us about Emily. Miriam joins me in everything I said in this letter.
    Your mother-in-law
    Adela Hobeiche

We know that Miriam wrote the letter because Adela was not literate in Arabic. The sentence, "Miriam joins me in everything I said in this letter," betrays the scribe's true identity. Also we are able to identify Miriam's handwriting from other letters with her signature.

Toufic remained in France a total of six weeks, vainly trying to cut through the red tape. Finally, the disconsolate groom booked passage to New York for the twenty-second of July, sailing on the RMS *Olympic*. He was resigned to the idea that he'd have a better chance to get Angèle's visa in America. When Toufic announced that he was going to have to travel back to America alone, Emily took him aside and said she would chaperone Angèle while he was gone. Toufic wasn't sure Angèle would appreciate that but thought it might be a good thing all the same.

Reluctantly bidding farewell to his wife and his sister, and leaving Angèle with most of the cash he had, Toufic boarded a train to Cherbourg.*

Toufic's in-laws became confused about the couple's travel plans, thinking that they had already departed for the States. In a letter Toufic received shortly after arriving at his Carthage address, Miriam humorously wrote,

> I know what to write her when she sends me a letter announcing her arrival. If she hadn't found a place on the ship we would have sent a carriage to take her so that she does not stupidly stay in Marseilles.

Of course, both Angèle and Emily were still in Marseilles, and why this confusion prevailed was surely attributable to the time it took for the ships to deliver correspondence. Based on the dates of the letters, it was taking from eight to fourteen days to make their trip between Marseilles and Beirut. Letters were obviously crisscrossing on the high seas.

Angèle and Emily, not knowing how long their stay in France would be, busied themselves by getting acquainted with other Lebanese in similar circumstances. The rumor mill was extremely active among the émigrés, and they were keenly interested in information about how people were circumventing those onerous laws to get into *Amreeka*.

Canada, with its enormous landmass, was known to be much more immigrant-friendly than the US. According to the rumor mill in Marseilles, a Lebanese priest in Montreal would help in sponsoring Lebanese immigrants, and Emily wrote him soliciting his help. Even though she had a Canadian visa, a single woman traveling alone would be no more welcome in Canada than in the US. From there, however, she hoped she would be able to get into the States.

*It was much more expedient to take a train from Marseilles to Cherbourg as a sea journey would have added two to three days to the time and 40% to the cost.

Angèle continued to press her case with relatives back in Lebanon. Like her brother Yousef, she was easily frustrated and given to outbursts of irritability. She proceeded to vent her frustrations to her mother about her husband's misadventures with immigration officials. She redoubled her pleas for help in obtaining the proper paperwork that would legally validate her marriage and for the needed letter of recommendation.

Now all Angèle could do was pass the time with friends she was making by taking in the sights of their new surroundings. To the women, most of whom were from small villages, the cosmopolitan Marseilles was indeed exciting, if not intoxicating. One of her new friends had asked her to be matron of honor at her wedding, which would take place as soon as her intended arrived from Africa. Another lady, by the name of Zakia Sickrey from the South Lebanon village of Rashaya, had forged a strong bond with Angèle. She was on her way to Canada to join her family, and the two had become like sisters.

According to Zakia, as reported by her descendants in Canada, the reason her family fled Rashaya for Marseilles was because of the Druze insurrection that had been going on for nearly a year. There were reports of raids, looting, and killings, and many chose flight to France, the Sickrey family among them. Zakia would be the last of the family members to finally make it to Canada.

Angèle especially enjoyed Zakia's company because she was well educated, had a penchant for poetry, and appreciated intelligent conversation. There would be sightseeing trips, and of course, shopping in the jewelry stores that were full of pretty bracelets, necklaces, and brooches. Angèle didn't concern herself about finances because her husband was a prosperous businessman and said he would be sending her money as needed. Angèle saw no need to be fiscally conservative and was relieved that her deprivations due to war and family poverty had finally come to an end. If there were any frugality genes in the Hobeiche DNA she, like her brother Yousef, hadn't inherited them.

Over the years, Angèle would recount her time in Marseilles in a progressively negative light, no doubt influenced by bouts of depression resulting from dashed expectations. On the one hand she would recount the wonderful times she had there and on the other would lament having been "deserted" by Toufic. Her feelings seemed to parallel those she had when she was sent off to school as a child.

Surely it was melancholia that led her to begin exaggerating her circumstances and ascribing them to her husband's ineptitude. As an example, as I was surprised to learn, Angèle always maintained that she had been abandoned in France for six months when in fact it was three months to the day after Toufic left before she laid eyes on him again. Time not only plays tricks on memory, but it also varnishes the truth, as I found out more than once during my journey.

*Triumphant Toufic returns to the US.*

# 29

*A trade without its master soon disintegrates.*

Upon arriving back in the US, Toufic quickly went from the docks to Grand Central and boarded a train for home. His sojourn had lasted a year and seven days and had given him a lot to think and report about to his friends in Carthage. He looked forward to seeing his friends Amin, Aziz, his partner Naja, and the rest of the Lebanese community, even his Uncle Seghaan. He was anxious to show them the many photographs he had proudly taken of his new bride.

It was nearly midnight when the train pulled into the Carthage station, but Toufic was wide-awake with anticipation. He was ready for the tumultuous greeting that a conquering hero would surely receive, but his beaming smile evaporated into a frown when he saw there was no one there to receive him. This was highly unusual, because he had written to Shukrullah, who had certainly informed the community about his travel plans. Hospitality, a cornerstone of the Lebanese character, was readily, if not compulsorily, displayed at every opportunity. Where was Naja who had seen the trio of travelers off with the boisterous equivalent of a twenty-one-gun salute? Perhaps it was well past Uncle Seghaan's bedtime, so he might be excused. But, surely, everyone knew he was coming.

His expectation of a triumphant arrival as the man who had captured the heart of a sheikha was dashed as he walked under the dim streetlights to his modest lodgings on the third floor of the Hippodrome block. At his apartment he was alarmed to find his roommate, cousin Naja, gone along with all his belongings!

The weary traveler reluctantly decided to try to get some sleep and tackle this puzzle in the morning. He tossed and turned all night long, and at first light he arose feeling more tired than when he went to bed. He got dressed, and without shaving, went down the stairs to street level. It was very early, and few of the town's residents were stirring. As if impelled by a sense of doom, he hurried across the street toward the Boston Sales Company store. When he arrived, the sight that greeted him sent him into shock. The store was empty, and there was a large For Rent sign in the window.

Toufic went up the two steps and pressed his face to the window to peer inside. Indeed, the room was bare, the fixtures that the suits hung on, the tables where he had neatly stacked the shirts, the cash register, everything was gone. His heart sank as he turned and walked briskly to his Uncle Seghaan's apartment. He knew the man was an early riser, so it was without hesitation that he marched up the two flights of stairs and banged on the door. Soon the dour uncle opened the door, and Toufic stalked in without saying a word.

*The cat and the mouse had agreed to run the house.*

Seghaan inquired about Toufic's new bride, adding that everybody was anxious to meet her. But Toufic had no time for small talk and quickly asked what in God's name was going on. Nobody had met him at the train, not even his business partner. And the store was closed!

Seghaan said he thought somebody had written him about what happened. He proceeded to give his nephew the bad news that his cousin wasn't a very good businessman. After Toufic left for Lebanon, Naja started getting behind in their bills. Seghaan couldn't restrain his urge to throw out an "I told you so" in the process. Naja, behaving like a modern American businessman, gave credit to everybody, his uncle continued, even people who didn't live in Carthage. When the suppliers came after Naja for payment and didn't get it, they cut off shipments. After Naja missed a couple of months' rent, the Boston Sales Company was evicted and went out of business. The creditors took whatever was left and sold it to pay the bills. "Your dear cousin Naja is back in Tupper Lake working in his father's grocery store."

His uncle, unable to repress a reiteration of the many admonitions he had given his nephew, would shake his head while reaching for one of the many Lebanese proverbs at his command. *They slaughtered the camel and left you with an ear*, he said. The uncle prattled on about the evils of trusting people and how "big ideas" lead to big disappointments.

Toufic was dumbstruck and depression quickly overtook him as his thoughts turned to his wife and her family who were under the illusion that he owned a thriving business. He still had to negotiate Angèle's passage, and there was the matter of the obligations that he had committed to his brother-in-law Yousef. He was expecting to call in his loan from the business, a business that no longer existed.

This surely gave Toufic a headache. I know it gave me one when I heard about it.

Toufic gave his uncle a rapid and abbreviated version of his visa travails, ending with his wife still in France. Seghaan opined that maybe it was just as well she didn't come with him. It was then that he told his uncle that he would have to go back into the tobacco shop with him. It would be popping corn for movie patrons and shining shoes of the businessmen, a definite comedown from the dry goods business. But he had to make a living, especially with the added obligations of marriage. A man had to earn his keep no matter how it might appear to the people back home in Lebanon, and Toufic felt that his new wife should understand.

After he left his uncle, Toufic retrieved his car, which had been cared for in his absence by Joe Solomon, and headed to Watertown, the county seat, to see if he could jump-start the visa process. As he drove he wondered what he would tell his wife and his brother-in-law. What could he possibly tell them?

Toufic arrived in Watertown and soon found himself in front of the courthouse, the same place where he had been awarded his citizenship two years before. He was directed to the Immigration Office where he inquired about a visa for his new bride. He explained to the clerk that he had gotten married overseas some ten weeks prior and his spouse had been denied a visa in France. His wife was waiting in Marseilles for him to send the papers so she could complete the journey to America.

Toufic displayed all the documents he used while on his trip, including his proof of citizenship, to the clerk. The woman asked for a bona fide marriage certificate, which, as we well know, Toufic didn't have. He was told he'd have to have it before they could process a visa application and to come back when he did.

Totally dispirited, he walked out of the courthouse and went to the post office to write and send letters to his wife and her family to tell them of the continuing paperwork problems and the need for a copy of the marriage certificate in English. He saw no need to trouble them about his business problems...just yet.

Uncovered in the trove of documents that my parents left behind after their deaths is a sworn statement, intended for the American Consul at Marseilles, that was obtained by Toufic from Carthage's village president and chief of police. In the affidavit, dated August 23, 1926, the two officials swore that Toufic had lived in the village for ten years, was a naturalized citizen, had never been arrested or given any trouble to the authorities, and had uniformly good conduct.

In his desperate attempts to gain entry for his bride, Toufic thought to duplicate the practice used in his homeland where a letter from the village sheikh attesting to a person's good character was required for visa purposes. Just how his good character would influence the American Consul in France is speculative at best, but it shows Toufic's anxiety by his leaving no stone unturned to facilitate a reunion with his bride.

*Angèle in Marsielles.*

# 30

*To go away is within one's will but to return is not.*

Two weeks had passed since Toufic's departure when Angèle received a letter from him. He needed the marriage certificate in English and said she should inform her family how important this new detail was. Toufic, although never effusive, seemed even more reserved to her in his letter. She later thought she might have been imagining things.

Angèle immediately wrote her sister reiterating the need for documentation while also subconsciously hinting at her developing depression. She was homesick and wondered aloud if she hadn't made a mistake by agreeing to leave Lebanon (i.e. get married). She also began what would become her lifelong habit of sending gifts along with her letters. This time it was a bolt of silk cloth she had purchased from a shop down the street from the hotel, which was included in a package with her note.

After mailing the parcel, she decided to have her picture taken to send to her husband and relatives. The photographer that had been recommended was a man named Mathieu on the Boulevard Baille. He posed her standing with her hand on a simple wooden chair in front of a backdrop of flowers shrouded in a bright mist. The photo would be rendered as a postcard, as was customary in that time, and would be ready for pickup the following day.

Angèle liked the picture so much that she ordered six copies. She would send the first one to Toufic and the others to her family and close friends in Lebanon. She took the picture postcards back to her hotel and penned the following inscription to her far away spouse on the back of one of them.

> My heart told me that if my loved ones would like to see me and kiss me, to give them this picture as a present. For if it is difficult for us to be together, this picture is the best gift.

Angèle was a bit shy about the love note to her husband, so she didn't sign

215

her name or mail it as a postcard but put the message in an envelope to keep the inscription from unintended eyes. After posting the letter, she fell into a depression that would last for several days.

As Angèle pressed her worried family more urgently, letters continued to crisscross the Mediterranean on ships passing each other in opposite directions. Her relatives scurried to get the required documents and made several missteps in the process. Papers would be received which wouldn't prove satisfactory, and Angèle would write back asking for the correct documents while chastising her family for not being more careful. Tempers began to fray as her patience, not in abundance to begin with, began to unravel. Her dear friend Zakia had left for Canada in the first week of August, and Angèle's demeanor turned darker as she wondered if she and Emily would be stranded in Marseilles forever.

Zakia's departure served to accent the depth of friendship between the two women. The ambivalence Angèle was experiencing was mirrored in a letter she received shortly after Zakia arrived in Canada.

August 27, 1926
Dear Angèle,
I swear by the sisterhood between us that you haven't been out of my mind one single day. How can I forget the one who is dearer to me than my soul but cursed is the time that separated us. Now each one of us is in a different place after we have been together continuously. I do not suspect your sincerity and I have no doubt that you will keep the friendship of this sister even after a long time of separation.
We have reached Canada safely and met with all our loved ones. I hope that you and Emily will arrive safely, too. This country is very pretty, very civilized and rich. It includes the best of what the combined efforts of nature and human hands can produce. But all that does not lessen the longing I have for my beloved country and for the loved ones whom I miss very much.
Sincerely,
Zakia Sickrey

A week passed before Angèle got another letter from her sister Miriam.

4 September 1926
Dear Sister,
I kiss you from a distance. You have been sending silk. You don't need to do that.
Why didn't you say from the beginning that you needed the signature of the Bishop and the Patriarch? We had sent you the paper as you first asked from Fr. Hanna and Fr. Elias. We did this too. When you receive them call me by phone. Not in French, but in Arabic. Send a copy of the

paper that you prefer more, so that I'll write it to you.

The family's growing frustration with the need for "papers" was becoming more pronounced The appetite of the yawning maw of bureaucracy seemed insatiable to them. Papers were obtained, sent, rejected, and returned, with requests for more.

From her husband, Angèle was also receiving more insistent letters about the need for the proper documentation from Lebanon. She began to feel as if she was being squeezed in a huge bureaucratic vise, and she continued to question her decision to set sail on this marriage voyage. A note from her brother extols his personal efforts at easing her dilemma, and as we will see again and again, seizes the chance to mention his expenses—a recurring theme in his correspondence.

> 6 September 1926
> Dear Angèle,
> Kisses. I received your letter dated August 21. Concerning the papers for the baptism, good conduct and place of birth, etc. I have sent my mother to do that for you. I gave her 10 Syrian pounds for her pocket money and another 10 pounds for the automobile that will take her to Bekirki to get your marriage papers... I would have gone, but I think that my mother is capable of doing it by herself.
> Yousef

Although she still had the company of her sister-in-law Emily, Angèle never spoke of her in the same tones as she did of Zakia. My impression is that she didn't think Emily, or anyone in the Kmeid family for that matter, was her intellectual equal. Over the ensuing years, she often demonstrated that attitude with her other sister-in-law Christine. Angèle was also feeling a little constricted by Emily's presence. The woman apparently took her chaperone's duties a little too seriously for Angèle's liking.

As one might imagine, a group of young ladies touring Marseilles with no obvious male attachments began to draw interest from the eligible bachelors in the Lebanese colony. Not long after Toufic left, males in the commune began approaching Angèle and her companions. There was a well-to-do gentleman by the name of Tobias Steed, staying at the same hotel, who took notice of Angèle. When she heard of his interest, Angèle told her companions to inform him that she was a married woman, but this didn't seem to deter him.

As a young woman who had now convinced herself that she had been abandoned by her spouse of less than four months, Angèle was flattered by the attention. And, as is usually the case in these situations, people began to gossip. Angèle felt it necessary to tell Emily to pay no attention and added that people liked to talk because they didn't have anything better to do. It seems, however, that Emily took notes and relayed her concerns about the goings on in Marseilles to her brother.

The ladies in the group enjoyed having Angèle in their company, both because of her impressive command of French and her Beirut-acquired cosmopolitan demeanor. Only a few of the other ladies were bilingual and most came from small villages in the mountains of Lebanon. They treated her like the sheikha she was and catered to her whims. And, needless to say, Angèle liked it.

One day, the aforementioned Steed approached Angèle as she was pouring yet more letters into the correspondence stream. Steed began by addressing her as Mademoiselle, and Angèle didn't think quickly enough to correct him because she was truly flustered by the encounter. Steed introduced himself and said he couldn't help but notice her around the hotel and wanted to make her acquaintance. Attempts to get a proper introduction through her companions had come to naught. He thought they were protecting her for some unknown reason and added that he was a countryman in transit, as he assumed she was.

Angèle noted that the man was handsome and well spoken but she quickly excused herself and headed for the elevator. The gentleman was not easily deterred as he followed and gently took hold of her elbow. As she turned to look at the man again, a familiar voice called out, "Angèle!"

"Edmond!" Angèle exclaimed. The sudden appearance of her cousin nearly caused her to faint. Edmond spoke sharply to the man holding Angèle's arm, causing him to abruptly release his grip. Steed, confronted by the towering figure of Edmond, saw discretion as the better part of valor, bowed slightly, said goodbye, and quickly withdrew.

Edmond took the man's place with his hand on Angèle's arm and led her to a large sofa in the reception area. The persistent suitor told his cousin that he hadn't been able to eat or sleep since she left. He had heard of her immigration problems and knew her husband had left for the States. "What kind of man would leave you here alone?" he asked. He then added, "To be accosted by strangers?" He explained that he still wanted her to come away with him.

It was an emotional moment, and Angèle was touched by her admirer's ardor and tenacity but said, as she looked around to see who was watching, that she was a married woman now and couldn't possibly entertain entreaties from him. And, had he forgotten what she had said about their families? They would both be disgraced and disowned. She couldn't have that.

Edmond didn't care. He said they would go to Africa where Angèle could get a divorce, and they would then marry. He pleaded for her to come with him.

Angèle became downcast as a rush of mixed emotions took hold of her. She had already begun to question her union with the absentee husband and had her fill of the ensuing bureaucratic nightmare. She thought hard and long before she slowly let words escape from her lips. "No," she said firmly, "my family would be disgraced." And, besides, her husband had gone to great expense for her.

Edmond continued his pleading with a few choice invectives about that peasant husband of hers, whom, he said, wasn't fit to shine her shoes. She couldn't possibly go to live with him and added he couldn't let her do it.

She reiterated her refusals in the gentlest tones possible, saying they had to think of the relatives, especially those in religious life. It would be positively scandalous. "No, no, they could not do it!"

Edmond rose and took Angèle's hand in his and kissed it, holding it as long as he dared under the circumstances. He then bowed, said goodbye, and was gone.

Emily had witnessed this encounter and couldn't wait to report it to her brother. Many years later, in the heat of an argument with his wife, Toufic shouted, "Maybe you should have gone to Africa!" When I asked my mother what he meant, she smiled and told me the story about her last encounter with Edmond el Khazen.

In a letter to Angèle dated 2 November 1926, Miriam verified Edmond's travel plans.

Our cousin Edmond left for Africa and did not tell anyone.

On several occasions while in Lebanon, I tried to verify this story with Edmond's descendants. I found that, after a short sojourn in Africa, Edmond had returned to Lebanon, married and raised a family. Among his progeny was a surviving son named Farouk. Repeated attempts to speak with him proved fruitless. His wife was wary, despite being told that Farouk and I were second cousins through his father's first cousin, my grandmother Adela el Khazen. Lebanon's patriarchical society, I discovered, is so ingrained that maternal relationships are not even documented, much less acknowledged. Family trees record no women's names. This also made my research more difficult.

Nonetheless, my trusty guide Samira Menassa wouldn't give up the hunt for the elusive Farouk. One evening she announced that she had finally found him, and he owned a restaurant in Kaslik. She insisted that we jump in the car and drive down there immediately. It was already past 9:00 p.m., and thinking it was too late, I suggested that we go the next day. "No, no," she declared, "the Lebanese have a tradition of dining late, so this would be the best time to catch him." Thus, off we went to Kaslik to a little restaurant called La Creperie.

When we arrived, Samira marched up to the bar and asked if Farouk el Khazen was about. With a wide smile, she turned to me, and pointing to a diminutive fellow who was seated at a table in the bar area, announced, "There he is!" Frankly, I was elated because all of my previous attempts at making contact with Farouk had ended in failure. I would now get the chance to interview my mother's spurned lover's son. We sat down to speak with Farouk and quickly found that he spoke excellent English due to having spent twenty years in the US as a restaurateur.

I began the interview by relating to Farouk how I had tried in vain to contact him on my previous visits and how happy I was to finally meet him. He said he never knew that I was looking for him. I also related the story of how my Grandmother Adela was taken from the convent and how my mother had gone to the States, etcetera, etcetera. He listened intently and said he found this to be a very interesting story, one he had not heard before. I finally came to the point and asked if he knew what his father had done in Africa after he had left France. He looked surprised and said that to his knowledge his father never went to Africa. It was my turn to be surprised and blurted out, "Edmond el Khazen never went to Africa?" To which he replied, "My father's name was not Edmond!" "Aren't you from Kfar Debiane?" I asked. "No, I'm from Ghosta," he replied.

At this point Samira burst into paroxysms of laughter and exclaimed, "We've got the wrong guy!" Indeed, we had found another man with the identical name, a relative no doubt, but surely not the right one.

Much later I finally met up with Farouk, the son of Edmond el Khazen. It turned out that he didn't speak English, knew nothing about any romance between his father and my mother, and didn't even know that his father was ever in Africa.

The search for truth takes many twists and turns, and this episode proved to be one of them.

# 31

*Pride was the cause of the angel's fall from heaven.*

T HE WAITING GAME IN MARSEILLES CONTINUED, and the ladies busied themselves with trips to shops, the zoo, and the cinema. Things were happening in the world. Rudolf Valentino died shortly after the women saw *Son of the Sheik*. All were saddened but Emily seemed overly distraught, which concerned Angèle.

Locally, the French were abuzz about their currency taking a dive. The franc was under attack, having fallen to 49¢ to the US dollar. This was beneficial to Angèle because the American dollars Toufic was sending her were worth a lot more, although this didn't measurably affect her disposition. Letters from Lebanon tried to calm an obviously dispirited Angèle. The following note from her brother Yousef is one of the most telling in the collection.

11 September 1926
Dear Sister, May God keep you safe,
Kissing you from a distance with affections and longing to see your face.
Dear, I swear by God that I really felt sad for the kind of letters that you have been writing to me. Particularly when you say that you would like to come back to your family if the situation allows and if your family considers you as you were before. You have written a few statements of this kind that broke my heart. Angèle, if you are joking, I am not. And I mean it when I say that I am suffering from missing you. Our separation has depleted my strength, believe this, and if I felt otherwise I wouldn't have said anything. This way you are adding to my sadness, furthermore you compose statements that might be intended as jokes, but in fact these statements become arrows that tear at my heart.
Thank God I am still confident that you have stepped in the right direction. Our hearts are your home wherever you are, and our homes in fact are yours, not ours...
My mother, Miriam, and Khalil are fine and send their kisses. Dahabiya is in Baabda alone... You haven't told me anything clear about Toufic's

221

state of affairs and if he has sent you letters and what he said in them about your travel and when that will be…

Angèle, and we can only guess at how seriously she was entertaining the idea, was considering returning home and asking whether or not her family would take her back as she was (before marriage). There was no doubt that she was in the throes of a deepening depression, and this was obviously distressing Yousef. Cynically, we could say this was because he had a lot riding on the union and wouldn't want to lose his brother-in-law's largess.

Eleven weeks after Toufic had departed, Angèle finally got clearance to book passage to the States. She bid her friends and Emily goodbye as she boarded the train that would take her to Paris and then on to Cherbourg. Emily would arrive in Canada two weeks later.

Ambivalence, the birth of which was mainly due to the prospect of traveling even further from home, bedeviled Angèle. Trying to decide whether to travel east or west had enervated her. And, the train ride through the lovely French countryside did little to assuage her feelings.

In Cherbourg, she boarded the White Star Line's RMS *Homeric*, the same liner Toufic had taken to Europe a year earlier. The ship was making biweekly trips between Southampton, Cherbourg, and New York. The voyage would take six days, arriving at a pier in New York on the evening of September 22. It would be too late to debark, so Angèle would spend the night aboard.

Because she was traveling second class she wouldn't have to process through Ellis Island and was spared the anxiety that the steerage-class immigrants would endure. However, she had a different set of worries—reuniting with a husband that she had been away from longer than they had been together. She also had another concern—she thought she might be pregnant.

*He who marries a girl from a noble family*
*should be able to treat her as well.*

The anxious Toufic drove from Carthage to New York City in his Buick roadster, accompanied by two of his Lebanese compatriots, Tamer Astafan and Aziz Elhage, both of whom owned grocery stores in Carthage. They had come along because they wanted to take in the heavyweight prizefight between Jack Dempsey and Gene Tunney being held the next evening in Philadelphia. In the morning they would take the train to Philly, leaving Toufic by himself to fetch his wife.

At long last the lonesome bridegroom would see his wife again. The next morning he drove his car down to the pier at the mouth of the Hudson River and found the White Star mooring slip. He parked the Buick and walked down the wharf, intending to board the *Homeric*. An agent of the line stopped him, asking where he thought he was going. Toufic explained that his wife was aboard, and he had come to meet her. The agent told him he'd have to wait until she got off. No amount of explanation or exhortation sufficed, and the agent simply repeated that he'd have to wait for her ashore.

Toufic was visibly agitated. He had waited all this time to see his bride, and now she was so near and yet so far. He walked back down the pier along the fence that separated him from the ship. When he had gone about fifty feet he looked back and saw that the agent guarding the passenger gangplank was not looking his way. Seized by impulse, Toufic took matters into his own hands. He jumped onto a shipping crate next to the fence and catapulted himself over the fence to the other side and traversed a passageway being used to off-load luggage. He quickly found his way to the promenade deck and began searching for his wife. After navigating nearly the entire length of the ship, he spotted his bride relaxing on a deck chair, seemingly in no hurry to get off the boat. He sauntered up behind her and gently touched her shoulder. His startled wife turned abruptly to see a grinning man standing behind her.

Angèle was taken by surprise and asked, "Who are you?"

Toufic was shocked and crestfallen as Angèle studied his face. It still hadn't dawned on her that this man was her husband. She began to laugh, much to Toufic's annoyance. "Is it you?" she finally asked.

"Of course it's me!" he answered and reached down, grasped her arms, and lifted her up from the recliner so he could give her an embrace. Angèle rose, seemingly reluctantly, and let Toufic give her a hug and a kiss on the cheek. "I'm sorry," she said, "I didn't recognize you. It's been so long since I saw you."

Toufic was disappointed but smiled and said, "I probably should have sent you my picture so you wouldn't forget me."

Together they found their way down the canvas-covered gangplank to claim Angèle's luggage and get her processed through customs. The gate agent that had frustrated Toufic's first attempt to board the ship lifted his cap and scratched his head while giving Toufic a quizzical look. But he said nothing as the couple passed through the portal at the bottom of the gangplank.

It took less than a half hour for Angèle to be processed since she was one of the last passengers to leave the ship. Her husband, in a role reversal, acted as the interpreter, for Angèle understood barely a word of English. This made her feel uncomfortable, although she knew not why. Toufic took hold of her luggage and led her to his Buick roadster, which was parked on the street. He put her baggage in the rumble seat and drove back to the hotel. They would have the night together and await the return of Toufic's friends the following morning.

Toufic and Angèle got reacquainted over dinner. Angèle tried not to seem overly impressed with New York City. To her, she said, it was not much different from Marseilles or Paris. She wondered about these people Toufic said had came with him and what was this prizefight they went to see. She had heard of such things but couldn't understand why anyone would go to such lengths to attend them.

After dinner Toufic took his wife on a trolley car to Times Square, and they spent an hour or so looking in store windows at, ironically enough, the latest fashions from Paris.

The next morning the fight fans, elated at Gene Tunney's upset of the Manassa Mauler, Jack Dempsey, joined them for the trip home. Toufic had apparently given little thought to how they would all fit in the single-seat roadster for the trip home. Crammed into the front seat of the Buick for the ride back to Carthage, the four travelers began the 350 mile journey over two-lane roads. They started at seven in the morning and were well along the road to Albany when they were jolted by a clattering noise. Toufic pulled over to the side of the road and got out to find that one of Angèle's suitcases attached to the running board had slipped from its restraints and spilled its contents all along the roadside. The bedeviled Toufic and his friends walked up and down the highway, retrieved and re-packed all the items, and re-tied the suitcase to the running board more securely. Angèle suddenly burst into laughter, to the puzzlement of her companions.

How funny it was she would reminisce years later. Here she was jammed into the front seat of a car with three men, two chain-smoking strangers and her husband who was trying to delicately shift gears between her legs, luggage falling off the car, and on an endless trip to only God knew where. There were long, lonely stretches without even a house to be seen, and she thought she was in some godforsaken wilderness. America's landscape was not as pretty as the mountains in Lebanon, she mused.

When they arrived in the village of Carthage, Toufic dropped his companions off and took his wife to the house where they would be staying. It was the same house on Furnace Street, owned by Uncle Nasief, where Toufic had spent his first years in the country. Aunt Sadie was still there, although Christine had long since departed to Tupper Lake. This would be where Angèle would first set up housekeeping in America.

Toufic's relatives greeted the new bride warmly, with kisses on both cheeks. Everyone wanted to know about her trip and any news she had from the old country. The dinner table was set with fine china and silverware for the welcoming feast. Angèle was impressed with her husband's arrangements. Aunt Sadie, who was helped by Tamer's wife, had labored all afternoon preparing a sumptuous meal. The group sat down to a dinner preceded by appetizer dishes that covered the entire table. It reminded Angèle of the finer restaurants in Beirut where *mazza* (appetizer) dishes were a tour de force of dining. Aunt Sadie served several entrees, and the meal concluded with coffee and baklava. It was a most satisfying repast, deliciously prepared and served, and Angèle complimented the two women who had prepared it.

The remainder of the evening was spent with a stream of visitors coming by to pay their respects to the sheikha. Placed at the center of attention of these peasant women with their callused hands and simple clothes, Angèle was in her glory. Her educated use of the Arabic language held her audience's attention, and as a result, a few turned bashful and hesitant to speak. Everyone complimented Toufic on what a lovely bride he had, and how lucky he was. Toufic beamed with pride.

The evening concluded, much to the satisfaction of everyone, including Angèle. After Aunt Sadie retired to her room, Angèle reminded her husband that this wasn't quite what she expected because he had said they would have a home of their own.

Toufic demurred, saying that this arrangement was temporary and that there had been a business setback that he would explain later. Angèle was tired and would postpone thinking about all of this until after she'd had a good night's rest.

When Angèle awoke the next morning, her husband was not in the room. She got dressed and went downstairs, and Aunt Sadie, who was preparing breakfast, mentioned that Toufic had already left for work. She quickly noticed the china and silverware from the previous evening had been replaced with mismatched odds and ends. Aunt Sadie explained that they wanted the reception to be nice for her, the china and silver borrowed for the dinner party, had to be returned that morning. Angèle was taken aback and many of the good feelings she had from the evening before began to evaporate. "We don't even own a good set of dishes," she thought.

The New World's heralded prosperity had begun to lose its luster.

# 32

*A husband is not a flower with which to decorate your head.*

TOUFIC CAME HOME EARLY IN THE AFTERNOON TO LOOK in on his wife. He had arranged with Uncle Seghaan to take the afternoon off in order to show Angèle the town that she was to call home.

Angèle was puzzled that her husband was now talking as if he was partnered with his uncle and not his cousin Naja. Toufic told her it was a long story but that the dry goods business went bankrupt in his absence, and his cousin owed him money from that venture. He had to go back to work with his uncle.

Angèle was curious as to what kind of business it was, and Toufic became evasive, as the moment he dreaded had finally arrived. He said, rather minimally, that they sold newspapers, magazines, and tobacco.

For Angèle the revelations were coming too fast to be absorbed. She asked if there were any more surprises because a) they didn't have their own house, b) he was in a different business than she had been told, and c) a cousin now owed him money. One thing he failed to mention was that, although Naja had agreed to repay him, he had serious doubts he would see the money anytime soon.

Angèle's tone both surprised and disappointed Toufic, and he told her not to worry because he would take care of it. "I'll take care of it," (it came out as "I'll t'kare it") was a phrase that I heard many times over the years from my father. He decided to distract Angèle with the Lebanese custom of visitation, taking his bride around town to meet other members of their community. Toufic explained that the people they would visit were all from his village of Bqaatouta and that, for the most part, were very nice and looking forward to meeting the sheikha.

As he drove his wife around Carthage, Toufic pointed out the few sights of interest. There was State Street, the Hippodrome Theater, and St. James

Church. Toufic neglected to direct her attention to the small store next to the theater where he and his uncle made their living.

After her sojourn in Marseilles, the little upstate New York village of Carthage looked small, and she said so. It would be big enough for them, Toufic said, and continued to drive his bride up and down the various streets and across the Black River to West Carthage. The view when crossing the bridge looked picturesque, and had Angèle been in a better frame of mind, she might even have mentioned that.

Finally, when the touring was done, Toufic stopped at the house of his first cousin Monera, Uncle Seghaan's niece from his mother's side of the family, who was very gracious and highly deferential to Angèle. After the appropriate amount of fawning over the new arrival, she asked if Angèle knew what a scamp her husband was in the old country. She brought up the church bell ringing prank and said that their priest had to take the clapper out of the bell so they could have some peace. Other stories Monera told embarrassed Toufic, and Angèle became aware of how little she really knew about her husband.

Monera then asked if Angèle would be available to write a letter for her to the old country. Angèle was willing to oblige because she knew that literate Lebanese were at a premium in this little town. Her appearance on the scene as an educated member of the community would be warmly welcomed.

The next stop was to see Shukrullah Mobark, who boarded at Aziz Elhage's house. Victoria, Aziz's teenage wife and the "apple" of his eye, was also a gracious hostess and greeted the couple warmly. Angèle was surprised by the stunningly made up, expertly coifed young woman. She certainly didn't look like a peasant girl from Bqaatouta who was discovered by her future husband up an apple tree. Victoria had quickly learned and adopted the intricacies of American beauty products.

The next morning, Angèle wrote several letters to family and friends in Lebanon. As the return correspondence would reveal, her letters didn't succeed in glossing over first impressions of her new surroundings. She then thought to take the letters to her husband's store and have Toufic address the envelopes and post them. The business section of town was only a block's walk from her new residence.

It was a pleasant fall day as the area was enjoying what the natives strangely called "Indian summer." The leaves on the trees, many of which had fallen to the streets, were arrayed in brilliant shades of magenta, red, orange, and yellow.

When she arrived at the main intersection of the town, Angèle saw the traffic to be a mixture of automobiles and a few horse-drawn carts loaded with crates of goods being taken to stores up and down State Street. A policeman stood in the center of the intersection, directing traffic. The large bank on the corner with its huge clock hanging on the side of the stone and brick building was impressive. She had never seen a clock that big, even in France, and checked the time with the petite watch that was pinned to her lapel. It was a few minutes before noon.

She recognized the marquee of the Hippodrome Theater in the distance and headed toward it. Toufic and Seghaan's storefront was rather narrow, and she stopped at the entrance and peered inside. She suddenly recoiled at the sight that greeted her. There was her husband Toufic stooped over in front of an elevated set of chairs...shining some man's shoes!

She turned, and quickly hurried up State Street to get away from the scene she had just witnessed. Slowly regaining her senses, she found herself in front of the St. James Church. She hurried up the long walk and up the steps to enter the church. After dipping her fingers in the holy water font, auspiciously held by a life-size angel, she entered and took a seat in the front pew. The church was cool and effected a tranquility that served to calm Angèle. She knelt to pray.

A middle-aged priest entered the sanctuary and busied himself at the altar, opening the tabernacle and placing a ciborium (a container designed to hold the consecrated wafers for the Eucharist) inside. When he turned to leave he noticed Angèle, the only person in the church. He didn't recognize her as one of his parishioners, so he descended the altar steps and spoke to her. "Hello," he said, "and who might you be?"

"*Je ne parl pas Anglais,*" Angèle responded, stifling a sob.

"Ah," the priest brightened. "*Parlez vous Francais?*"

Angèle was surprised and elated. "*Oui, oui,*" she said. The priest was Fr Alfred H. Valiquette, OSA, originally from Quebec, Canada, and who had become pastor at St. James one month before. He had come to the States to go to college and subsequently joined the Order of Saint Augustine, which serviced the Carthage parish. Thus began a friendship that lasted until the priest's death in 1949. She would even name one of her sons after the priest, and he would also go on to become a priest of the same order.

After a short conversation, Angèle asked the priest to hear her confession. Once inside the booth, she poured out all her frustrations, including what she had just witnessed. She explained how degrading this was and that her husband had deceived her and brought her to America under false pretenses. The priest tried to be consoling and told Angèle he had heard about her husband's business misfortune. "It was not his fault," he said, "He's a good man and there is no shame in shining shoes." He counseled that she should try to adjust to life in America and reach an accommodation with her husband. "Things will get better soon," he said. The confession concluded with a mild penance, which Angèle performed before leaving the church.

Angèle felt that the meeting was providential, and although she was far from mollified, she walked out of the church in a better frame of mind.

Given how often she spoke of it, this event plagued my mother for the rest of her life. My relatives in Lebanon never heard this story and labored under the illusion that their in-law was a "respectable" businessman. Mother always admonished her sons to never shine shoes when tending the store. Like my father, however, earning money was more important to me than disapproval from my mother, so I shined shoes anyway.

*Sheikh Yousef with his second wife, Nahde.*

# 33

*Life is full of misery, and most is caused by women.*

ANGÈLE BEGAN TO SETTLE INTO HER LIFE IN AMERICA, yet she remained concerned with the events taking place in her homeland. Her extravagant brother Yousef was lush with the largesse from his new brother-in-law. Toufic had given him a check for $1,000 and told him the remainder would be forthcoming after he straightened out his affairs in the States. Yousef doled out his riches parsimoniously to his mother and cousin Wadih, as part of the agreed upon finder's fee. They had no idea then that Toufic would not be able to meet the remainder of the obligation.

A problem in which Angèle found herself embroiled was her family's unhappiness with Yousef's affair with the lady Dahabiya. Angèle met the woman when Yousef brought her to her wedding and he never failed to send his sister Dahabiya's regards in his letters. It was also rumored that Dahabiya's mother was not enamored with her daughter's choice of a womanizing, soldier lover.

Dahabiya was a strong-willed woman, not unlike her paramour, who would do whatever her whimsical whims desired. Likes were supposed to repel, and yet again, they defied the laws of physics. The surprise, in Angèle's seeming acceptance of the relationship, is that, in addition to the woman's reputation, the Hobeiches were opposed because of the couple's cohabitation before marriage. That's something that I would have thought that Angèle would definitely never approve of. Perhaps the woman kindled a symbiotic empathy in Angèle's awakening feminine emancipation.

Her brother never failed to include a story about his lover in his letters and even noted her need for notoriety. In one note he wrote,

Kisses… Dahabiya had a tattoo on her arm, she decided to put some acid

233

on it to remove it and burnt her skin. Dahabiya wants to know whether you have received the crochet that she sent you and whether now her work is now famous in New York. If you saw her these days you wouldn't recognize her because she has recently gained so much weight.

Certainly, a Christian woman having a tattoo back then was a bit rare, and being a member of an art colony wouldn't be proper resume material for inclusion in the Hobeiche clan.

When Angèle persisted in asking her family questions about the woman, she was flatly told to discontinue her inquiries. Adela wrote to say,

> I cannot tell you anything about Dahabiya, but if you want me to be your mother do not send her anything and whatever Yousef tells you, do not believe him.

Yousef was undaunted. He wrote Angèle that he was proud of his girlfriend's bravery, as she had repelled robbers one evening while he was away.

> ... some of the people in Marjeyoun thought because I was away from the house and Dahabiya was alone they could rob the house thinking that a woman cannot stop them. Dahabiya wasn't afraid... When she awoke, two of the robbers put their hands over her mouth to strangle or gag her. She immediately grabbed one of them by the testicles and with her other hand took her gun and fired four shots at them. One was wounded and died the next day.
>
> Now she is like a monkey, she thinks she is a heroine and we cannot keep her from practicing shooting every day.

Angèle received a letter six months later wherein Yousef agonizes that Dahabiya was gravely ill. I suspect that he chose to write in French to keep certain prying eyes from reading the contents.

> ... Arriving home I found Dahabiya sick. When I asked her what was wrong, she told me that she had been sick for the past month but did not mention it so as not to upset me. I learned that her illness included a continual loss of blood. I asked the doctor what the cause was and he said that the blood came from a tumor or swelling the size of an egg located at the base of the abdomen.

He continued pouring out the details to his sister as though he had no one else in whom to confide. Yousef recounted the many tests they both endured (they apparently suspected a sexually transmitted disease) and said the results showed no illness. An ominous note was sounded when the doctors recommended the start of sixty-seven days of radium and radiation therapy. The saga continued

234

for a few more months with periods of optimistic remission.

Angèle then learned that her brother had married Dahabiya quite suddenly when Miriam wrote,

> We hope Khalil will be next to marry because Yousef is already married. What a shame. I'll write you more about it. Do not ever send them anything, neither to him nor to the lady. He is upset with Khalil because he told him, 'Who is this woman whom you married?'

Yousef was reportedly still on good terms with his mother—at least for the time being. But Miriam and Khalil were very upset with him and Angèle's sister cautioned her not to say anything.

> He does not write to me and I do not write to him. Do not ever tell Yousef I've told you anything about this affair.

The optimism that Yousef expressed to Angèle was short-lived and soon Dahabiya was again gravely ill. Yousef "made an honest woman of her," Angèle later commented about his marriage to Dahabiya shortly before her death. The Hobeiche family had no regrets that this affair was finally over. Her sister Miriam wrote,

> We know nothing except what you tell us. My mother's comment was that four devils came to take her body and her spirit. She thought they were thieves.

Angèle's brother Khalil wrote a one-liner claiming that he was glad they were "finished" with Dahabiya. This comment exemplifies the depth of negative feeling the family had toward the woman.

Angèle, however, displayed a sense of Christian charity that the rest of the family seemed to lack. Among her saved correspondence was a letter from Fr Toubia Turk acknowledging the receipt of a $5 mass offering for the repose of Dahabiya's soul.

# 34

*A rightful claim does not die with the passage of time.*

THE LETTERS FROM HOME ARRIVED IN CARTHAGE AT their greatest frequency in the period between 1926, the time of Angèle's arrival in the US, and 1930. Angèle's sister Miriam penned most of the notes for her mother, and their frequency made me wonder how a professed nun managed to have so much free time to be at home to write letters and care for her mother. Angèle was constantly worried about Adela and was anguished over her inability to do more to help. Money, a commodity that people in the religious life were supposed to forsake, seemed to be on Miriam's mind, nearly as much as it was on her brother Yousef's.

Angèle had a lot of other things to worry about during this period. There were continuing problems with her sister-in-law Emily, her husband's occupation and lack of earning power, and the possibility that she might again be pregnant (her first pregnancy ended in a miscarriage).

Adding to Angèle's worries was the land dispute that arose after her Uncle Rashid's death. The family regent, who saw them through the war years, was wise enough to see that his nephew Yousef was not to be entrusted with family property. "Yousef has never had money that he does not need," his sister Miriam once wrote. Thus Rashid's will deeded one of the Kattine houses to Yousef's younger brother Khalil.

Fabiana, Rashid's sister, claimed that her brother gave her the property on his deathbed and she initiated a long and acrimonious dispute to confirm her claim. The case was finally settled in Khalil's favor, but not without creating a lot of bad blood. Angèle, who followed this dispute from afar, could finally subtract this item from her long worry list.

Angèle, however, remained gloomy over her circumstances in the "Promised Land" of America. Her letters to family and friends had gone from qualified optimism to outright despair. She continued communicating with her friend

Zakia in Canada, and in one letter, enclosed a note from her brother Yousef. The newly minted second lieutenant was having a time of it in South Lebanon with the fractious Druze. He had been involved in skirmishes where he was wounded in a narrow escape.

Zakia to Angèle, 22 October 1926 – By a happy hand I received your letter and I thanked God that you are in good health along with your husband whom I respect as I do you. I have read in your letter your kind words that were like medicine to the wounds of my broken heart...

Angèle never forgot her fear of the Druze during the 1925-26 revolt and often said, "If it were not for the French, they would have killed us all." And from the letters, we see that Zakia also shared those feelings.

Haven't they [the Druze] been satisfied with all the innocent blood that they have shed? But they are still at their wrongdoing, they have eyes but do not see, they have ears but do not hear. Haven't they seen how many thousands of men have been killed and how many homes have been destroyed? Haven't they heard the screaming of women and children? But their belief is that they will be reborn in China [an allusion to the Druze belief in reincarnation]...

Angèle was proud of her brother's exploits, though she would never admit this to him. She would, however, not be hesitant to bask in his perceived glory, and Zakia's comments about his heroism helped her do that.

Angèle you should be happy that your brother is safe. Truly he is to be thanked and remembered for his courage. I am proud of my courageous brother in religion who defended his country and his people.... I read your brother's letter in front of some of my compatriots who happened to be here at our place. First, they were very happy for his safety. Secondly, they said in one voice long live the brave man who loves his country.

The two women also commiserated about their unhappiness. At this point we don't know why Zakia seemingly suffered the same anxieties and second thoughts as Angèle. The first of December brought a surprise letter from Zakia's father that revealed the source of the woman's despondency.

Yousef Butrus Sickrey to Angèle, 26 November 1926 – Zakia will soon be in your rank. i.e. married... Zakia will be getting married soon to a young man, Toufic Haddad, from Rashaya, [the same hometown in South Lebanon as Zakia's] but he was born in this country. We would love very much for you to attend the wedding of your friend. Zakia told me that you are her dearest friend...

This letter came as a surprise to Angèle because Zakia had not previously talked about marriage. A letter soon followed from Zakia that begins with a poem, a common device used by Lebanese letter writers of the period.

> *From Sudbury I send my regards*
> *From Sudbury I show my respect*
> *From Sudbury I send my longing for you*
> *  the daughter of my great country*
> *My immigration has lasted long, Angèle*
> *While others enjoy it over my unhappiness*

> Dear Angèle,
> I tell you that my soul is very unhappy to the degree of death. But I have to drink that cup, hoping that God will take it away from me because I hate to drink it. I keep praying. I have even fasted three days in honor of the Virgin Mary hoping that God will answer my request and will have mercy on me and will see my tears that fall on my cheeks like the dew on Mt. Hermon…
> Your friend the miserable Zakia Sickrey

When Zakia's family in Canada was asked about this letter, they were thoroughly surprised. From all they had observed and knew, Zakia had a happy marriage, blessed with several children, and lived a long and fruitful life. I suspect Zakia's family felt the same about my mother.

A letter dated a year and a half later from Sudbury, Ontario, told of continuing unhappiness and longing for the homeland. Both women had given birth to their first child, Zakia to a boy and Angèle to a girl. It is patently obvious from the correspondence that we have two sympathetic souls commiserating with each other. The language between the friends was uninhibited, even at times sounding like communications between lovers. Zakia's poetry, like most poems and sayings in foreign languages, loses the beauty of rhythm and rhyme when translated into English. Her writings often referred to Christ and the Virgin, giving voice to a profound religious belief.

> I kiss you from the distance with longing that cannot be described, and I offer you my love that is coming from an anxious heart, anxious to see your beloved face. I have received your kind letter carrying to me verses of love and friendship, which indicates your love, so I rejoiced when I learned that God has given you and your baby daughter good health. I thanked Him for his generosity:

> *If I had to describe you with my pen*
> *  it would betray me,*
> *And my tongue will not be able*

239

*to count all your good qualities.*
*Your good deeds are continuous*
*and your kindness is always fresh.*
*May God keep you in good health, happiness and safely.*

Dear friend, you have mentioned that I might not like long letters. Why not, especially since your talk is like honey coming from your mouth and like the sweet fragrance of basil that permeates the air and like medicine for my wounds. Let us each give time its due and let our hearts whisper to each other...

From her prose and poetry I see many of the same characteristics that I saw in my mother. I could easily understand why they became such close friends.

As time passed, the letters became less and less frequent as distance and familial obligations inevitably superseded the bonds of friendship. Communications were reduced to the obligatory Christmas card and news of great import, such as births, deaths, and war. Almost exactly fifty years after they first met, Angèle made the trek to Canada for a last visit with her friend, where they had the opportunity to reminisce about times past, something both women enjoyed immensely.

Unfortunately, according to her daughter-in-law Claudette Haddad, all of Zakia's personal possessions, including photographs, letters and documents, were lost when the basement of her home was flooded during an extremely cold winter, when the water pipes burst. Otherwise we might have had access to some of the letters Angèle had sent to her.

Zakia's life concluded on January 29, 1998, a few weeks shy of her eighty-eighth birthday.

# 35
## *To expect death is worth than death.*

ANGÈLE'S COMPLAINTS TO HER FAMILY CONTINUED TO mount. The winter weather in Carthage, although brutal at times, certainly was not worse than the damp cold of Kattine. Her empathetic mother, responding to her daughter's continued pining for home, was feeling her misery from afar.

> Miriam to Angèle, 2 November 1926 – ...I received your letter yesterday, but this time we were not happy because you say 'I wish I were in Kattine, how pretty Kattine is.' We do not know why you say that. Is it because of the cold weather there? Are you upset with someone or is it because you miss us? We do not know. Please tell us what is making you so upset. When you say such things you make us worry. Your mother does not need this. Whenever your name is mentioned she sheds tears. Are you lonely and have no one to keep you company?
> Now we would like to know why you are unhappy. Is it because of the snow and cold? I cannot say more now because I am busy making you a tablecloth...

Angèle was unhappy about her husband's occupation and couldn't bring herself to tell her family the source of her discontent.

Miriam, meanwhile, seems to have been contemplating leaving the convent for a romance with the widowed postal worker Francis Yahyoushi, who was giving the Hobeiche family special attention. He delivered letters and made sure packages weren't tampered with or stolen. Angèle vehemently disapproved of Francis' interest in Miriam, so much so that it caused the sisters to become estranged for a short time.

> Miriam to Angèle, [no day/month], 1927 – When you first left, I used to worry who was going to send me blue paper [carbon paper used in making embroidery patterns], but God does not forget anyone. He sent me Francis who is always bringing carbon paper. He even sends me designs but the poor guy, his wife died. Now he is looking for a bride.

Taking women for brides from religious environments, as we saw with Adela, was hardly unheard of in Lebanese society. In a letter that arrived after the start of the New Year in 1928, it is obvious that Angèle had heard rumors of the potential relationship between Miriam and Francis. In fact, I don't think Angèle ever really approved of her father's method of courtship either, even though she was a product of that union.

In one letter Miriam scolds Angèle for not referring to Francis by name. This would have been typical behavior for Angèle—not speaking in the first person of people she didn't like or of whom she didn't approve. Her dissatisfaction seemed to stem from the rumor that Miriam and Francis had gotten engaged, which it turned out, wasn't true.

But, after hearing the gossip, Angèle, as she often did, vented her displeasure by penning some denigrating remarks to her friends, this time about the smitten Francis. The commentary ultimately reached the offended man's ears, and he felt compelled to respond. Francis wrote,

> ...I have read the letter you have sent to your sister, and I understood all that was in it. For that, I will answer that my mother's milk is good and I come from a good origin...

That was the last anyone heard from Francis, although Angèle later learned from her sister that he eventually remarried.

A letter to Toufic carries the first mention of a serious health problem for Miriam. She was put in the hospital with a "stomach ailment" and returned home to recuperate for three weeks. The doctors didn't know what was causing her abdominal pain. Adela to Toufic,

> ...The doctor thought she had appendicitis, but it wasn't that. It was only a small problem with her kidneys. Now she is better.

Five weeks later Miriam sends a short note telling Angèle,

> ...I haven't been feeling well but now am feeling better, thank God...

With all the correspondence that told of the illnesses of Angèle, Miriam, Adela, and even Khalil, no one was prepared for what came to pass in the spring of 1929. The initial letter informing Angèle of the tragedy is not in the collection, but her response to the news evoked the following from Adela.

> Adela to Angèle, 17 April 1929 – My dear daughter Angèle, God protect her from all evil.

After kissing your eyes many times with anxiousness and warm tears, I tell you that I received your letter to Yousef and me. I was alone in the house and felt bad to know that you are feeling depressed for the death of Miriam. She broke my heart. Nothing can compensate for her loss for me. But God chose her and my only consolation is you and your brothers, hoping that I'll die between your arms. Yes, it is a great catastrophe. This is how she died:

It was the first night of Christmas Lent. We gladly stopped eating meat. Around mid-night, Miriam felt a pain in her stomach and had a strong nervous attack. We called the priests and nuns but then she felt better. They went back to their rooms, but then she felt pain another time, so we called a doctor. But she died shortly after leaning on my chest at 4 a.m. Later we understood that she had appendicitis. [Originally diagnosed as such nine months earlier but dismissed by another doctor who said it was kidney stones.]

Two bishops came to her funeral. She was young [twenty-six years of age]. Everybody in Ghazir cried for her and attended her funeral. I have submitted to God and asked him to give me patience. I know that Miriam is in the lap of Mary and Jesus. Please pray for her. I would like you to accept God's will and to endure and be patient. We Christians should not feel sad when we lose someone. God created us, so as to live for him and die for him and to receive eternal happiness in the kingdom of heaven...

One tragedy followed another in this family, and it made one wonder what was coming next.

# 36

*That which is hidden is that which never takes place.*

THE HOBEICHE FAMILY GENUINELY LIKED TOUFIC'S sister Emily, whom they met during her brother's courtship of Angèle. She was quite often mentioned her in their early letters. Adela, Miriam, and even Zakia, who had only made her acquaintance in France, also inquired about her. Angèle, however, didn't seem interested in reporting Emily's circumstances as seen from the absence of commentary.

How Emily survived the famine and plague during World War I that slew the rest of her family is a mystery that I was never able to unravel. Toufic had begrudgingly let his surviving sister tag along with him and his new bride as they traveled from Lebanon to France. Angèle's reticence, when questioned about her sister-in-law, was but one indicator that she was unhappy about the situation. Both she and her husband had noticed Emily's increasingly odd behavior, but once the journey began there wasn't much they could do about it.

Then, suddenly and without warning, Emily's name disappears from the correspondence. From the few stories that were passed down about the woman, I deduced that there was great consternation about her personal behavior. Emily had emigrated to Canada under the auspices of a Lebanese priest there. She remained in Montreal for some fifteen months until Toufic traveled north to smuggle her into the States, to live with him and Angèle in Carthage. When stopped at the border, he recalled with a chuckle, "I told them she was my wife." Once in Carthage, the atmosphere soon soured, and Toufic sent her to live with sister Christine, who was now in Tupper Lake, New York. However, even the mild-mannered Christine, who had since remarried, couldn't abide Emily's bizarre behavior. "Emily," Christine said, "claimed we were trying to poison her." An exasperated Christine sent her back to Toufic.

In those days mental illness was something that families were ashamed of and tried to hide. As a youth, I remember visiting a Lebanese family who had a mentally disabled child. The young girl burst into the living room unannounced, much to the consternation of her parents. Her father scolded the girl and promptly banished her to a room hidden from view. It didn't take long for me to understand that families concealed such misfortunes because they thought it somehow reflected badly on their bloodline.

After discussion with his immediate family, Toufic agreed that Emily belonged in a mental institution, and he had her committed to the state mental facility in Ogdensburg, New York. A problem soon arose when authorities discovered that Emily, as an undocumented alien, was not entitled to institutional care at state expense. Because the immigration laws were specifically designed to keep out people who might become wards of the state, Emily was not eligible for permanent residency either. She had been in the States a total of only three months and would now have to be sent back to Canada.

Toufic was unable to return Emily to Montreal due to the press of business and his wife's condition—she was about to deliver her first child. He persuaded Shukrullah Mobark, who, had business in Detroit, to take Emily with him and escort her back to Canada.

However, once in Montreal, Emily faced the same problem she had in the US, that of becoming a ward of the state, so her sponsors were forced to send her back to Lebanon. Upon arrival, she trekked up the mountains to Bqaatouta to the house where she was born. She must, even in her diminished capacity, have been eager to see and experience the familiarity of her ancestral home, the home she had shared with her departed parents and siblings.

When I was in Bqaatouta, I asked cousin Amin Kmeid if he remembered Emily. Indeed he did and told me some of the problems she encountered upon her return.

Bad news travels fast in the villages of Lebanon, and all of Bqaatouta soon heard about Emily's sickness. When she returned home, the cousins who had taken over the house denied her entry. They claimed that Emily had a contagious disease that could be communicated to their children, and didn't want her anywhere near them. The lady of the house drove Emily away— once by pelting her with stones.

Thus, Emily became a homeless person in her hometown. She roamed the town, sometimes sleeping in stables or out of doors, completely at the mercy of benevolent townspeople. Mercifully, for Emily, this situation would last only a few months.

An excuse one could offer for this cruel behavior is that ignorance, superstition, and the lack of medical knowledge in 1930 didn't permit rational behavior when confronted with mental illness. However, as we see time and again, even in America today the mentally ill are turned out and made homeless, and this seems to have been no different in Lebanon. Soon, word of Emily's plight reached Kattine, and Yousef wrote a letter from his St. John's Hospital bed where he was recovering from an accidental gunshot wound to the leg.

> Every time I decide to go up and bring Emily back with me something tragic happens. I haven't seen Malik [Toufic's first cousin and best man at his wedding] for a month now, and we were both planning to go to Emily. Imagine what bad luck.

The next time we hear about Emily is in the following letter, which details the tragedy.

> Yousef to Angèle & Toufic, 14 August 1930 – My dear sister and brother-in-law, Concerning the will and registration of property [in reality Toufic's property], this is the story: The late Emily did not write a will when she was alive. After her death a will does not become useful because no one believes that the dead can write a will. What I have heard and what I am still trying to find out is that when Emily died, they kept her body at home [could it be that they were no longer worried about contagion?] for a while. During that time, a woman went to court and said that she was Emily Kmeid and would like to sell her property to the man who accompanied her (I do not know his name and do not want to know). They brought in witnesses to verify that the impersonator was Emily Kmeid, and the sale was carried out. I am still trying to verify the truth of this story. But I am doing this slowly and secretly. It does not matter how long it takes, because once we find the truth the perpetrators will face imprisonment.
>
> Emily couldn't have written a will because she was mentally ill. This is why she was sent back from the U.S. [and Canada]. Doctors here said the same thing about her mental health as doctors in America. Even if she had written a will, it would be neither valid nor legal. They had to bring in an impersonator to consummate the deed.
>
> I wrote to you about Emily's death earlier in this letter and I report to you now that her ailment was tuberculoses in the brain. In her last days I used to visit her regularly in the hospital. I even asked her to come and stay with us in my home, but she would not accept. I gave her some money (from God and from you). Tuberculosis of the brain is not contagious [apparently Yousef heard of the reasons her relatives gave to deny her entry]. She went back to Bqaatouta when I was in the Bekaa near the Syrian boarder on a military mission and had to stay there for a

while. There I heard about her going to Bqaatouta, but when I returned I learned that her relative kicked her out of the house and he and his wife did things that no one would do to his enemy [stoned her]. I wrote a letter to Wahib's wife telling her that I did not want to write to Wahib so that he can't say he has a lot on his mind. I told Nahia [Wahib's wife] that I was writing to her because I know that she is wise and loving and told her to go to Toufic's cousin and to tell him to take Emily back home and to put her on his head [be responsible for her] and on his wife's head otherwise I will go up and break his head and his wife's head. Nahia's answer to my letter came with the solution saying that Emily died before she received my letter. Her death was caused mainly by her sickness in addition to the maltreatment and suffering that those people inflicted on her. Then what did you want me to do after she was dead and buried? Now it is her brother's [Toufic's] turn to act and to deal with his own people, because if I do, I will go up and give them a beating for what they did. Along with the witnesses, they will be sentenced from 5 to 15 years imprisonment. I wonder if they did this on their own or they were incited by someone else to do it. I hope to be able to tell you more about this story and to verify the truth and to find out how it really happened.

Emily had passed away, and as Yousef relates, the vultures swooped in to pick over her bones while the body was still warm. Emily had taken all the abuse this earth could offer and gave up her spirit in the month of July 1930. She was twenty-five years of age.

When I was sitting in Amin Kmeid's parlor listening to this story, he told me of the appearance of a mysterious glow from atop the makeshift grave where Emily was laid to rest. He claimed it was an apparition that was visible intermittently, and I couldn't help wonder if those people who had mistreated the poor woman cringed in fear.

Thus, the saga of Emily's demise was added to the tragic ledger of obituaries that both families were accumulating.

*Brothers Khalil & Yousef Hobeiche.*

# 37

*The son of the brother becomes the enemy of the sister.*

THE RELATIONSHIPS BETWEEN THE HOBEICHE SIBLINGS were intricate and passionate. Each of the members of this Lebanese clan had their own perceptions, frustrations, and prejudices that would often clash and cause dissention. The enigmatic Khalil, the youngest of the four, appears and disappears regularly in the correspondence.

Adela had a special affection for her youngest child, certainly not uncommon in many families, regardless of ethnicity. When I inquired of the few Hobeiche elders in Lebanon that remembered Khalil, they spoke of his physical prowess—greater than his brother Yousef they said. The premium placed on physical strength is common in societies like the one found in the Lebanese mountains.

Growing up during the war, Khalil was deprived of schooling between the formative years of eight and thirteen. Subsequent to the war, the family was struggling to make ends meet, so he went to work instead of returning to school. At times he made self-effacing comments about his not being as well-schooled as Angèle, saying,

> ...If something is omitted in my letters, I should not be blamed, because I am not as educated as you are, but I blame you for omissions in your letter...

Despite disparate personalities and an obvious sibling rivalry, Yousef often extolled Khalil's strength, such as in this letter to Angèle.

> Tell him [Angèle's eldest son Delor] also that his Uncle Khalil lifted two pipes of the IPC [Iraqi Petroleum Company] each one weighed one-ton for which the Manager of the company in Homs [a city in Syria] gave him a hundred dollars. Tell him also that Khalil used to lift his truck when it was fully loaded.

The brothers did come together, however, in opposition to their relatives in the quarrel that arose about a plot of land in the Hobeiche compound after Uncle Rashid's death. The dispute was resolved in Khalil's favor, even though it took several years to adjudicate. The rift between the relatives endured for many years, and those on our limb of the family tree gleefully trumpeted their victory when the dispute was finally settled. Yousef wrote,

> ...Fabiana [Yousef's aunt and litigator] fainted and had to be carried out to the car. Now she is still sick and I hope she will die soon and Sheikh Eugene [another relative] will attend her funeral and will eat a big meal at the table at the home of Rizkalla [Fabiana's husband]. He will be breaking bread as much as he wants and the eyes of your Uncle Rizkalla will be wide open watching. Can you imagine Yousef sitting there breaking bread and ordering people around and Rizkalla crouching in the corner crying?

The rocky relationship between the overbearing Yousef and the gentle Khalil struggled to endure. Angèle and Miriam clearly sided in favor of Khalil, the baby of the family, and they always mentioned him fondly in their letters. Angèle received a photograph from Khalil showing the stern-looking brothers—who had apparently declared a temporary truce and looked none too happy about it.

In another note, Yousef writes with his caustic sense of humor, again complaining about Khalil.

> ...What shall I tell you about Khalil, he is the heir to Assad [an uncle who reportedly left the religious life, got married, and fled to Palestine]. Asaad now wears a nightgown made of red material and has a hole in it where he puts his head through, and when Khalil comes to Kattine, he is going to be wearing a shirt made of sackcloth embroidered with old rubber tires [not sure what this metaphor means].

Khalil acquired a trucking business that took him far from home, to places such as Iran and India. He mentioned working for the British owned Iraqi Petroleum Co., but we do not know in what capacity. The first letter he sent to Angèle after her arrival in America was actually dictated to Yousef— apparently at one of those times when they were on speaking terms.

But, in the next letter, he is apparently on the outs with Yousef again, and asserts his pride in the lineage he bears.

> ...I want to tell you a piece of good news and that is Sheikh Yousef Namatallah Hobeiche [a sarcastic reference to his brother] wrote me a

letter blaming me for not visiting him when I was in Beirut. He also asks me about all that happened. My answer to him was better than his letter to me and was that my brotherly love to him is still there. But such subservience I do not approve of as long as I retain my honor and consider myself Khalil, the son of Sheikh Namatallah Hobeiche. All I desire is his good welfare. That was my letter to him...

Khalil's feuding with older brother Yousef continued for several years. Although away from home for long periods and an infrequent letter writer, Khalil still found time to complain about his brother's follies—his extravagant spending, domineering ways, and even about his ideas concerning marriage. In February 1933 he wrote,

> Nine months ago when I was in Persia I sent you a number of letters, but did not hear from you at all. I am not blaming you but Yousef *did not leave us any brains in our head* [a Lebanese idiom meaning drove us crazy] so as to know what to do... We were hardly through with Dahabiya when we fell into Hourieya [a rhyme that abases both the departed Dahabiya and the home of Nahde Hobeiche, the girl Yousef married a year after his first wife died]...
>
> If Yousef writes anything to you do not say anything at all, but send us a family picture so as to please my mother. I told Yousef that I was thinking of getting married. He was furious and really angry. Now I am asking you what do you think? It does not matter what he thinks...

Although quite common among siblings, we see in the correspondence from both brothers how neither approved of the other's choice of female companionship. Khalil was not fond of either of Yousef's wives and apparently—despite his earlier claims of wanting to get Khalil married to keep him out of trouble—Yousef objected to Khalil's love interest. Khalil, despite his claims of not caring what his brother thinks, goes to great lengths to keep his affairs secret from him. Their mother Adela did not approve of any of her prospective daughters-in-law either (an inclination mimicked years later by Angèle with her own sons). That Khalil would listen to his mother in affairs of the heart contrasts the brothers even more. Yousef, on the one hand, didn't care a whit what his mother thought about his choices, while Khalil seems to be overly sensitive to her wishes.

Angèle's expressed desire to return to Lebanon, due to her continuing homesickness, was quite unnerving to Khalil, and he enthusiastically endorsed the idea. He offered to pay her way if money was a problem. Angèle was expecting her fourth child at the time.

From time to time Khalil had complained about being ill, but never mentioned specifics. Angèle finally received her last letter from him, which contained foreboding news about his health. He writes,

> ...I had written to you [last] from Kirmanshah telling you that I was going home, and as usual, did not go. This delay is from God. Since that date up till now I have been at the American Hospital for an operation. Thank God the operation was successful, but now I am not working, and I won't be doing anything for a while...

None of the relatives in Lebanon know what his ailments were, not that there wasn't a good deal of speculation. Cousin Namatallah said that Khalil was spying for the English and had been poisoned, but there is no substantiation for this surmise.

In early 1939, Khalil perished at the youthful age of thirty-three years, just ten years after his sister Miriam's death. He lived on in the correspondence even though his reputed Herculean strength failed him in the end. Yousef wrote in May of that year,

> I thank you for your letter and for asking about us all. Khalil, you did not ask about him. Have you forgotten that we have a brother who gets upset if you do not ask about him? I tell you he is resting in peace and happiness. You ask me to continue to pray for his soul, I agree with you but our prayers cause constant suffering for us and are a menace to God because He does not want to listen to us, neither when we are thanking nor when we are praising. If He wanted to listen to our prayers, He would have listened to that poor and desperate woman whom we both know has suffered so much with us and how often she carried you and Khalil on her loving wings and flew in the countries of God and thanked God for keeping you near her.
> In answer to her thanks to God, He snatched from her Miriam and Khalil when she had just opened her eyes on them. This means that God punished her for her prayers and for her suffering. It was a punishment like the way that people punish the criminal by hanging, and hanging is less painful than Adela's catastrophe. You, you know how much Adela suffered because you were with her while I was wandering around, totally crazy and uncaring: a child who neither knows nor understands. In spite of all that, I shall pray and pray until God has mercy on me and takes me away from this world. How can I enjoy life after losing Khalil?

The family grieved over Khalil's passing even more than that of his sister Miriam. I distinctly remember the event because I saw my mother weeping uncontrollably while sitting in the stairwell of our home, death letter announcement in hand. She did not say what was wrong, but the news seemed to drain the life out of her. In some way she blamed Yousef for Khalil's demise. He had taken advantage of his younger brother by misappropriating his money, and she felt that the lad had to work much harder because of it, contributing to his ill health and untimely death. Yousef, trying to bury his grief, threw himself into his work.

Yousef to Angèle, July 23, 1939 – My dear, in justice neither my family nor I can remember anything or deny anything that Khalil did for himself or us. The matter is in the hands of Him, in whose hands our souls are also held.

My dear, since January I am depressed and I'd love to run away from home so that I will not have to hear or remember. I ask to be sent to far away places like the Alawite [region in Syria] area or any other place. Here I am now at the Cedars in B'sharry. I came with some soldiers who are now busy opening a road that will connect B'sharry with Baalbek. By God I work at digging harder than they do so that I will tire myself out and forget everything, but the memories are dragged along and stay with me.

Yousef continues his lament when describing the receipt of a colorized picture of his departed brother, sent to him by Angèle, who had it retouched by photo studio in the States.

Today as I was sitting in my tent, writing and keeping busy, I saw the mailman bringing me a parcel. I recognized it before I received it. The minute I saw the word glass on it I immediately understood what was inside it and my eyes froze and my heart jumped. The mailman, a soldier, was frightened and jumped back while the signature book fell from his hand. I then regained my senses and signed his book and asked him to leave me in peace. I opened the parcel, which was wet with my tears. I removed the picture, put it aside and would not look at it. Now it is the end of the day and the picture is on the bed. I will send it to be put facing the other picture, which I have framed so that no matter which way we look we see what we are glad not to talk about its details...

Years later, Yousef continued to write about the departed Khalil.

Let us go back to your letter where you were surprised at how much weight I have lost and how I have changed. You are right I have changed very much. But think, now I am fifty years old and I have been a soldier running around suffering and enduring for thirty-one years. In addition to this, the death of Khalil took a heavy toll on me.

Thirty-one years of running between the countries of the east, wounds and suffering in addition to Khalil's death. Khalil's death left me alone suffering. I miss the light of his face, his strong arms, his beautiful youth, his rare sense of helping and giving. That alone should change my shape and my figure.

But, as we have seen, death was a frequent and premature visitor to the Hobeiche and Kmeid families. Khalil was only the latest to be added to the long ledger of bereavement.

*Adela el Khazen Hobeiche.*

# 38
*The man makes the money, but the woman builds the home.*

ADELA EL KHAZEN HOBEICHE PROBABLY DIDN'T THINK her life was terribly notable, even though she came from a notable family. Her unanticipated marriage was not made in heaven. And, despite her obvious religious fervor, the combination of upbringing, social mores, and extenuating circumstances, caused her to experience great frustration in life. The conditions Adela and many others faced during World War I were abominable. The marvel of it all was that she managed to survive with her immediate family intact, all without the aid of her husband, while 50% of the Lebanese population perished.

When Adela's children wrote about their mother, they lamented that she was doing things that she oughtn't be doing. On one occasion Miriam had written to Angèle,

> ...I think I told you she fell after she picked the silk cocoons [from the boughs hung on the walls of the cellar]. But God was merciful in that I was home. Otherwise, no one would have found her...

Adela would have been fifty years old at that writing, certainly not elderly by twenty-first century standards, but, after a life of comparative hardship, not as spry as she might have been. Six weeks later she reportedly fell again, this time from a grape vine. (Many grape vines in Lebanon are taller than trees, winding their way upwards to the roofs of two and three-story homes. Some have been pruned and nurtured for hundreds of years.)

The death of Miriam, who looked after her, and Khalil, who provided her main financial support, greatly grieved Adela. Now these duties fell to Yousef, who was busy with his military career and pursuing pleasures of the flesh. Her remaining daughter, Angèle, was 6,000 miles away, married to a man whom she'd presumed was wealthy but was not, and pining to return home.

After Miriam's death, Angèle became unceasingly concerned about her mother's welfare and Yousef's ability and willingness to care for her. Adela, despite counseling Angèle to adhere to the patrimonial conventions of their culture, had a mind of her own. There was bound to be friction between her and Yousef as both had strong-willed personalities. And, we find Yousef quite often put in the position of defending himself and intimating that his mother was too difficult to cope with. Often times Adela stayed with Yousef and his family, but she never seemed pleased with the arrangement. Yousef writes to Angèle,

> You ask me to take care of my mother, and not to leave her alone, and to find someone to take care of her if she refuses to stay with us and decides to live alone in the house. This is a new problem that is very difficult for me to solve when you know well that I am able to solve any problem no matter how difficult it is. Problems are usually solved by a lie or by the truth, by goodness or by ugliness, by trickery or by frankness, but your mother's problem cannot be solved except by the devil when he takes my soul and saves me.

But it seems that Yousef had reason to be exasperated with his seemingly capricious mother.

> My mother [Adela] left us and went to Kattine in October and we do not know how or why she left because she does what she wants. She gets upset whenever she wants to and then gets pleased by herself and for no apparent reason. I bought her clothes in Baalbek at a time when my financial situation was not so good. She returned them saying that she did not need them. Then she began saying that I do not buy her any clothes, so I bought her a coat and a suit of the best material. She said that I cheated her because the material was of a low quality so I returned them to the store and Nahde [Yousef's second wife] and I took her to the market by force so that she could choose whatever pleased her. She bought a dress for 360 piasters [$1.20] to the meter, but when we got home she said that she wished she had kept the ones I had bought her before. So once again I returned what she had bought, after a big quarrel with the merchant. After that she ran away. A month ago I went home to take there a hundred olive plants and saw her in the house. I gave her a few piasters, not much, and came back without asking her any questions. I do not know whether she is coming back to us or not.

The intimation, of course, is that Adela is suffering from dementia, which for a woman in her early fifties is certainly premature. Yousef's mother was obviously stubborn and hard to please, a trait we might assume contributed to her husband's migration to the US. Such behavior is not uncommon among depressed and unhappy people entering their senior years, although I sometimes wonder if this was not a genetic Hobeiche or el Khazen trait. My mother exhibited those same characteristics, well before reaching fifty years of age.

Adela's letters, perhaps filtered by the writers she employed, do not betray any diminished capacity, but she does talk of other physical ailments, and also laments growing old. The much-discussed reunion between Adela and Angèle in America had become impractical because of Adela's advancing age. And it was unlikely that Angèle could return to Lebanon as she was raising five children in a rented house during the Great Depression.

Adela continued to hold out hope that her daughter would return to her native land, and Khalil's death made her yearning even stronger.

Adela to Angèle, May 30, 1939 – Concerning your coming here, I am waiting by the hour, and I am worried about the expenses that this will incur. But I do not know what to do because I miss you very much. I'll just leave it to God and he will take care of you. May He inspire you to do what is best for you…

Yousef's frustration with Adela was mounting, although his children, Marie, Namatallah, and Jouhaina, seem to be fairing better with their grandmother than he.

…Everyday the children force her to eat what is good for her and they make her go to bed on time. They take her places. Namatallah [Yousef's son and father's namesake] and his sisters know what she likes more than we do. Whenever he comes home from school he tells her, grandma I am working hard at school, but I forget that I'm tired when I see you. Jouhaina [Yousef's youngest child] tells her, "I feel sorry for those who do not have a grandmother like you. I don't think I love my mother as much as I love you." Marie tells her that, "My brother and sister are attached to you, and they do not go with me to school unless you push them away. Please do not be nice to them, so that they will follow me to school."

Only a month later, Yousef seemed at the breaking point.

Every time she [Adela] is up there [in Kattine], we have to pay twenty pounds [about $7] for a car to go and have a big fight, and tear up the mattresses so that she will come with us and against her will. Moreover, every time she goes she alienates the partner [sharecropper]. This means we have to go to him, beg him and kiss his ass to return with a thousand compliments.

Ask your mother about this. Food: I do not think Abdallah Fadl

261

el Khazen [Adela's father] brought to his house half a *ratl* [2.5 kgs] of meat and seven tins of butter every year. Sleeping: It is better not to speak about this. Doctors: Four instead of one come to our house. Servants: Two and a soldier. Plus I am a servant and Nahde is a maid and Namatallah is a waiter, and Jouhaina is her servant also.

All the markets in Tripoli are at her disposal. Two dressmakers are near the house. Nahde is a dressmaker too. Last month we had to return a pair of shoes that she had chosen, four times until she was satisfied. What is there in Kattine? Where is the butcher, where is the tailor, where is the doctor? There is no one to give her a glass of water to drink, no one to heat the water for her to wash her feet.

If someone strangled her or if the devil came and took her, no one would ever know about it up there. During the day maybe someone will visit her as long as she has coffee, nuts, soap and matches. But at night, who will sleep in her house, she does not know, and neither do we.

You tell me that I should find her a maid. Angèle, in Kattine there are no maids and a stranger will not stay in Kattine. I am willing to pay twenty pounds per month for a maid if we find someone who will stay with her. But even if we pay fifty pounds we will not find one.

War seen through field glasses is easy [A Lebanese proverb that demeans Angèle's concerns while remaining away from the field of battle].

A seemingly harried Yousef would say in a following note,

…My mother is a righteous woman, a saint, a benefactor, but unfortunately she has a bad temper to the extent of madness…

In the early 1940s, it becomes obvious that Adela is in declining health. Although only beginning her sixth decade of life. She was known, in an act of grieving over Khalil's death, to repeatedly strike her head against a wall until her face swelled up beyond recognition. Outward expressions of grief are common to the Lebanese culture, but Adela's response was at the extreme end of this spectrum. In mid-1941, while Europe was engulfed in war, Yousef related the following about his mother's condition.

My mother had some kind of a growth on the right side of her face below the eye near the nose. It is the size of an egg and hard to the touch but does not hurt her at all. She has had it for six months and will not accept having it removed. She even would not accept to see a doctor. She is hard headed and this attitude increased after Khalil's death, I think there is something wrong with her mind. Finally, I took her by force after a few swear words. She had five x-rays and the doctor took a piece of the growth to examine it. I was worried that it was cancer, but thank God it was not. The doctor said it is a sack-like blocked vein where the blood has accumulated. Although there was nothing to worry about, I kept her in a hospital near our house. The doctor operated on her to remove the growth. He removed it from the inside between the upper jaw and the skin of her face. After thirteen days her wound healed because her blood is clean and her health is strong. We brought her home and she stayed in bed for fifteen days. After she got better she confessed that this growth was caused by hitting her face, which caused the vein to be blocked. Now it is beginning to grow again in the same place, but since we know the reason if it gets bigger the doctor will cut it from outside this time and remove the whole thing...

But, despite Yousef's optimism following the second operation, the lump on Adela's face reappeared.

Lebanon was fortunate in that World War II did not cause hardships that would compare with those of the First World War. The biggest complaint Yousef voiced was the length of time it took for mail to be delivered. He mentioned that it took on the order of three months for a letter from America to reach him. And he finally confesses to Angèle that,

> ... there is something I feel I have to tell you and that is that mother has not been well for the last two years. Her sickness was caused by the growth on her face. She has had 31 X-rays, and the best doctors have seen her including army doctors. She has had three operations and in the last surgery they removed half the bones of her face, but that did not cure her and she is getting worse. The doctors told us that it is cancer, but we did not tell her...

What followed this bad news was a series of letters from Angèle, renewing the accusations that her brother was not providing proper care for their mother. She suspected that he put his personal pleasure before familial obligations.

In 1945, Adela el Khazen Hobeiche died of cancer at the age of sixty-eight. Her death reopened up the floodgates of recrimination between brother and sister. Yousef, in blistering anger writes,

> ...My mother is my mother before being your mother by nine years [actually seven years]. I did not look for a disease to give her...

Then, in defense of himself, Yousef mentions the woeful expenses he had to bear for his mother's care. His exaggeration is obvious.

> ...Your mother's sickness cost me five thousand pounds [$1,700]. I mean five thousand pounds, and this means five thousand pounds. It is money counted and paid to doctors and hospitals. And if I were not the head of the fire department at that time and had ambulances and other cars at my disposal, I would have had to pay for transportation to bring my family to visit her and to move her back and forth to the hospital at a cost of at

least a thousand pounds, I mean a thousand pounds, that is a thousand pounds. Add this to five thousand which makes the sum six thousand pounds...

Concerning her death, the funeral and the expenses for that, ask Fr. Butrus Hobeiche for a list of the expenses that he received and spent out of his own pocket for the funeral, ask him how many priests and how many bishops were there in addition to the large crowds from the adjacent villages who came. Yesterday the mother of Sheik Kisrwan died. Ask which funeral was better. Was it the mother of Kisrwan the owner of two hundred thousand English gold pounds or your mother's? My mother's funeral cost me two thousand pounds although many priests, who are my friends, did not accept to be paid.

The many cars and the cars that belonged to the government that carried the casket from Tripoli to Ghazir, can you estimate what its cost would be if the deceased were not your mother. What else do you need from me? If you were in my place Angèle, would you have done all that? No, by God you would not. Leave people alone and do not increase their unhappiness.

Yousef couldn't close this long diatribe without taking issue with his sister's penchant for criticizing and passing judgment.

You take life with arrogance, stupidity and nervousness. You appointed yourself as the Great God. But if you have any memory you should know that you have a brother whom you should approach in a different way. You sound as if you are afraid that I might ask you to pay me some of the money that I have spent. Be assured, *yaa* [common expression meaning you] Angèle, it is not me who asks for anything... I swear on the cross that I do not need you and I do not need anybody else. I am living like a king. Ask anyone you know and they will tell you about our style of life. Be assured and if you need anything from me ask me for it. But if you have something else on your mind we will divorce each other immediately. I will consider that death has severed this brotherly relation as it has separated us from the others. We were four brothers and sisters, now we are two and it does not matter if one remains as long as life is going to be the way that you have stated. Have you understood what I am telling you?

However harsh their correspondence, Angèle and Yousef never stopped communicating. Their anger always seemed to fade with time, and although neither would forget the other's perceived slights or insults, the strong familial attachment endured.

Adela certainly would not have wanted her death to be the cause of a family feud. Her letters were never maliciously critical of her children, perhaps because she was not actually writing them herself. However, the events leading up to her demise stressed the remaining family bonds to breaking.

The Hobeiches of Kattine were heirs to a familial rank accustomed to the accouterments of wealth, although they never seemed to have any. No doubt this is why their disputes often centered on money. It colored their judgment, influenced their personal family relationships, and affected their social intercourse with others. Living like a sheikh had consumed Yousef's thinking. Having a respectable occupation for her husband had nagged Angèle. Instead of a blessing, the notable rank could well have been a curse, at least for the Hobeiche clan.

# 39
*He who lengthens his stride, falls down.*

Sᴴᴇɪᴋʜ Yᴏᴜsᴇғ Nᴀᴍᴀᴛᴀʟʟᴀʜ Hᴏʙᴇɪᴄʜᴇ, ᴀs ʜɪs brother sometimes sarcastically referred to him, was certainly a complex character. He was a raconteur and a rogue. He could charm and he could chafe. He could be eloquent and he could be profane. He was a master at repartee, never at a loss for a pungent rejoinder or appropriate bon mot. Exceedingly proud, he was one who believed, because of the accident of birth, that he was destined to live like a "sheikh," and pass that birthright down to his children. He wrote to his sister,

> I decided to give my children status and to have a house worthy of being called a Sheik's house, a house that will reflect the lives of our grandparents. I have worked hard to build a house, buy property and improve the land that was left me by my parents in order to make a future for my children so that they will not live the way we lived in poverty and misery, with a simple mother, without a father and under the mercy of Uncle Rashid. I want my children to have a future where they can live like real sheikhs, prominent in their environment with people listening to their words.

Living like a sheik, in Yousef's mind, involved not only material accoutrements but social acceptance as well. "Looking good" was paramount, but being listened to was also important. Sheikh Yousef tried to live up to the expectation of his station whenever the situation provided an opportunity. I'm reminded of the lines uttered by Sir Lawrence Olivier in his screen portrayal of Shakespeare's *Richard III*: *Since this world offers no joy to me but to command, to check, to oe'rbear such as are better person than myself, I'll make my heaven to dream...*

Yousef certainly loved to command, check, and overbear while dreaming of better circumstances. He never passed up an opportunity to "show off" whenever the occasion arose. As children, my siblings and I heard of Uncle

Yousef's many larger than life exploits. Emulating this bravado, mother cautioned, would not be tolerated. She strongly believed that self-praise was no praise at all. This dictum had such an impact on me that throughout my youth, and for a long time thereafter, I'd actually be embarrassed were I ever paid a compliment. Yet, Yousef used every opportunity to "show off," as if it were the divine right of sheikhs.

Attending funerals was just such an occasion where the sheikh could enlarge his presence, even if it involved the death of a long-time adversary. His father's sister, Fabiana, with whom Khalil had the lengthy property dispute, passed away, and despite Yousef's rancorous relationship with her and her family, he asserted the duties of his station at her funeral.

> Our Aunt Fabiana died two months after her sisters [both nuns] as a result of her falling down and breaking her leg... Her children did not tell anyone about her death and prepared to bury her quietly in Mar Elias, Ghazir. No one from Ghazir came to the funeral contrary to our mother's funeral where everyone from Ghazir and the adjacent villages came and carried her casket through the streets and then returned to church. I went there and took with me seventeen officers and four cars filled with my friends. They all attended the funeral and looked good in the church. When I got to Ghazir and noticed that there was no one there, I sent a messenger to tell the dignitaries in the village that if they were upset and if they had no respect for the deceased and her children and her brother [Yousef's father], they should not forget that she is my aunt. Right away all of them came down to the village apologizing and attended the funeral. They were able to do that because I did something secretly to delay the ceremony one hour to give the people of Ghazir time to receive my message. Anyway, we improved the situation as much as possible.

And Yousef knew how to make an entrance, even if it meant he had to dig deep into his own pocket.

> ...I went [to the funeral of Fr. Toubiya Dahdah who had returned from Cincinnati after retirement] in the most luxurious car, a Buick limousine with six seats. Renting such a car costs four times as much as a regular car. I arrived at Ain Aljaa like a king, my car was parked in the courtyard of the village and everyone gathered around with great surprise to look at it, and I was very well received. All the attention was directed towards welcoming me during the funeral. People from nearby villages ran towards me to salute me. There were three bishops: Hanah Hajj, Elias Richa and Abdalla. The minute I entered into the room they stood up with everyone else and did not sit down until I did. The Dahdah's came to thank me for the style in which I arrived, which was different from anyone else. And they all admitted that what I did was in respect for the deceased and his relatives...

The bearing that Yousef chose to affect was evident in all his photographs. The pictures of Yousef in my mother's collection show him only in military attire. In one such photo, Yousef's posturing as a leader of men is obvious. The inscription reads:

> In Rachaya El-Wadi, after we arrived to defend it the year 1925 with my legion. My legion was composed of thirty volunteers. It was the day we ended the siege of Dahr El-Ahmar by 400 rebels; we captured ten men, and won 30 Machine Guns, and 6 fighting rifles.
> This is my picture standing on the roof of a building after I gathered my legion for the photograph. Six of my men were killed today.

Strangely, the letters in Angèle's collection contain sparse mention of Yousef's military exploits. We know he wasn't bashful about boasting so it is believed that Angèle forwarded those letters to friends such as Zakia. She could simultaneously inform them of the goings on in Lebanon, while priding herself about her family, something she often did out of their presence. The only exception to the above is the following report sent to Toufic.

> I have not left the barracks for a month now. Who is more courageous the Sharkas [Circassians from Jordan] or the Lebanese. On the 20th of August 1926 we were ordered to go to the border between Lebanon, Shams [Syria] and Palestine to clear insurgents from the area. We immediately went without hearing one soldier complain or saying that he was sick. We walked for three days (850 kilometers) and we used to sleep at night at the top of Jabal Sheikh [Mt. Hermon], which is 2,358 meters above sea level, think how cold it was. We slept without covers because we were ordered not to carry anything with us so that we will not be delayed and to join the other groups coming from Shams and Knaitra. We reconnoitered all of Mt. Hermon from Hasbaya to Shibaa, Knaitra, Majdal Shams until we reached Houla in Palestine and we then returned to Marjeyoun and now we will go back to Hasbaya. I haven't heard any of the soldiers complain that he was tired. I was there, yaa Toufic, on the hardest roads before I gave my orders to the soldiers to disperse in a well-studied plan. I immediately saw that they dispersed according to the plan from which the devil himself cannot escape. Although their number is small, I want you to tell the Americans about them and see if they have soldiers like them. We protected Lebanon and eradicated all the insurgents. The people went back to their villages and homes and I hope things will be calm forever.

The life of a career soldier had its privileges, as well as many disadvantages. Yousef spent nearly his entire career under the command of French officers, with whom he often disagreed. Professional military men from a different culture could not abide a man who spoke his mind and often disobeyed orders.

In 1931, Yousef was severely disciplined and suspended from service for six months for organizing a lottery for his own benefit. There were reports of several lotteries being run—for sheep, a gun, and a phonograph. Where these "liberated" items came from one can only guess. The suspension without pay hit Yousef where he hurt the most—in his purse. Finally, through the intersession of the Maronite Patriarch himself, who wrote a letter on his behalf, Lt. Hobeiche was reinstated.

Although there were several notations in the records about Yousef's strength and enthusiasm, he continued to rankle his French superiors. Officers with names such as St. Martin, Reynier, Hassetche, Lacroix, and Pontiex wrote critical reports. Other Lebanese officers were also named along with Lt. Hobeiche as doing the same things he was accused of. "Unfortunately, such practices are accepted among these men," one French officer complained.

"Wherever Hobeiche has passed there is a story," an evaluation in 1935 said. In another, dated a year later, Sheikh Yousef was deemed to be a "terrible example for his comrades and subordinates. Recommend he be discharged from the Special Troops, made non-active and retired from service."

It is a wonder with all the reprimands he received that Yousef had time to engage in all those battles. He was wounded on several occasions and awarded over two-dozen medals and citations. And his fame spread far and wide in the mountains of Kesrouan.

Some twenty-five years later, Yousef was still obviously confident of his physical and military prowess. He boldly wrote to Angèle,

> Your brother is a lion do not worry about him.

Despite his prominence, at least among the villagers in his home environs, Yousef's financial condition was never far from concern. In 1945, he began a series of exchanges with his sister that talked about his need for a "power of attorney," one that involved Angèle's rights as co-heir of the Kattine property they inherited after the death of their mother. He wished to get clear title to the Hobeiche estate and pressed his sister for the legal document to do so. But Angèle was reluctant, for she feared that Yousef would sell the property, or find some other way to misappropriate the asset.

> Yousef to Angèle, 7 June 1945 – …He who reads your letter would think that I am an ass and do not know who the concerned person is in the property. 'Jeha [the idiot savant foil in many Lebanese folk tales] grew up and started to teach his aunt,' yaa Angèle? My letters, which I have sent to you concerning the power of attorney, why don't you read them

well? If you have read them well and understood them, why don't you act accordingly? If you have understood it why don't you send the power of attorney? Were you afraid that I would trick you and take away your property from you? You are suspicious of me, yaa Angèle. Stay like that, stay like that, God bless you.

These were strong words, indeed, but not at all unusual, for Angèle could certainly provoke such an outburst. My siblings and I, as recipients of letters of rebuke over the years, knew mother's proclivity for critical commentary well. Yousef, like his sister, didn't take reproach kindly and never shrank from returning the favor. Perhaps it was the experience with Aunt Fabiana years before that caused Yousef to write about relatives fighting over the land.

7 June 1945 – My dear, I do not think that we will ever disagree over property especially that it is, which as you well know, not worth any disagreement, and two people cannot live on the income it yields, because of its insignificance. But the coming days are not like the old days and people have different characters and you have children and I have children and who knows that after we die what the devil will do to their minds. They might start to fight and look for the old books [records]. Based on this, if we wish peace for our posterity, we should divide the property now so that each one will know what his share is so that when we die our children will live in peace and the devil will not have anything to do with them. How many brothers and sisters who loved each other, found their children were exactly the opposite. And how many fathers saw their children fight among each other over trivial matters…

But Angèle stubbornly refused to give over her property rights to Yousef, which prompted the following response:

I am not giving up the idea that I am upset with you or that I am furious at what you did to me concerning the power of attorney. I asked you for it and then I will return it to you to be certified. No, by God I shall never forget your deed, which the least I could say about it is that it is stupid and shows total unawareness of the facts. You said that he who is in America does not care about property any more. For you this is true but for us here this is nonsense. If we were in America, we would have said the same, but here we cannot say that because we are not in America and we do not have stores and businesses [referring to her husband Toufic supposed prosperity] that will make us give up a piece of land and do something else instead. If we continue as our fathers and grandfathers used to do and let this and that rob us our property, take advantage of us and take away what is around us, then how do we eat, drink, buy clothes and take care of our children.

The battle continued for nearly a year before an armistice was declared.

271

Angèle always maintained she would give her brother clear title, and after he had made many improvements to the property, she did. Once he had retired from the military and settled into the role of gentleman farmer, Angèle's fears that her brother's spendthrift inclinations would lead to ruin abated. After turning fifty, Yousef signaled this change when he began reflecting on his past.

> 12 March 1947 – You start your letter by asking about Nahde, my dear
> I am a sinful man and my age of fifty compels me to go back in memory
> and to meditate and my meditation reveals to me that I am accountable
> for 'breaking the leg of St. Ephraim's cow' this is why all that bothers me
> and breaks my heart on this earth is God's punishment for what I did
> in the past. If St. Ephraim got what he got for breaking a cow's leg, I
> remember that I have broken many legs, cow's legs, goat's legs, and many
> other animal legs in addition to many men's legs and I ended by having
> my wings [clipped] and my fingers broken. And I ask God that make that
> the limit and add no more.

Yousef alludes to the legend of St. Ephraim "The Syrian," who in his youth abused a cow by pelting it with stones. He was subsequently converted from his sinful ways after a stay in prison on a different charge, for which he was not guilty. When he appealed to God to save him, an angel appeared to remind him that, although he was not guilty of the current offence, he needed to be asked, "What about the cow?" Ephraim immediately promised to fulfill a religious vocation if he was saved from prison, and the rest, as they say, is history.

But Yousef, unlike St. Ephraim, had a hard time mending his ways. He also had his eye on Toufic's property in Bqaatouta, and he besieged both his sister and brother-in-law to give him control over it.

But Toufic was not to be as magnanimous as his wife. He had fallen out with Yousef a few years after the marriage and ceased writing him entirely. Despite the lack of response, Yousef hammered away by flaunting the current condition of Toufic's property.

> In fact they [Toufic's cousins] asked me to go to Bqaatouta and see how
> the property was left after all the destruction. They told me that it was
> a shame that you should neglect your sister's land that way. Nothing is
> left of the *horsh* [forest]. All the oak trees and even their roots have been
> stolen, because a quintal of wood (trunk, branches, roots) is worth fifteen
> Lebanese pounds [$5] and each oak trunk weighs a quintal and a half if
> not two. The walls of the terraced gardens have fallen down and the stones
> have been taken to other people's property and the house is beginning to
> fall down… There isn't a single tree, a wall or perimeter on your property
> now.

Those who remained behind in Lebanon, relatives or not, calculated (no doubt correctly most of the time) that the emigrants were never coming back and they could do what they wished with their properties. But Toufic had his own plans for his land, and all of Yousef's rhetoric went for naught.

In his later years, as noted above, Yousef did indeed become a gentleman farmer, to a large extent like his father before him. And, also much like his father, Yousef struggled financially. Six years after my first trip to Lebanon in 1971, I visited Yousef for the last time. I could see how the years had taken their toll on him. He wasn't nearly as spry as he once was, and had taken to walking around in his kimono and stocking cap. He had stopped paying his usual soldierly attention to his appearance. Just two years later, his son Namatallah wrote to his Aunt Angèle with bad news.

My father has a growth in the larynx. After taking a biopsy and testing it in the lab, the doctors decided it was malignant and is cancer and needs to be removed. But my father's health especially his weak heart and lungs do not permit surgery. His heart is swollen and his lungs are filled with water. The X-rays and the medications are not giving a positive result. This has been going on for a year now but now his health is continuously deteriorating. One time he looks like it is the end then he recovers and gets better again. We took him to different hospitals but finally we have decided to keep him at the Military Hospital for they can get him to take his medicine and food, because lately he has been refusing to take medicine or eat his food.

The doctors at the Military Hospital gave the same diagnosis as the ones at the private hospitals, but when I found him in a state of despair and nervousness, I decided to take him home where we will take care of him. We have asked a doctor to come and check on him every three days but whenever things get worse we call him and he will come.

When he spoke to you on the phone he was all swollen. But now and after the treatment, the swelling has disappeared from all parts of his body, thank God. But you should see him now he is skin and bones. Jouhaina comes from Kuwait every now and then and when we ask her to come, she spends a week and then returns.

My mother and I have worked out a program for taking care of my father. We alternate days and nights in nursing him and in cooking. When he was semi-conscious, he was calling your name. He kept saying, "Angèle, where is Angèle, she is standing, give her a chair," he was talking to you as if you were in front of him and that prompted me to call you and say, "*haram* [poor one] you, Namatallah, should let Angèle come and make his last wish come true." I did not want you to feel sad since I know well what the heart of Angèle contains, but this is life and this is God's wish.

Pray with us and tell Kail and Alfred [sons of Toufic and Angèle who are priests] that their uncle is in dire need of their prayers and I shall not slacken my efforts in preparing him to meet his God as a good Christian.

I kiss you many times from this distance.

When I spoke to Namatallah on my next visit after Yousef had passed on, he told me that his father did not go gently into that dark night. He was as imperious on his deathbed as he was in his youth. On his last day, as he was lying on a hospital gurney with myriad tubes sticking out of his body, he cried out with all the strength he had left and said, "I am Sheikh Yousef Hobeiche son of Sheikh Namatallah Hobeiche, they cannot do this to me!" And with that pronouncement he yanked all the tubes out of his body. Yousef expired shortly thereafter at age eighty-two.

*Toufic Traad Ellis, circa 1935.*

# 40

*If partnership was a blessing,*
*every two men would marry one woman.*

WHILE GROWING UP, THE ONLY FATHER I KNEW WAS the one who ran a cigar store. There was no domestic dad, one who read to you or tucked you in with a goodnight kiss (in fact, mother wasn't like that either). If I wanted to see or talk to my dad, I went to his store.

Once, when I was twelve-years-old, I stopped by the store to ask my dad for a dime so I could go to the movies with a few friends. "A dime!" he exclaimed in front of a store full of customers. "You know how hard I have to work for a dime?" I pleaded and begged as my friends waited for me outside. "Friends," he scoffed and thereupon peeled a dollar bill off the wad he kept in his pocket, and pointing to the portrait of the father of our country asked, "Whose picture is that?" "Oh, that's George Washington." I replied, "Everybody knows that." "Well, remember this," he said, "He's the only friend you've got!" The customers laughed, and Toufic, reveling in a point well made, finally gave me the dime and off I went. Just recalling that episode reinforces the indelible impressions my dad made on me. Toufic had come to believe that his best friend was money—it would not betray him—and, if he could amass enough of it, he could well do without any human friends.

I knew my dad had been injured by life's experiences. His early life in the small town of Bqaatouta had limited opportunity for a lad who had heard of *Amreeka*. So, he came, counting on his relatives in Carthage to help him get started earning a better living. He had been a trusting fellow, somewhat on the naive side, never considering that members of his own tribe would take advantage of him.

When the Boston Sales Company sank on its maiden voyage, drowning most of Toufic's life's savings, it changed him. The burdens he assumed with the Hobeiche family were not dissimilar to the obligations he had with his own family before their untimely demise. The humiliation and guilt he suffered turned the fun-loving youth into a suspicious, untrusting, and driven man who denied himself the simplest pleasures of life.

Bad news travels fast in the hills of Lebanon and the news of my dad's business setback was no exception. Reports soon crossed the ocean to Bqaatouta and the gossip gathered there soon made its way down to Kattine. His mother-in-law Adela heard the rumblings and began asking questions. Adela to Angèle,

> We heard that Toufic is broke, and had to sell his store, and you have never mentioned a thing... Now everyone I meet asks me. I tell them I do not know. Please tell me about Toufic's work and if this is true.

What happened to Toufic was obviously not an isolated incident. The seemingly prosperous immigrants who returned to their home country in search of brides couldn't have realized they were putting their hard-earned American fortunes at risk. A short time later, Miriam wrote to Angèle,

> I want to tell you this piece of news. The daughter of Dalal got married a month after you left, to a very rich man. She went to the U.S. where her husband had a partner in his store, and the partner had robbed Dalal's husband. She lost her mind because of this incident.

The crowning insult for Toufic came when it was reported that Wahib, the matchmaker back in Lebanon, who was unhappy with the returns on his matrimonial efforts, was a prime gossiper, gloating over Toufic's setback. Yousef had warned Toufic to cut his ties with Wahib, who had apparently kept a gift that Toufic had meant for him.

> Yousef to Angèle, 25 October 1926 – Concerning Uncle Wahib, *kuss ummu* [a sexual derogation involving one's mother], I can't but ask him to give me the gun and I will write to him now a few words asking him to take warning from the son of Butros Waked No.3 [when Yousef wanted to make the point that he should be feared, often he said that he was also "the son of Butros Waked," a Hobeiche of legendary strength]. He has been armed for a while and enjoyed it, power to him. Tell Toufic if he has money to distribute, let him send it with an honest man to distribute to the poor. And if he does not have money he can do without, he does not have to give Wahib anything at all. If I find out that Toufic gave Wahib anything, I will be very, very upset. Toufic might say, 'It seems Yousef is running my life,' on the contrary. I am not telling him what to do, but giving a piece of advice only, for God's sake, so that he will give the money

to the poor and not to a dishonest man like Wahib. Let Wahib and his people say whatever they like, I assure you that after receiving my letter, he is going to shut his mouth.

Toufic's long business association with his Uncle Seghaan came to an end in 1937. The decision to dissolve the partnership was spurred by the planned renovation of the business block on State Street where the shop was located. The old Hippodrome had been defunct for several years, having been replaced by the Strand down the street, and the block was to be remodeled and new storefronts created. So, Hannah & Ellis were evicted and the old uncle decided it was time for him to retire. He was then sixty-six years old, had no family responsibilities, and saw no reason to continue working.

Toufic was more than happy to finally strike out on his own and assumed Uncle Seghaan would give or sell the store's fixtures to him. Imagine his shock when he found that his partner had already sold the display cases to one of the Maroun brothers who had a store down the block. "Can you imagine that?" he told me years later. "He sold the cases out from under me!" One more slight to add to the litany he had endured over the years at the hands of relatives.

The uneasy relationship with his uncle would be an on-again and off-again affair. This did not deter the retired Seghaan from dropping by Toufic's store on a daily basis. He would sit in one of the shoeshine chairs and comment on the comings and goings of Carthage. My father didn't seem to mind and on occasion would ask his uncle to tend the store while he took a bathroom break.

Toufic never forgot the losses he suffered, nor at whose hands they were delivered. When I asked my father fifty years later about the details of what happened to the Boston Sales Co., he became visibly agitated, and with his eyes flashing said, "He gave away the business." And then he disgustedly said, "I don't want to talk about it!" Those scars were deep indeed.

The few interactions that I observed with his cousin Naja were always cordial, if somewhat reserved. Incidentally, Naja died unexpectedly of a heart attack at age forty-eight while on a long road trip to pick up produce for his grocery store. Toufic had the casket brought to his home (at his expense) and a wake was held there for the Carthage Lebanese who all knew Naja. The body was then shipped to Tupper Lake for another wake and then shipped back to Carthage for burial.

When his Uncle Seghaan died a few years later, Toufic made all the funeral arrangements, and we believe, defrayed many of the expenses as well. When extenuating circumstances prevailed, Toufic believed that Lebanese traditions trumped inner feelings and he did the right thing.

A few days after Christmas in 1947, after my father began closing his store for a few hours on Sunday afternoons, I suggested the family go to the movies. Pop confessed to me that he hadn't been in a theater in over twenty years. He was fifty years old at the time. It was so memorable that I even recall the movie we saw *Golden Earrings* with Marlene Dietrich.

Pop was not totally unlike my mother, as one might imagine, for he could also be a stern taskmaster. Although I enjoyed working in the store among all those magazines and newspapers, I was not permitted to read them when customers were in the store. When Pop came back from lunch or working in the garden and saw me reading a newspaper or a magazine, he was quick to admonish.

"But there are no customers," I protested.

"If there aren't any customers do something else. Sweep the floor or straighten out the magazines. There's always something to do," he would say.

But when I took up the broom to sweep the floor under his watchful eye, he would shake his head and say, "That's no way to sweep a floor!"

He would then seize the broom from my grasp and proceed to show me the right way to administer those long gentle strokes that would keep the dust down while herding the dirt into a neat pile for pick up and disposal. I have to admit that, although I was amused by this display of correct sweeping, because I ended up not having to actually sweep the floor, I was careful not to make my glee too obvious. (Years later, whenever I caught myself relaxing, I would suddenly think that there must be something I should be doing.)

Pop had three rules that he drilled into my head more than once. The first was: "Never discuss politics or religion." The second: "Always greet customers when they come into the store." And the third: "Always say thank you when a customer gives you money." No doubt these rules had held him in good stead, but I have to admit I violated them on many occasions, especially the one about religion and politics.

I often marveled at my father's usually upbeat attitude, given that he labored such long hours and lived with a perpetually unhappy wife. But, he always greeted his customers with a smile and was regarded by all as an affable and congenial person.

For most of his working life, Pop opened his store at seven in the morning and closed at eleven at night, seven days a week, 365 days a year. He also was continually looking for fresh sources of revenue by offering new items for sale in his cigar store. He acquired such items as books for rent, ice cream, ballpoint pens, antacid pills, aspirin, and even condoms, which were secreted in a compartment inside the cigarette display case. The latter item was for his regular customers who were too bashful to ask for them at the local drugstore. This was in a since-forgotten puritanical era when sanitary napkins came in a plain brown wrapper and well before prophylactics were freely placed on drugstore shelves. During the 1940s, my dad also sold treasury balance lottery tickets and football pools, both of which were illegal but winked at by the local authorities.

The treasury balance racket was run by an organized crime syndicate in Utica, New York, and in Carthage even the local police chief's wife bought them at my dad's store. The tickets contained numbers that used the last five digits of the US Treasury balance and people could look up winning combinations in the daily newspaper. What the syndicate didn't take into account was the simmering political situation that existed in the summer of 1948. Former prosecutor, district attorney, incumbent New York State Governor and presidential candidate, Thomas E. Dewey, was seeking to embellish his already substantial reputation for being tough on crime.

This was also the summer my father was incapacitated due to a gall bladder operation, and I was placed in total charge of the store. One fateful Saturday morning in June of that year I noticed a state trooper's car pull up and park in front of the store. Although troopers often frequented the store and my dad was on a first name basis with many of them, it seemed curious because the two officers just sat in the car. I soon came to understand why.

Promptly at 10:00 AM, they emerged from the patrol car and entered the store. One of them confronted me and told me they were there for the lottery tickets! I, of course, feigned ignorance, but to no avail, and was told to give them up or they would start searching for them. I was in a panic because I thought I was going to be arrested and would have a criminal record for the rest of my life. I quickly decided to give them the tickets that were in a small cigar box, even though there were many more hidden in a different place in the store.

Pop's store was also a drop off point for tickets that would be picked up by a courier and taken further north to lottery sellers in Star Lake and beyond. The troopers didn't know about those, so after handing me a subpoena to appear before a grand jury in Syracuse two months hence, they left to pay a visit on my recuperating father at home. When he came down the stairs in his bathrobe, his first thought was they were just friends paying a courtesy sick call, so he was quite shocked when they handed him a similar subpoena for the same grand jury.

This incident became the talk of the town, as all the state's newspapers played up the story of Governor Dewey smashing the extensive gambling ring. Try as I might to be excused from the grand jury appearance, even writing a letter to the district attorney claiming that I was going into the service with several of my friends (which I really had no intention of doing), I was not to be excused. In September, my dad and I boarded a bus to Syracuse some ninety miles away to appear before the convened grand jury.

I waited anxiously in the anteroom while my father went in to testify. He was in and out in less than five minutes. I was summoned next, and the prosecutor apparently decided to have some fun with me to liven up his audience. The jury room was intimidatingly large, and had several people in attendance in addition to the judge and twelve impaneled grand jurors. "Raise your right hand..." a bailiff intoned as I was administered the oath. After being duly sworn, the DA, a dapper young man obviously on his way up the proverbial ladder, asked me about trying to get out of appearing in front of the grand jury.

"You didn't want to come and see us?" he asked with a smile. He was being quite jocular and asked my age and what grade I was in at school. I replied that I was seventeen and had graduated high school the previous June. He smiled and said, "Kind of backward aren't you?" to the amusement and laughter of the crowd.

After several minutes of this style of light-hearted banter, he produced a front and side view mugshot, complete with a string of numbers below, of the man who used to bring the lottery tickets to my dad's store. He then asked if I recognized him.

"That's Sam Ross," I noddingly replied.

Sam was a large, suave, ruddy-faced guy of about sixty who dressed in custom tailored suits, wore a felt fedora over his neatly combed crop of gray hair, and always had a long, fat cigar clenched between his teeth. He used to chat me up in the store when he came by to pick up the money and pay off the winning tickets, which were scant to say the least. One time he even suggested that I get myself a cheap car, a "flivver" he called it, and he'd give me my own route to peddle lottery tickets. I was really interested, but my dad quickly put the kibosh on that idea.

"Sam Ross!" the DA exclaimed. "Don't you know this man to be Samuel Rosencrantz?"

"No," I said, "that's Sam Ross."

Apparently the DA didn't know Ross' alias, just as I didn't know his true name was Rosencrantz. He wasn't happy with my response, and what had been an amiable and humorous session suddenly turned very serious. He then pulled a lottery ticket from his pocket with a flourish and waved it in front of the jurors and me.

"Does this look like the ticket you sold to Sgt. Hamilton of the Bureau of Criminal Investigation?" he demanded. I knew I hadn't sold any tickets to people I didn't know, so I peered at the specimen and said, "I don't know, they all look alike, don't they?" At that point my antagonist shouted, "I REPEAT, DOES THIS LOOK LIKE THE TICKET YOU SOLD TO SGT. HAMILTON OF THE BCI?!"

I quickly responded, "Yes sir, that's the one, for sure that's the one."

When I finally exited the jury room, my dad asked what I had been doing in there for twenty minutes. The DA, who had followed me out, put his arm around me and told my dad, "You have a fine boy here, Mr Ellis." I guess he was feeling a little guilty about beating up on me. My dad smiled and nodded, relieved that this ordeal was now over, even though he had lost a fairly good source of revenue. In any event, the lottery ticket furor soon died down, and when the presidential election was held a couple of months later, Thomas E. Dewey, the crime-busting heavy favorite, lost.

Toufic began to soften a little after he turned fifty. In 1950 he bought a new Chevrolet, his first new car since the Buick roadster. This was a momentous event because he had been without an automobile since before World War II. The grueling routine had finally begun to wear on him, and he began closing on Sunday afternoons from one to four. He justified reducing his hours by saying there was little business then anyway. This time off would be used to take Sunday afternoon drives with his wife, a pleasure they both had foregone since they began raising a family.

In many ways I was like my father—a trusting, happy-go-lucky youth—who was rudely awakened to the realities of life after entering the armed forces during the Korean War. When I was thrust among street-wise New York City kids in a barracks at Fort Dix, I quickly found that a naïve, gullible small town boy was no match for big city youths. They borrowed money never to be repaid, and goldbricked with abandon. It didn't take me long to develop a hard-shelled distrust of new acquaintances. I could empathize with my father's outlook on life.

One slight that stuck in Toufic's craw was the treatment of his sister Emily after she returned to her home in Lebanon. He was also quite upset about the abuse of his property back in Bqaatouta by the people to whom it had been entrusted. They paid him no rent and actively contributed to its disrepair. It was the house his father had built, and to him these acts were a desecration of his family's memory. In 1958, my mother finally got her wish to send her youngest child Khalil, her brother's namesake, to Lebanon to study. In a letter home to his dad, Khalil describes the state of his father's property.

> I went to Bqaatouta it is very nice... The next thing I saw was the house where you were born. There's nothing left to it but a few stones on top of each other. I took a picture of it. We walked a little further on, and we saw the [your] house. It really looks nice from far away, and your land was the most beautiful land I ever saw, a thousand times better than Kattine. From the house you can see all the Mazra'a, the long road, the deep valley. It's really beautiful. In Kattine you see a mountain in the back, a mountain to the front of you, and a mountain to the east and west of you. But in Bqaatouta you have the most beautiful view, and in spite of its farness [distance] you can see Beirut and the sea. As we walked further on, we began to see how the land had been neglected for so long. The stones that made the terraces were falling down. The woods have all been cut down. I was told that the front of the house had a vineyard. Now, there is nothing but a few grape leaves. The water in front of the house is polluted and dirty. As we got nearer the house, we could see that it was falling down. (I forgot to tell you that the roof was tin.) I wanted to go inside the house, so we did. We knocked on the door because ibn Jafail [the son of Toufic's first cousin] lives there with his wife and kids. From what I saw of the house, it was divided into four rooms. One to sleep, eat and receive people, and the other three for the animals. Also, the balcony was for a kitchen. We didn't stay long. We took some pictures and then came back to Malik's house. To tell you about the land, father, it is terribly neglected and wasted...

Toufic didn't need further verification that his relatives were not to be trusted, and he vowed to go back one day and set things straight. In 1965 he finally saw his way clear to return to Lebanon after an absence of nearly forty years. While there, he often wrote back to his wife bitterly venting the disdain he felt for his countrymen in general and his relatives in particular. The purpose of his visit was to sell the property that had been neglected all those years. The letters express feelings my father never voiced at home, perhaps because it was the first time that he had the luxury to reflect on his life. He also exposed a religious bent that was also never observed in Carthage. In Bqaatouta he went to church, made confession, and took communion. This was from a man who worked every Sunday in his store and seldom found time to go to church.

Toufic to Angèle in November 1965 – I was planning to finish everything today, but something happened and I could not do what I was planning to do. My cousin [Mansour] was not serious and just fooling with me. I realized his intentions and felt upset and left unhappy and told him that I did not want to sell to him after all. Whether I sell or not, I am tired of their lies. I will be at your end this month if nothing from God happens. I am tired and I have just buried my sister [Emily] and I have not paid Hanna my board at his place. I still have not been to Baalbek or the Cedars. And here everyone wants *baksheesh* [tips], I mean a bonus for their work and your family is impertinently asking for *baksheesh* and they are saying how stingy I am but I am turning my ass to them. Let them say whatever they want to say…and do not either ask me anymore or write to me anyway.

The people in Lebanon believed that anyone who went to America automatically became rich. I don't think our relatives ever really knew or appreciated how much my father struggled to feed and clothe his family. He was not receptive to their pleas, had enough of their duplicity, and was not about to reward their perfidy.

Toufic to Angèle, 20 November 1965 – I had told you that I will soon finish my business and travel to you as soon as possible, but the man who wanted to buy was not able to obtain the money. I have been promised, that during this week, if he is truthful, I will be able to finish the sale. I have put it in my mind that I will not leave unless I sell the property. I should like to spite my relatives and your relatives to teach them not to talk about me and that nothing good comes out of lies…

I have already spent five travelers' checks and I have four left, I hope God helps whoever lives and returns to this beautiful country for it is a bastard nation where the child does not know his father or his brother. I do not feel sorry for any of my relatives or your relatives even if they die from hunger because they expect a person to give them everything he has…

When I first read those words I was shocked and believed they were from a frustrated man who didn't really mean what he said. Toufic had always seemed proud of his Lebanese heritage (whenever anyone called us Syrians, he corrected them and told his kids to do the same) but obviously struggled with his co-habiting American identity. Whenever there was a crisis in Lebanon, and there were several over the years, Toufic took the lead in Carthage, collecting and sending money for relief.

His words, however, brought to mind the time he took me to the hospital, at age eleven for a tonsillectomy. The admitting receptionist asked my dad what our nationality was. Without batting an eye he said, "American." Both the receptionist and I looked at him quizzically while he added, with an impatient glance, "We're citizens aren't we? Of course we're American."

Toufic felt that he had paid his dues and had earned his American identity. He worked for everything he ever got out of life and had no patience for those who were looking for a handout. Whatever little he garnered from his labors came from hard work, so why couldn't his relatives do the same, including his children?

Toufic had a lifelong problem remembering names and took to calling everyone John, even his kids. His store was across the street from the Augustinian Academy, our parish school, and many of the students often stopped in to buy soft drinks, candy, or comic books. He didn't even try remembering their names, and after calling them all John, they took to calling him Toufee (Americanized spelling) John.

Lunch, when he partook of it in our early years, was brought to him by his children. He would wolf down his meal, in the back of the store behind one of the magazine racks, while watching closely as one of us kids manned the counter. Supper would be handled the same way. After he became confident that his progeny were sufficiently trained to manage the store by themselves, he would walk home for his meals. When my siblings and I were grown and had left home, Pop would have Uncle Seghaan spell him while he tended to fixing his house, working in his garden, or making his *arak*.

In spite of his demanding schedule and his wife's stern and somewhat cool demeanor, Toufic fathered six children. In retrospect, I wondered when he had the time or the energy to accomplish that feat. Occasionally, when he wanted to give his wife a respite from raising the large family, he would send the older children to summer with his sister Christine at Tupper Lake.

I loved going to Tupper Lake because I looked up to my older cousins Philip and Eddie. And Aunt Christine doted on us, something we weren't at all used to at home. But she didn't have an easy time of it either in her marriage to Octave LaBrie, a French-Canadian-Native American, with whom she quarreled regularly. All his nieces and nephews loved Uncle Octave because he played the fiddle, joked a lot, and was great fun to be around. Unfortunately, he took to drink to drown out Christine, who in her latter years became an increasingly harpy wife. More than once I heard Aunt Christine in the heat of argument call him a lazy bum and a "goddamned Frenchman." Undaunted, Uncle Octave would shoot back, "You don't know how lucky you are. If you'd married one of your own kind, you'd have been dead a long time ago!"

When Christine was hospitalized with a stroke at the age of eighty-two, I went with my father to visit her at the hospital in Tupper Lake. I've only seen my father moved to tears a few times in my life, and this was one of them. He brought me into her room with him, leaned over his sister and said, "Look who I brought with me. Raffee." Christine opened her eyes and in a wavering voice repeated "Raffee". It was the last word she spoke before she passed away.

Toufic endured a lot to realize the American Dream, the dream he had wanted so desperately when he was a young lad working in a stone quarry and orchards of the mountains of Lebanon. If you had asked him if he were happy, he would have said yes—given a loose definition of the term. He didn't seem to expect much from life, and therefore, wasn't really disappointed with it. As long as he could feed his family and able to put away a little for the inevitable rainy day, he was indeed happy.

After fifty years as a storekeeper, and when the income from the daily grind was no longer needed, Toufic retired. His days were spent taking long walks, working in his garden, reading the Arabic language newspaper, listening to a short wave radio, and sitting on his front porch smoking his beloved pipe. Toufic continued to be a student of current events in the Middle East, listening to short wave reports from Egypt, Kuwait, Syria, and Lebanon. He was always informed and ready to engage in conversations about the goings on in that turbulent area of the world.

As Toufic's health inevitably declined, alarms would go out to his progeny, summoning them to make the trek home for their final goodbyes. I personally dreaded the phone call that would beckon me home, and one day it came.

"You'd better get up here," I was told by my sister. "This could be it."

So, I booked a flight from Orlando to Syracuse and rented a car for the drive to Carthage. I arrived at the homestead late in the evening, and since I couldn't see my dad until the next day, I did what Lebanese do when they gather on these occasions. Having mastered the preparation of a few ethnic Lebanese specialties, I threw myself into making *humus*, *baba ganough*, *mjaddra*, and *zatar* for the gathering clan. The family sat around talking, eating, and reminiscing about Pop to pass the time.

When we got to the hospital the next day and went into my father's room, he was asleep. I was surprised at how well he looked. I bent down to give him a kiss on the cheek, as is our custom, and as I gazed at him with a tear in my eye, he opened his eyes, looked straight at me and said with a grin, "Too much garlic, John!" Everyone burst out laughing. My heavily garliced *humus* was evidently secreting through my pores. Pop's heart may have been failing, but his sense of humor and smell were not at all diminished.

After a long period of decline Toufic died in his ninety-fifth year of congestive heart failure. His heart was exhausted and unable to pump out the fluids that had built up in his lungs. He was laid to rest in the St. James Catholic cemetery, underneath the black granite headstone that he had proudly prepared years before with his original family name of Kmeid inscribed thereupon.

*Angèle Hobeiche Ellis, circa 1960.*

# 41

*When livelihoods were distributed, one was not satisfied.*

Fate's optometrist had fitted Angèle with a pair of defective glasses that gave her a distorted outlook on life. This warped view often guided her pen in writing things that caused great consternation to the recipients. When Angèle first arrived in the States, her family was sympathetic to her complaints, but showed some empathy towards Toufic. They knew how difficult Angèle could be and in one note to her brother-in-law, Sr Miriam tells him to take his wife in hand.

> ...If Angèle wants to keep nagging you, give her a few slaps and tell her you married her without olives or figs [without a dowry]. If she does not shut up, ask her about this statement. She knows what it means...

Those patrimonial precepts were hard to shake although this mood didn't last long and the tide soon turned in Angèle's favor. Toufic, she often lamented, was not the man her family thought he was. This must have struck a responsive chord in Adela because it so closely mimicked what had happened to her—marrying a man who was not who she thought he was. Her family soon began siding with her against her husband.

> Miriam to Toufic, 19 May 1928 – I am beginning to write this letter and my heart is shivering with poison. I am upset with you, especially since *sitt* [Miss] Angèle wrote two months ago saying that she is going away...

> Yousef to Angèle, 12 June 1928 – I tell you that I read in the papers that divorce is on the increase in the U.S. Since your husband does not allow you to come here, why don't you divorce him, rid us of him and come back so that we will see you. Damn be the devil! What do you say? I was also planning to send you a bottle of water from the river Jordan, but because I am hoping that Toufic will be kind hearted and will answer my letter positively, I stopped everything until you come here.

Miriam to Angèle, 18 July 1928 – Your words have become very harsh. It seems you are hiding my letters because of Toufic. I do not blame you anymore because I know the truth [the truth Miriam knew had to be from gossip passed down the mountain from Bqaatouta]. One's hands are tied when one has a disease in the home.

Adela to Angèle, 5 September 1928 – I was happy to know that you want to come here, but I am worried that you are not feeling well. Listen to me. Come before winter; do not spend the winter there. If you get sick, America cannot do anything for us. This is what your brothers and sister think, too. When you wrote and said you were going to the hospital, Yousef wrote to you and asked you to come here. Try your best. If you come immediately by sea, it will be better. Even if it takes a long time, 30 days, it does not matter. Do not spend winter there.

Toufic hadn't really changed, but his financial circumstances and the Hobeiches' perception of him certainly had. It took nearly ten years before talk of Angèle's return home diminished in the correspondence. Toufic, who had initially been a frequent exchanger of letters with his in-laws, finally gave up writing them altogether. He sensed what was going on and refused to participate.

No matter how unhappy she was, mother did her duty as she had been taught. She had children as was expected and reared them as she had been reared, with a firm and unyielding hand. When she received word that someone had gotten a letter from the old country, she scurried to their home, often with me in tow, to read the letter and write a reply. Many of the Lebanese women, if not totally in commiseration with her, tried to allay Angèle's unhappiness. Indeed, most continued to be deferential, at least in the sheikha's presence. They came to her house to help cook meals and listen to her ventilate. She did not, indeed could not, adequately express her appreciation for these kindnesses.

Angèle's early actions showed her husband that she was an independent, driven woman in a rush to absorb everything American. She wanted to quickly learn English and to learn how to drive a car. This didn't make people happy on the Lebanese side of the ocean. Adela wrote to Toufic,

We were happy to receive your letter, but it seems all you think about is the car and all we hear is that Angèle is learning to drive and she is not satisfied with your car. She is driving somebody else's car. This does not please me. What I like to hear is that you have made a house or you have saved money to come back to your country. This is what will make me happy. But even if Angèle is stupid and insists to drive a car, I know that you are intelligent and should not let her do whatever she likes to do. She wants to have fun, okay, but should that include a car? ...

Incidentally, her brother Yousef never learned how to drive either, choosing to be chauffeured wherever he needed to go.

Angèle brought the many tales of her family and country's history with her to the New World. Storytelling, an integral part of her life back in Lebanon, was a talent that must have been passed down to her from mother Adela. Thrust into Depression-era America a few short years after arriving in Carthage, Angèle used those skills as a form of entertainment for her rather large brood of six children. This was before that art form declined as a way of passing down folklore and tribal history. Mother was blessed with a prodigious memory and could faithfully recount tales of the hardships of the First World War, her family's renowned history, and various other folk tales that often took the form of poetry and song.

Learning English was another item that was at the top of Angèle's list. She'd heard there was a retired Irish schoolteacher, Miss Kate Traynor, who gave private lessons in English, so she soon engaged her. I remember Miss Traynor in her latter years as a short, stout spinster type who had a lot of fine blonde facial hair, and who lived in a big house on State Street. Both Kate and her sister Clara never married and lived to ripe old ages in the "harsh" Carthage climate. Kate was ninety years old when she died in 1969.

I asked mother how she paid for private tutoring, and she confessed to having bartered some of her jewelry for the English lessons. The Lebanese ladies, my mother included, treasured the gold bracelets that adorned their forearms for they were an indication of their net worth. These prized possessions were always on display at weddings and funerals.

Angèle's willingness to give up any of her rings or bracelets in exchange for intellectual independence made me appreciate her determination all the more. The eager student mastered the English language to a degree that allowed her to hone her already sharp tongue in yet a third language. She was able, and indeed often inclined, to trade jibes with natives using their own vocabulary. On one occasion, after the local paper had printed an article about Angèle being a "Syrian Princess," her English teacher commented that "There are only two kinds of people on this earth: Those who are Irish and those who wish they were Irish." Angèle quickly responded with, "I heard that St. Patrick drove the snakes out of Ireland. I didn't realize he'd sent them all to America."

But, often, Angèle could be circumspect in her correspondence. In a letter from her sister, Miriam says that they are puzzled about Angèle's admission that she had fallen and later that she was ill. Apparently Angèle did not want to disclose that she was suffering from morning sickness. Her suspicions that she was pregnant after leaving Marseilles were correct, but two months later she suffered a miscarriage and told her family only that she had been ill. Now she was carrying another child and didn't want her family to know her condition. Could it have been that, in the event she miscarried again, she would be displaying a weakness by not being able to carry a baby to term? Or, could it have been that she would be admitting intimacy with a man she had been denigrating to her family, from the first days of her marriage? The proud Hobeiche clan abided neither physical nor emotional weakness very well.

Angèle always suspected her brother Yousef was mismanaging the care of their mother. Despite Adela's cancer, she always maintained that her mother had died of a broken heart—over the loss of her son Khalil, the baby of the family.

It's hard to imagine how a woman in her depressive state endured the untimely deaths of those she dearly loved, especially her sister Miriam and her brother Khalil. After her brother died, she vowed to have another boy to be named after him. My curiosity was aroused because all through the years I lived at home, my parents slept in separate bedrooms. I asked mother how this pregnancy came about. In a burst of ingenuousness she said, "I tricked your father," and would say no more. But she got her wish, and a son who would be named Khalil was born eighteen months after his namesake's death.

As a parent, Angèle was a stern taskmistress, just like her mother before her. She expected her children to do their duty and strive for perfection as she had been taught to do. She needed to prepare her offspring for a cruel and unforgiving world, and no matter how well they did in school, it wouldn't be good enough. I once came home from school with a perfect score on the New York State Regents exam for Trigonometry and proudly proffered it for mother's affirmation. "Is that the best you can do?" she asked. "No, Ma," I said, "I'll try harder the next time." I also remember my sister Theresa signing up to take French in her first year of high school, thinking that since mother was fluent in the language, she would be a great help to her. When her mother decided that Theresa couldn't even pronounce *bon jour* correctly, my sister rued her choice.

Angèle's offspring accepted this treatment, for deep in their hearts they knew that mother, in her own way insofar as she was capable, loved them and only wanted what was best for them. It was the way she had been brought up, and it never occurred to her that she should behave any differently. Her children understood that.

Writing letters was a passion with Angèle and among her correspondents was a Lebanese Maronite bishop in Cuba. During World War II, she did her patriotic duty by often penning V-mails to many of Carthage's Lebanese servicemen stationed in various war zones around the world. Each one of them showed their appreciation by visiting her whenever they came home on furlough. She also wrote several articles for the Arabic language newspaper *al Hoda*, which was based in New York City. If something didn't sit right with her, she invariably redressed her concerns by dropping a line to the editor of the newspaper or manager of the radio station. And her pen could deliver pungent prose indeed.

Whatever money she could cajole from her husband, or as we all suspected, cadge from his wallet while he soundly slept, she put in envelopes to send back home. The relatives in Lebanon still spoke of her generosity whenever I visited there. I continue to believe, however, that they never really understood the lengths she went to or the sacrifices she made to deliver a few dollars to them.

This spirit of generosity was manifest in other ways as well. Depression era hoboes frequently walked the New York Central Railroad tracks that passed behind the home we lived in during the 1930s. They would often knock on our backdoor looking for something to eat. Mother, remembering her wartime experiences back in Lebanon, didn't have the heart to turn them away, so she bade them to sit on the back stoop while she fetched a meal for them. At the very least they would get some hot soup served up in a Mason jar.

Angèle was so starved for intellectual interaction that she had a hard time turning anyone away from her door. Vacuum cleaner salesmen, Jehovah's Witness missionaries, drummers from specialty importers, and even a few Lebanese con men gained entrance to our home.

An historian once asked me if we had the envelopes for the cache of correspondence we discovered after mother's death, which would have made them eminently more valuable. I had to answer in the negative because Angèle's charity also extended to several overseas Catholic missions with whatever small offerings she could muster. One way she supported them was with cancelled postage stamps. She cut the stamps from all the envelopes and sent them off to one mission or another. I assume they were then sold to collectors around the globe.

I have often remarked to my siblings that reading the saved correspondence was like listening to one side of a telephone conversation where you have to deduce what the other party is saying. After reading and studying the letters many times, I was able to construe from the responses what mother was writing and thinking, even though I couldn't actually see her words.

The letters to Angèle revealed a sub-rosa pride in her children that was never displayed to them. It seemed as if she and her brother Yousef played a game of "dueling children." Yousef always acknowledged the accomplishments of Angèle's brood, but then would proceed to recount the somewhat better accomplishments of his own offspring.

It took Angèle twenty-two years after arriving in America to finally make a return trip back to Lebanon for a reunion with her brother Yousef. One can only imagine the simultaneous joy and heartache of that reunion, followed, of course, after an appropriate grace period, by the inevitable clash of wills, just like the old days. And the stories my cousins told of her visit on my first trip to Lebanon in 1971 verified this.

Angèle never wavered in her religious fervor, and the family's vocational torch was passed when four of her six children chose the religious life—two nuns and two priests. This affirmation of her spirituality seemed to have made Angèle's life worthwhile, and she was accordingly quite proud. She beamed gloriously when in the presence of the many clergy at professions, ordinations, funerals, and other functions that flowed from those career choices.

In her later years, Angèle's sight began to fail, and this plagued her. She had spent a lifetime reading, writing, sewing, and creating fine needlework, and when she could no longer do those things, she became even sadder than before. She began reflecting on her past sins in preparation to meet her maker.

On a visit I had with her in her last year, she told me she needed to talk over some things. She then proceeded to dredge up a forty-year-old event that occurred shortly after I was married, wherein she explained why she didn't want my wife Loretta and me to stay at the old homestead. She said she was worried that her thirteen-year-old son would observe us newlyweds in the throes of passion. Little did she know how remote that possibility was given my wife's unease at staying there in the first place. It wasn't so much that Mom was apologetic, but she just felt the need for me to understand so I wouldn't think badly of her. The sad part is that I clearly remembered the event because my wife and I ended up spending the night in one of the local hotels.

This puritanical preoccupation with matters sexual, real or imagined, carried over in other areas as well. Once when my father was in need of someone to tend the store and unable to find anyone else, he pressed his wife into service. He soon came to realize what a mistake that was. Upon his return he found that Angèle had thrown out all the girlie magazines, such as *Penthouse* and *Playboy*, along with all the aforementioned condoms.

Angèle maintained her mental faculties and her stubbornness to the end, much to the chagrin of her caregivers. In the last two years of her life, she often spent time at the convent of the Sisters of St. Joseph where her daughter and designated caregiver Sr Angèle, nee Theresa, resided. She had to have thought about her mother staying, and being cared for, at Sr Miriam's convent. This was but one of many parallels between her life and that of her mother.

Angèle's yearning for her homeland had transformed Lebanon into a romanticized version of the land she was initially quite anxious to leave. Her wistfulness about home intensified as the years passed by. I have often thought that her—and her fellow expatriates—pinings were a bit delusional. Surely they had to be exaggerating, or their memories were playing tricks on them. I wondered how a country that was so willingly abandoned by so many could ever compare with this great land of America? Why did they leave if they remembered it so fondly?

So strong had these feelings become that Angèle wrote a poem about wanting to return to Lebanon. The verse verbalized her love of nature and her heartfelt longing for the Lebanon of her youth.

## I'd Like To Return To Lebanon

I'd like to return to Lebanon to see the young ladies of the village at evening time promenade on the roadway trading witty tales, their laughter resounding through the neighboring hillsides and valley below.

I'd like to return to Lebanon in the evening to enjoy the horizon filled with stars and falling meteors as we say, "God preserve you as he preserves us."

I'd like to return to Lebanon to pass the evening on our vine-covered patio, grapes dangling overhead while we stay seated, reaching effortlessly, to take, taste and taste endlessly.

I'd like to return to Lebanon to call my friend across the valley; our conversation is cordless with bell-like clarity.

I'd like to return to Lebanon to prepare a picnic of my favorite foods, endive and other herbs.

I'd like to return to Lebanon during the silkworm season when the mulberry trees are full of berries, tastier than strawberries.

I'd like to return to Lebanon at harvest time, to ride the animals as they circle round and round separating the wheat from the chaff. A ride more exciting than in a Cadillac.

I'd like to return to Lebanon when they transform grapes into a savory syrup, which we scoop into our mouths with mulberry leaves gathered for this tasty treat.

I'd like to return to Lebanon to climb from one fig tree to another, taking from them their multicolored, delectable fruit.

I'd like to return to Lebanon on the first of September for it is during the early rains that an abundance of escargot surface, with baskets and lanterns we gather all we can carry home.

I'd like to return to Lebanon in the wintertime to sit around the fireplace warming ourselves, cracking and munching on acorns much in the same way we feast on chestnuts in this foreign land.

I'd like to return to Lebanon to pass the evening with the neighbors all around to tell stories and talk about the history of Lebanon.

I'd like to return to Lebanon at noon when ladies dressed in fine apparel commence their neighborly visits to sip coffee, inhale the *nargelie*, tell tales and return contented with the latest news from around.

I'd like to return to Lebanon to gaze at the full moon in all its splendor, encircled by an array of jeweled stars.

I'd like to return to Lebanon to hear again the monastery church bells announce a new day, echoing their call of the faithful to pray.

I'd like to return to Lebanon to go up on a hill to breath in the fresh air and from there view the vast sea, with its ships coming and going and I say to myself, "Maybe they are carrying an immigrant longing to return to Lebanon just like me."

Angèle succumbed to congestive heart failure in the spring of 1994—a few months short of her ninetieth birthday—from the same causes as her brother Yousef and her husband before her. Nineteen priests, two of them her sons, gathered to concelebrate her funeral mass. Her obituary and the above poem were published the Beirut newspaper *al Anwar*. Angèle's ashes were carried back to Lebanon by four of her children and placed in the same sarcophagus with her brother Yousef, in the family crypt at Mar Elias Church. Her wish to return to Lebanon was finally fulfilled.

*The first three Ellis Children. From left, Theresa, Raffee, Delor.*

# Afterword

*The ignorant person learns at his own expense,*
*the wise one learns at the expense of others.*

WHEN I WAS GROWING UP IN THAT SMALL TOWN OF Carthage, many things that nearly every kid now takes for granted were considered luxuries in our typically Lebanese household. Things such as toys for Christmas, a radio in the living room, a shower in the bathroom, or a family automobile were amenities unknown to us in the Depression era 1930s. We didn't think that sheets made out of flour sacks, or bread and milk with a little sugar for breakfast, were all that unusual either. I didn't realize it then, but our family was constantly skating back and forth across the blue line of the poverty rink. My siblings and I never knew until much later in life how much my father struggled during the Great Depression. In spite of this, we were happy and never went hungry.

These same circumstances, or worse, surely applied to millions of others in the United States during that period in our history. This narrative is but a small ripple in a tsunami of immigrant stories, the vast majority of which have been drowned by the tides of time. My story is not about remarkable people or remarkable lives, but has the unique advantage of having been accumulated in a variety of documented ways and thus could be told with detail and accuracy.

As the children of immigrants, my siblings and I just wanted to fit in, to be ingredients in that celebrated melting pot where many diverse cultures and national origins blend together to form the strong alloy of Americanism. At times it appeared that the "real" Americans (always referred to as *Amarkaan* by the Lebanese immigrants), those who came earlier or from more "respectable" origins, didn't want us cast into that fabled pot with them, and we were not allowed to melt and fuse with them.

What this environment did to me was magnify in my mind the differences

301

between others and myself. It didn't make me unhappy, just subconsciously wary in social circumstances. But, the subtle class divisions that are learned and reinforced at school, easily subvert the melting pot paradigm of America.

To say I was reluctant to embrace my Lebanese heritage understates my feelings by quite a margin. Once, when Shukrullah Mobark was visiting my mother, he asked me if I wanted to learn the Lebanese mother tongue. I replied in no uncertain terms, "No." The old boy was aghast. In retrospect, he should have been.

As the months and years rolled by my Lebanese heritage, no matter how hard I tried to shake it, would come back to haunt me. "You goddamned black Syrian," the Greek storekeeper from across the street yelled at my brother and me on more than one occasion. (When I related this to my father, he told me to respond by calling him a goddamned Turk. This was, I surmised, supposed to be the ultimate insult to a Greek.) To the kids from the Sand Flats (an "other side of the tracks" part of town), we were a bunch of "niggers" or "cat-lickers," a play on the word Catholic. To others we were just "black bastards."

Some slights took a little longer to sink in. A barber once suggested to me that another practitioner up the street would be "better" at cutting my hair. My boyhood school chums were always welcome in our home—to play cards or even share snacks—but somehow the favor was never returned. As a result, attempts to deny my ethnicity only served to reinforce it, and I would have to grab on to it as an anchor to keep from drowning in a hostile social world. Perhaps this is why so many immigrants in America, to shield themselves from the economic and social hardships of assimilation, hang on to their customs and talk so fondly of their forsaken countries, even if they are only fooling themselves.

Growing up in this environment, there were times when I wished my father were more prosperous, like the fathers of some of my friends and classmates. At other times I wished he had been able to come watch me play basketball, a sport I excelled at in high school. When men came to his store the day after a game and told him how well I had played, I wished he could have been there. But, the store had to come first in his scheme of things, and I thought I knew why.

When I took the time to reflect about my dad's past, how he had crossed an ocean at the age of sixteen, not knowing the language, the land, or what lay in store for him, I wondered if I could have done it. When I thought about how he struggled to make a decent living in a strange country to feed his large family, I wondered if I could have done it. And when I considered how my dad with all his struggles lived to see his six children garner ten college degrees, I had to admit he had been pretty damn successful.

When the Korean War commenced and I entered military service, I found myself thrust together with a rainbow of ethnicities. There were many for whom the concept of the great American melting pot was also meaningless, and their attitudes certainly affirmed that. To a youth from a small town, living in close quarters with savvy, big city boys became an experience all its own. From a kid with a ready smile, eager to make friends, I became a wary, selective, and suspicious, if not a somewhat misanthropic, young man in two short years. This was when I began to understand what happened to my dad.

Wherever I was stationed, I would head to the nearest city on weekend pass and instinctively search for restaurants that served the kind of food I was used to at home. The culture of my ancestors, as represented in the food they ate, became a refuge for this homesick kid. So it was that my ethnicity kept drawing me back, even though I had loudly protested that I wanted out.

One thing that didn't change for me upon entering Uncle Sam's Army was my mother's continued adherence to the strict rules imposed on me in childhood. Whenever I was home on leave and stayed out late, mother would be there to greet me no matter what the hour. "But when I'm away, I stay out as long as I like," I protested. "It doesn't matter," she would reply, "when you are here you obey my rules." Of course, I stayed out late anyway, just as I did when I was in high school.

A small consolation was that she no longer threw the tantrums she had when I was a tardy teenager. Back then, when locked out, I resorted to all manner of trickery to gain entrance to the house, including the use of an assortment of skeleton keys, throwing pebbles at my brother's bedroom window, and climbing over the second-story railing of the back porch. Invariably mother would be out of her bed like a shot as soon as I hit the top step of the second floor. She berated me so loudly that my father would ask me to try and behave better so he could get some sleep. Once she even overturned the mattress on my cot so I couldn't go to bed. Whatever she imagined I was doing out that late certainly didn't meet with her approval.

Despite chafing under these disciplinary encounters, there were many things I learned from my parents, often whether I realized it or not. My father emphasized the need to be absolutely disciplined in money matters. When paper towels first came out, after wiping his hands, Pop would dry it on a radiator rather than throw it away. As a recycler, he was way ahead of his time. Much to my mother's chagrin, I shined shoes avidly in his shop

303

because my father let me keep all the money I made, and the majority of my earnings went into my savings account. I also peddled papers, worked in grocery stores, and even as a grease monkey in a garage.

When I finished high school, I had amassed the princely sum of $600 at the Carthage Savings & Loan. After graduation, my dad asked me what I was going to do, and I responded that a lot of kids were going to college, so perhaps I should too. He told me to take my savings and go to college and when I got my report card to bring it to him. If it looked as though I would make something of myself, he would help me. If not, we'd both be better off. When I finally went to college a few years later, it was with the help of the GI Bill, and I never took a dime from my dad, even when he offered. It seems I had inherited some of that Lebanese pride as well.

It wasn't only my parents who came from that "old school." Many of the nuns at the Augustinian Academy were molded in the same forge. When my high school sojourn was nearing completion, the principal stopped me in the hall one day and asked me the same question about my future that my dad had. I told her that I would like to study mathematics in college. Just then my math teacher was passing by, so the principal asked her what she thought of my career choice. "He'll never make it," she responded. This was from a teacher who saw me get all As and a couple of perfect scores in New York State Regents exams in mathematics!

In retrospect, I think this was an attempt at reverse psychology, something that would make modern day guidance counselors cringe. But, perhaps it worked because I did end up getting a science degree with a major in mathematics.

If there is one thing kids sense instinctively, it's who likes you and who doesn't, and that includes nuns and priests. That is not to say that there weren't a lot of nuns who were great and fair teachers and priests who were awfully nice, and I remember them fondly. But it should not come as a shock to anyone that members of religious communities are subject to normal human foibles. Some were obviously brought up in racist homes, and that inevitably carried over in their vocations.

Prejudicial treatment exists, and manifests itself at odd times and in odd circumstances, even in those religious societies whose members aspire to higher spiritual ideals. A few of the nuns, it seemed to me, swung their rulers a bit harder on us boys with dark hair and "dubious" immigrant heritage. I distinctly remember an incident in seventh grade when Sr John Matha hit me over the head with a geography book. I can't remember what indiscretion I was guilty of but it startled and enraged me, so I promptly arose and announced that I'd had enough and left the building. Soon one of my classmates came looking for me. "She wants you to come back," he said. Finally, I reluctantly returned. The next day, my mother came to school and in front of the class, coerced me to apologize to the nun. She assumed I'd gotten what was coming to me. The happy ending was that Sr Matha never laid a glove on me for the remainder of my time in the seventh grade.

Some of the priests were curt and less tolerant of mistakes made by altar boys coming from the lower strata of local society. I remember, after serving mass for the visiting Maronite priest Fr Spheir, who was at most five-feet-two inches tall, one of the tall parish priests rather fatuously asking him if all people in Lebanon were as short as he. "No, no," he quickly replied, with his hand on my shoulder, "this boy's uncle is quite tall, taller than you in fact." To this day I still chuckle when I think of that incident, mainly because of the stereotypical misperceptions many individuals have about different people from different parts of the world.

As the old saying goes all good things must end and so my eight-year journey for the truth of the tales and legends I had heard while growing up also came to an end. It was a trek that took me places I never dreamed I would go, to meet people I never would have met, and to discover things I never would have known. In retrospect it was a long, enjoyable, and worthwhile trip.

BIBLIOGRAPHY

Abinader, Elmaz. *Children of the Roojme*. Madison, Wisconsin, University of Wisconsin, 1991.

Akarli, Engin. *The Long Peace*. Berkeley, CA, University of California Press, 1993.

Antonious, George. *The Arab Awakening*. New York, G.P. Putnam's Sons, 1946.

Debbas, Fouad. *Beirut, Our Memory*. Beirut, Lebanon, Naufal Group, 1986.

Fawaz, Leila Tarazi. *Merchants and Migrants in Nineteenth-Century Beirut*. Cambridge, MA, Harvard University Press, 1983.

Freyha, Anis. *A Dictionary of Modern Lebanese Proverbs*. Beirut, Librairie Du Liban, 1974.

Goudard S.J., Joseph; Jalabert S.J., Henri. *Lebanon: The Land and The Lady*. Beirut, The Catholic Press, 1951. Chicago, Loyala University Press, 1966.

Haddad, Emily Marie. *Mt. Lebanon to Vermont*. Rutland, VT, The Tuttle Co., 1916.

Hourani, Albert; Shehadi, Nadim; Editors. *The Lebanese in the World: A Century of Emigration*. London, I.B. Tauris & Co. Ltd., 1992.

Khater, Akram Fouad. *Inventing Home*. Berkeley and Los Angeles, CA, University of California Press, 2001.

McGilvary, Margaret. *The Dawn of a New Era in Syria*. New York, Fleming H. Revell Company, 1920.

Moghabghab, Faddoul. *The Shepherd Song on the Hills of Lebanon*. New York, E.P. Dutton & Company, 1907.

*Morton Allen Directory of Steamship Arrivals*, Baltimore, MD, reprinted: Genealogical Publishing Co., 1998.

Naff, Alixa. *Becoming American: The Early Arab Immigrant Experience*. Southern Illinois University Press, 1985.

Nehmé, Moustapha. *Fleurs Sauvages Du Liban*. Beyrouth, Liban, Conseil National de la Recherche Scientifique, 1977.

**Archives**

Ellis, Angèle. Letters collection, 1925-1980.

Ellis Island Foundation, History Center, Ellis Island, New York.

Ministry of National Defense, Lebanese Army Headquarters, Beirut, Lebanon.

Presbyterian Historical Society, Philadelphia, PA.

U.S. Department of Census, Washington, D.C.

## Acknowledgements

ALTHOUGH MANY PEOPLE MADE CONTRIBUTIONS TO the development of this work during my journey, special mention is due to the following persons. First of all I owe a great debt to my mother who saved most of the correspondence she received from relatives in Lebanon. Virtually all began with kisses from wherever they were.

I also wish to thank Dr Hadia Harb of the Lebanese American University, Beirut, who in a true labor of love faithfully translated the letters from their original and somewhat archaic Arabic script. Without her help this work would not have been possible. Fr Kail Ellis, OSA, at Villanova University, aided immeasurably with research materials and encouragement for the continuance of this labor, especially during periods when thoughts of giving up arose.

Madame Désireé Joseph was not only my hostess on many occasions while doing research in Lebanon, but acted as chauffeur and translator and introduced me to information sources that would have been otherwise unknown to me. Mme Samira Menassa helped greatly with introductions while also acting as chauffeur and interpreter.

My good friend Dr Khaled Diab spent many hours with me translating the books I brought back with me from Lebanon. Translations from the French were provided by Dr Paula Hoche who without a doubt "thinks in French." Elias Choueiry at the Jafet Library of the American University of Beirut was always ready to answer questions or look up references for me. Finally, I must thank my wife Loretta and daughter Diana, both of whom spent many hours reading manuscript drafts and providing valuable suggestions.

The authors of the many books I accumulated that aided me in forming opinions and understanding the social, political, and economic situation of the country of my ancestors, and to whom I owe a great debt, are listed in the bibliography.

As in any effort that spans the time period that this work took to produce, many others helped along the way, some with a story or an anecdote and others with just a name or reference. They are not mentioned here, but I give them my heartfelt thanks nonetheless.

nargelie, 40, 41, 298

O

Ottoman | Ottomans, 37, 40, 44, 60, 61, 65, 67, 70-3, 78-80, 82-4, 114, 123, 125, 129, 139, 156, 158, 162, 164, 202

P

Peasant's Revolt, 47

Peddlers, 119, 142, 145-6, 151-3, 164

Phoenicia | Phoenician | Phoenicians, 141

Picot, Georges, 73, 85

Presbyterian, 60, 69, 78-9, 153-4, 157, 159

R

Réglement, 40, 70, 72, 162

Remittances, 119

RMS Homeric, 222-3

RMS Olympic, 204

S

Saydet el Becharra (convent), 54

Scherer, George H, 157

Second Punic War, 142

Sericulture | silkworms | silk, 48, 55, 57, 66, 90, 110, 117, 119, 120, 179, 197, 216, 259, 297

Shadiach, Yousef , 72

Sickrey, Zakia, 205, 216-7, 238-40, 245, 269

Sidon, 84

simsar, 110

Solomon, Monera, 228

sousse, 195

Spanish Flu, 84, 159, 163

SS Phoenicia, 144

St. James Church, 142, 144, 228-9, 288

Sykes-Picot-Sazanov Agreement,

73, 85

Syria, 47, 54, 60-2, 65-6, 70-72, 83, 132, 157, 162, 181, 201, 251, 255, 269, 285, 287

Syrian Orthodox Religion, 79, 101-2, 154, 184

T

el Tabashi, General Armand, 94

The Empress of Ireland, 132

Tripoli, 78, 83-4, 93, 99, 262, 264

Turkey | Turks, 44-5, 59, 65-6, 70-72, 78-81, 83, 114, 129, 132, 134, 139, 152, 153-7, 162, 164, 202

U

Utica, New York, 138-9, 142, 144-5, 167, 281

V

Volstead Act, 170

W

Wilson, President Woodrow, 162

World War I, 29, 69, 95, 135, 158, 163, 179, 201, 245, 258, 262, 292

World War II, 262, 282, 294

Y

al Yahshushi, Francis Nassif, 19, 25, 54, 84-5, 241, 242

Young Turks, 40, 69-70, 72, 80, 123

Z

Zahle, 77, 159, 181

Zouaves, 77

Zouq Mikhail, 30, 33-4

*The author during the Korean War.*

Raff Ellis is a freelance writer whose father emigrated to America from Lebanon in the early part of the Twentieth Century. His mother was descended from a prominent Maronite Christian family and arrived in the United States in 1926. Ellis, a frequent traveler to Lebanon, based his memoir *Kisses from a Distance* on family documents, oral histories, and folklore tales. He is a former computer industry executive and the author of numerous magazine articles, essays, short stories, and technical papers. He lives with his wife Loretta in Orlando.